SCRIPTURE *and the*
ENGLISH POETIC
IMAGINATION

SCRIPTURE *and the*
ENGLISH POETIC
IMAGINATION

David Lyle Jeffrey

Baker Academic
a division of Baker Publishing Group
Grand Rapids, Michigan

Published by Baker Academic
a division of Baker Publishing Group
PO Box 6287, Grand Rapids, MI 49516-6287
www.bakeracademic.com

Printed in the United States of America

Library of Congress Cataloging-in-Publication Data
Names: Jeffrey, David Lyle, 1941– author.
Title: Scripture and the English poetic imagination / David Lyle Jeffrey.
Description: Grand Rapids, MI : Baker Academic, a division of Baker Publishing Group, [2019] | Includes bibliographical references and index.
Identifiers: LCCN 2018036382 | ISBN 9780801099625 (cloth : alk. paper)
Subjects: LCSH: Religious poetry—History and criticism. | Bible and literature. | Bible—In literature.
Classification: LCC PN56.B5 J44 2019 | DDC 821.009/3822—dc23
LC record available at https://lccn.loc.gov/2018036382

978-0-8010-9963-2 (ITPE)

Unless indicated otherwise, Scripture quotations are from the King James Version of the Bible.

Scripture quotations labeled NKJV are from the New King James Version®. Copyright © 1982 by Thomas Nelson. Used by permission. All rights reserved.

Scripture quotations labeled NRSV are from the New Revised Standard Version of the Bible, copyright © 1989 National Council of the Churches of Christ in the United States of America. Used by permission. All rights reserved.

The poem "Adam" is reprinted from COLLECTED EARLIER POEMS by Anthony Hecht, copyright © 1990 by Anthony E. Hecht. Used by permission of Alfred A. Knopf, an imprint of the Knopf Doubleday Publishing Group, a division of Penguin Random House LLC. All rights reserved.

The poem "Supernatural Love" is reprinted from SUPERNATURAL LOVE: POEMS 1976–1992 by Gjertrud Schnackenberg. Copyright © 2000 by Gjertrud Schnackenberg.

19   20   21   22   23   24   25   7   6   5   4   3   2   1

HH 03 9322467

CONTENTS

PREFACE

his volume of new and selected essays is threaded together to tell a
story to which I have committed my scholarly life over the last fifty
years—namely, of the magnificent fruitfulness of Holy Scripture in
the work of English poets, including dramatic as well as lyric poets from Caedmon to the present. T. S. Eliot famously, and in some considerable measure
rightly, said that "the Bible has had a literary effect upon English literature *not*
because it has been considered as literature, but because it has been considered
as the report of the Word of God" (*Religion and Literature*, 1935). There is
undeniable truth in this observation; indeed, it has been a working assumption
for most who have seriously considered the richness of biblical story, character,
and allusion in vernacular European literatures, including myself. Yet it is
not the whole truth. The history of literature since the Enlightenment bears
a persistent witness to the power of biblical language, idiom, phrase, poetic
style, and spiritual presence to move poets to evoke it even when belief has
ostensibly been lost. It is this second truth, of the power of Scripture to fire
the poetic imagination independently of prevalent religious authority, which
completes the design and labor of this volume.

I have sought to be at least a little like the "householder instructed unto the
kingdom of heaven" spoken of by Jesus in Matthew's Gospel, who "bringeth
forth out of his treasure things new and old" (Matt. 13:52). My principle of
selection has accordingly been one of which I hope others than myself may
approve; the essays assembled here are (to me and, I gather, others) among the
most satisfying of my career. I have linked them in such a way as to outline
a story basic to English literary history, especially as it pertains to lyric and
dramatic poetry, and also to bear witness to the power of Holy Scripture to
elevate the creative mind. Chapters 1, 2, 6, and 7 are new; chapter 4 renews
an essay I began some decades ago but never till now completed; the other

chapters are reworkings, some quite heavily, of earlier essays that have been well received and yet are now in need of both updating and, as I am regularly reminded, easier accessibility. For those of my readers who may wonder how I could seem to overlook in a book of this sort the epic verse of John Milton, my answer is simply that two of my former students, Dennis Danielson and Philip Donnelly, both eminent Miltonists, have written comprehensively and persuasively on Milton's biblical and theological imagination, and anything I could add here would be superfluous.

I am indebted to several publishers for their permission to incorporate work first essayed in their domains: to Oxford University Press for an extract from "Conclusion and the Form of the Personal in Modern Poetry," *Journal of the American Academy of Religion* 43, no. 2 (1975); to *Franciscan Studies* for permission to extract from "St. Francis and Medieval Theatre," *Franciscan Studies* 43, no. 21 (1983/1988); to Sage Publishing for permission to draw on "Courtly Love and Christian Marriage in the Court of Henry VIII," *Christianity and Literature* 59, no. 3 (2010); "Of Beauty and a Father's Love: The Recrudescence of Fatherhood in Recent American Literature," *Christianity and Literature* 55, no. 2 (2006); and "Communion, Community, and Our Common Book: Or, Can Faustus Be Saved?," *Christianity and Literature* 53, no. 2 (2004), a talk given at the Modern Language Association in response to being given the Lifetime Achievement Award of the Conference for Christianity and Literature in 2003 and largely preserved in its oral format; to Brazos Press for allowing me to reprint "The Beatitudes in Dante and Chaucer" from *The Sermon on the Mount through the Centuries*, ed. Jeffrey P. Greenman, Timothy Larsen, and Stephen Spenser (Brazos, 2007); to the American Bible Society for allowing me to revise "Habitual Music: The King James Bible and English Literature," which first appeared in *Translation That Openeth the Window: Reflections on the History and Legacy of the King James Bible*, ed. David G. Burke (Society for Biblical Literature, 2009); to ECW Press for permission to revise "Light, Stillness, and the Shaping Word: Conversion in the Poetic of Margaret Avison," from *"Lighting Up the Terrain": The Poetry of Margaret Avison*, ed. David A. Kent (ECW Press, 1987); and, finally, to *First Things* for allowing me to revise my essay "God's Patient *Stet*: Richard Wilbur at 90" (2011).

I have, of course, many other obligations of gratitude than can be represented adequately here. Dominic Manganiello, Graeme Hunter, and Michael O'Brien each offered suggestions on one or more of these essays at some point in the past, and poets Anthony Hecht and Margaret Avison of blessed memory, and with them Richard Wilbur, have each been a source of personal encouragement. My generous Baylor University colleagues Phillip Donnelly and Katie Calloway, and my Chinese colleagues Yang Huilin, Zhang Jing, and Liu Jiong, have offered thoughtful comments and suggestions. I am indebted also to my resourceful graduate assistant Caroline Paddock, as well as to Abigail Higgins, and last but so far from least as east is from west, to my wife, Katherine Bentley Jeffrey, whose sharp eye and not-so-frequent "stet" has led to many an improvement in what follows.

INTRODUCTION

This is a book about poetry in the English language, especially such as exhibits the particular indebtedness of the English poetic voice to an unusual muse or animating spirit—namely, the language and spirit of the Bible. The persistence of biblical overtures, even in the absence of a living faith in many a poet, is something that may be readily observed in English verse, even in late modernity, to a degree unparalleled in other European languages. In fact, while the painting of biblical subjects and painting that includes biblical allusions is much more a European than an English cultural phenomenon, precisely the reverse is true in poetry. Scripture is not only a chief source of subject matter in English for much of the language's history but, more profoundly, it has served as a perennial touchstone for the poetic imagination itself, lending thus to poetry in English a rich polyphony of harmonic voices and a distinctive spiritual character.

Those readers of poetry in English from its beginnings to the present who have also some familiarity with the Bible will have unavoidably observed its pervasive influence. Even an inexperienced reader will see how commonly biblical narrative serves as inspiration or foil for poets such as John Milton in *Paradise Lost*, John Dryden in *Absolom and Achitophel*, T. S. Eliot in "Journey of the Magi," or Howard Nemerov in "Lot Later," not to mention countless others. What becomes apparent to a more seasoned reader, however, is that the Bible has been overwhelmingly influential over much more than name and story; pervasive idiom, locution, meter, and parallelism, aside from more direct borrowings of line and phrase, all bear witness to a biblical foundation. Beyond all this, there is a presence in English annals of a conception of poetry itself in which, to borrow a phrase from Walter Benjamin, the poet construes his task as imparting a certain counsel concerning wisdom.[1] That

1. Walter Benjamin, *Illuminations* (New York: Schocken, 1969; 1978), 86.

English poetry (and, by extension, poetry written in English elsewhere) is distinctively biblical in this respect among European literatures has long been recognized by scholars as well as poets. What the eighteenth-century English poet Thomas Gray observed—namely, that in English "the language of the age is never the language of poetry," and further, that "our poetry, on the contrary, has a language peculiar to itself"[2]—is in no small measure attributable to the formation of British poetic tradition in the language of Scripture. Since the seventeenth century these echoes have been largely attuned to the King James Version (1611), easily the most favored translation in English by poets right through to the beginning of the twenty-first century. (So pervasive are its resonances in English poetry that many still think of the KJV as "the poet's Bible.") But the influence of Scripture begins much earlier.

The central purpose of this collection of essays will be to explore some of the ways Holy Scripture has shaped the English poetic imagination, not merely through subject, cadence, idiom, and various echoes of its diction, but by effecting something deeper in the consciousness of English-speaking poets from Caedmon in the eighth century to Richard Wilbur, Anthony Hecht, and Gjertrud Schnackenberg among our contemporaries. Essentially, this involves an attunement of the vernacular English poetic imagination to biblical poetics as a wellspring of inspiration. Though individual poets may well be unconscious of the ways in which, in Scripture itself, poetry shapes the biblical mind from Torah to the Revelation, the collective "voice" of our poetic tradition in English discloses a mode of imagination and creativity either inadvertently or advertently in dialogue with a precedent Voice. Understanding the English poetic imagination can accordingly be much assisted by first considering that precedent Voice—namely, the divine voice as represented not only in Torah but by the prophets, Wisdom writers, and psalmists in the Old Testament, and then by Jesus in the New. Reflection on both these matters now, overwhelmed as we are by a culture of flickering images in which "the very notion of a creative imagination seems under mounting threat,"[3] is necessary. If we are to enable a future for imaginative life after our collective addiction to the internet has exhausted its power to anesthetize, we will need somehow to remember "what things were like *before*"[4]—before poetry withered under the pressure of so many cheap substitutes for its rich nourishment of heart and mind.

2. Thomas Gray, *Letters to West*, quoted in *Princeton Encyclopedia of Poetry and Poetics*, ed. Alex Preminger et al. (Princeton: Princeton University Press, 1974), 629.

3. Richard Kearney, *The Wake of Imagination* (Minneapolis: University of Minnesota Press, 1988), 3.

4. Kearney, *Wake of Imagination*, 359.

one

POETRY AND THE VOICE OF GOD

Trying to find ways to think plausibly about the nature of the immortal, invisible God has been a major preoccupation from the burning bush through both Testaments and on down through the annals of Christian tradition. For Gerard Manley Hopkins, in "Nondum" (a poem which has as its epigraph Isaiah 45:15, "Verily thou art a God that hidest thyself"),

> We guess; we clothe Thee, unseen King,
> With attributes we deem are meet;
> Each in his own imagining
> Sets up a shadow in Thy seat;
> Yet know not how our gifts to bring,
> Where seek Thee with unsandalled feet.

Hopkins is conscious that only a few pages away in the Bible are explicit divine warnings against idolatrous comparisons (e.g., Isa. 40:25; 46:5), yet also that analogies abound (God is a Rock, a Fortress, a Consuming Fire). All analogies communicate, even though such insight as they gather must be at best, by definition, partial. When such biblical metaphors are tumbled in the imagination of theologians and commentators, typically the invisible, omnipotent God is still envisioned figurally. For example, in Christian tradition imaginative representations of God as architect of the universe draw not only upon the first chapters of Genesis, as we would expect, but on related phrasing in the New Testament. In Hebrews, Abraham, still in the wilderness and not knowing where he was going, is said to have "looked forward to the city that has foundations, whose architect [Greek *technitēs*; Latin *artifex*] and builder [Greek *demiourgos*; Latin *conditor*] is God" (Heb. 11:10). This New Testament metaphor interprets Genesis but also looks forward to the end of salvation history, in which all human flesh will see that God is *alpha* and *omega*, the first and the last (Rev. 1:11; 22:13). Yet this is far from the only kind of assistance within the Scriptures to imagining what God is like. A second kind of biblical metaphor for God speaks not just to his omnipotence and omnipresence but, more intimately, to his personal nature; in other texts he may present himself as a lover, a bridegroom, a father. Of this latter kind of self-disclosure, one *figura* in particular seems to provide a special register of meaning for our understanding of God in Scripture: God is a poet—as John Donne will say, he is "a very figurative and metaphorical God." *How* he speaks, not just *what* he says, becomes an important measure of who he *is*.

The Divine Poet

When people less familiar with the Bible think of the "voice of God," they often think of it in terms of "thou shalt nots" and similar moral imperatives. To the degree that we take the existence of God to be real, this is an entirely reasonable thing to do; indeed, it would be foolish in the extreme to do otherwise. When we look more closely at the full canon of Scripture, however, we soon encounter the voice of a God who speaks fulsomely and frequently in poetry, and that not in any such way as to mask the truth he utters. In the writings of the prophets, these divine poetic irruptions are so evident when the text is read aloud that modern editors can readily insert quotation marks around the speeches of God, even when these utterances are not clearly indicated by a prose transition, such as, for example, "Thus saith the LORD" (Isa. 50:1). If one is reading in an English translation, this qualitative distinction in expression is most clearly apparent in the King James or "Authorized" Version (which I quote here, though set visually so that its nature as poetry becomes more apparent). For example, words ascribed to Isaiah himself are sometimes followed by an antiphon, or response of the Lord, often both an answer to the prophet and an amplification. Here is a luminous instance: after he has praised the Lord as "exalted," the prophet notes despairingly the contrary, desolate condition of his people because of their sin:

> The highways lie waste,
> the wayfaring man ceaseth. (Isa. 33:8)

The answering voice of God then (beginning at 34:16 are several divine interjections) takes up the prophet's lament and turns it into an extended poem about divine restoration.

> And an highway shall be there, and a way,
> and it shall be called the way of holiness;
> the unclean shall not pass over it; but it shall be for those:
> the wayfaring men, though fools, shall not err therein.
> No lion shall be there, nor any ravenous beast shall go up thereon,
> it shall not be found there;
> but the redeemed shall walk there:
> And the ransomed of the LORD shall return,
> and come to Zion with songs
> and everlasting joy upon their heads:
> they shall obtain joy and gladness,
> and sorrow and sighing shall flee away. (Isa. 35:8–10)

A rather despairing utterance of Isaiah is in this fashion transformed into a promise of reversal, radiant with assurance of future hope. That poem then becomes a theme, returning again a few chapters later as a pilgrim song:

> Therefore the redeemed of the LORD shall return,
> and come with singing unto Zion;
> and everlasting joy shall be upon their head:
> they shall obtain gladness and joy;
> and sorrow and mourning shall flee away. (Isa. 51:11)

Sometimes the pitch and tenor of the divine Voice produces an effect when read aloud (even in English—try it in the KJV or NKJV) that occasions a thrill of the sort described by the ancient Roman writer Longinus as an effect of the "rhetorical sublime" (for which his compelling example is the *fiat lux* of Gen. 1:3). Rhetorical sublimity is, in fact, characteristic of the divine Poet's utterances in many places:

> Ho, every one that thirsteth,
> come ye to the waters,
> and he that hath no money;
> come ye, buy, and eat;
> yea, come, buy wine and milk
> without money and without price. (Isa. 55:1)

Following this particular divine exhortative outburst and its sustaining meta-phor, the prophet himself is inspired to versify, now in classic Hebrew paral-lelism, entreating his people to return from the poverty of their sinfulness to the abundance of the Lord's Way:

> Seek ye the LORD while he may be found,
> call ye upon him while he is near:
> Let the wicked forsake his way,
> and the unrighteous man his thoughts:
> and let him return unto the LORD,
> and he will have mercy upon him;
> and to our God,
> for he will abundantly pardon. (Isa. 55:6–7)

Strikingly, God himself may speak in poetry even when he is angry, as we see regularly in Jeremiah (e.g., Jer. 23:1–8), Hosea, and Amos, among other prophets; in such contexts the *adah* voice (of bitter condemnation) rather than the *teudah* voice (of consolation) predominates. Another powerful example of the elegance of God's poetic displeasure comes in the famous "whirlwind speech" in which he first rebukes Job, then his theological friends:

> Who hath divided a watercourse
> for the overflowing of waters,
> or a way for the lightning of thunder;
> To cause it to rain
> on the earth, where no man is;
> on the wilderness, wherein there is no man;
> To satisfy the desolate and waste ground;
> and to cause the bud of the tender herb to spring forth?
>
> Hath the rain a father?
> or who hath begotten the drops of dew?
> Out of whose womb came the ice?
> and the hoary frost of heaven, who hath gendered it?
> The waters are hid as with a stone,
> and the face of the deep is frozen. (Job 38:25–30)

The elegant poetry of God is here and everywhere expressive of his divine majesty and attendant authority. Human poets sometimes seek to echo it, howsoever imperfectly. Christina Rossetti, for example, in her lovely poem (and hymn) "In the Bleak Mid-winter,"[1] delights in the beauty of the simile

---

1. No. 187 in *The Oxford Book of Carols*, ed. Percy Dearmer, R. Vaughan Williams, and Martin Shaw (London: Oxford University Press, 1928; 1977), 398.

of "water like a stone," and Anthony Hecht quotes verse 28 as an epigraph to "Adam," as he probes the mysterious transcendence of divine fatherhood compared to its human analogue.[2] Both poets are clearly inspired by the beauty of the KJV's language, but also by more than just the words. Read aloud, their poems reveal that these authors are responding to the tug of something higher up and further in, something of the divine nature itself that is projected by the divine Voice. Their own thought, accordingly, is elevated, aspiring, yet remains circumspectly aware of the gap between divine and human poetry that remains. This reality is addressed many times in Scripture itself, nowhere, perhaps, more memorably than in the poem from Isaiah we have already briefly considered:

> For my thoughts are not your thoughts,
> neither are your ways my ways,
> saith the LORD.
> For as the heavens are higher than the earth,
> so are my ways higher than your ways,
> and my thoughts than your thoughts.
>
> For as the rain cometh down,
> and the snow from heaven,
> and returneth not thither,
> but watereth the earth,
> and maketh it bring forth and bud,
> that it may give seed to the sower,
> and bread to the eater:
> So shall my word be that goeth forth out of my mouth:
> it shall not return unto me void,
> but it shall accomplish that which I please,
> and it shall prosper in the thing whereto I sent it.
>
> For ye shall go out with joy,
> and be led forth with peace: the mountains and the hills
> shall break forth before you into singing,
> and all the trees of the field shall clap their hands.
>
> Instead of the thorn shall come up the fir tree,
> and instead of the brier shall come up the myrtle tree:
> and it shall be to the LORD for a name,
> for an everlasting sign that shall not be cut off. (Isa. 55:8–13)

This is magnificent poetry. Any translation that captures some measure of it (e.g., KJV, NKJV, RSV) makes it possible for us to hear, even in English,

---

2. Anthony Hecht, *The Hard Hours* (New York: Atheneum, 1967), 31.

something of its beauty and power. Those who can read the Old Testament Scriptures in Hebrew should know this quality more naturally and cherish it, but happily much of the magniloquence of the divine poetic voice comes through at least partially even in translation.

But what about the New Testament, which has come down to us exclusively in Greek? Well, here too Jesus speaks in recognizably Semitic poetic discourse, and his many quotations from the Old Testament are most of all from the Psalms, followed by Isaiah. When he teaches discursively, as, for example, in his Sermon on the Mount as Matthew records it (Matt. 5–7), he uses several of the Hebrew poetic devices of *mashalim* (figural speech, including irony, aphorism, paradox, proverb, and enigma). These, along with parallelism, are Hebrew poetic devices characteristic of the Psalms and Wisdom books, much better suited to stirring oratory than the rhyme and meters with which we may associate poetry in our own tongue.

It is important to remember that Jesus was not speaking to his disciples in Greek. Much as many parts of the world today use English for written, formal documents that had their first utterance in a native tongue, so in the first century AD important communications from various quarters were regularly sent abroad in Greek, the lingua franca of the Mediterranean world, and this includes the New Testament. Here as elsewhere, translation typically obscures the grace of the original diction, even while communicating its substance. When Jesus conversed with religious professionals, such as a Pharisee like Nicodemus, he would most likely have spoken Hebrew, since biblical Hebrew was basic to a Pharisee's program of study and a badge of his competence. In this case, nonetheless, their conversation exposes the partiality of Nicodemus's understanding of the Scriptures; when Nicodemus compliments Jesus on the evidences that God is "with him," Jesus unexpectedly replies obliquely, breaking into the mysterious poetry of God, and Nicodemus stumbles (John 3:1–21).

> Jesus answered and said unto him,
> "Verily, verily, I say unto thee,
> Except a man be born again,
> he cannot see the kingdom of God." (John 3:3)

Nicodemus interprets this literalistically, saying, "How can a man be born when he is old? Can he enter the second time into his mother's womb, and be born?" (John 3:4). The answer Jesus gives conveys an essential truth not apparent to Nicodemus in his prosaic mode of thinking:

"Verily, verily, I say unto thee,
Except a man be born of water and of the Spirit,
he cannot enter into the kingdom of God.
That which is born of the flesh is flesh;
and that which is born of the Spirit is spirit.
Marvel not that I said unto thee,
Ye must be born again.
The wind bloweth where it listeth,
and thou hearest the sound thereof,
but canst not tell whence it cometh,
and whither it goeth:
so is every one that is born of the Spirit." (John 3:5–8)

Nicodemus is confounded; he is not used to poetic discourse in discussing theological truth. Jesus has juxtaposed "wind" (Hebrew *ruach*; Greek *pneuma*) with "breath" or "spirit" (*ruach*; *pneuma*) in such a way as to reveal the register of deep metaphor in language itself, visible both in Hebrew and in Greek. Like Nicodemus, the contemporary reader is prompted to reconsider the way in which spiritual reality is inherent in the physical order, whether or not we are aware of it; poetic imagination breaks through the barrier of unreflective thinking.

When Jesus speaks to the largely unlettered, Aramaic-speaking crowds (it is evident that Jesus used both languages, Hebrew and Aramaic), he teaches by means of brief, enigmatic wisdom stories or parables recognized by the disciples as a native though not necessarily familiar form of poetic speech (cf. John 16:25). When they ask him why he speaks in this indirect way instead of using more direct propositional discourse (in the manner of the Law), the answer they get is at first baffling:

"Because it is given unto you to know the mysteries of the kingdom of
    heaven,
but to them it is not given." (Matt. 13:11)

That is, Jesus implies that his purpose in using fictive, figural, and enigmatic discourse is to conceal as well as reveal, so that only one who truly seeks his meaning will find it.

"For whosoever hath, to him shall be given,
and he shall have more abundance:
but whosoever hath not,
from him shall be taken away even that he hath.

Therefore speak I to them in parables:
because they seeing see not; and hearing they hear not,
neither do they understand.
And in them is fulfilled the prophecy of Esaias, which saith,
By hearing ye shall hear, and shall not understand;
and seeing ye shall see, and shall not perceive:
For this people's heart is waxed gross,
and their ears are dull of hearing,
and their eyes they have closed;
lest at any time they should see with their eyes and hear with their
    ears,
and should understand with their heart, and should be converted, and
    I should heal them.
But blessed are your eyes, for they see: and your ears, for they hear.
For verily I say unto you, That many prophets and righteous men have
    desired to see those things which ye see, and have not seen them;
and to hear those things which ye hear, and have not heard them."
    (Matt. 13:12–17)

Obtuseness to the *way* God speaks is here connected to a refusal to be brought into communion with him. At the end of the seminar that Jesus then gives to the Twelve on allegory and parable (13:18–52), Matthew observes, "Without a parable spake he not unto them" (Matt. 13:34). The "things which have been kept secret from the foundation of the world" (Matt. 13:35) that Jesus reveals are not naturalistically self-evident but are deep truths and, rather like secrets, hidden, coded, beyond the reach of our normally prosaic way of thinking. The form of their disclosure is in riddles, for whereas direct speech, especially concerning familiar things like the Law, might be shrugged off as redundant, it may be that indirect speech, the sine qua non of poetry, will fire the imagination in search of understanding.

Or not. For his chosen ones, eager to understand, Jesus will patiently explain to them how to grasp the mysterious yet so memorable way he speaks, but he will not do so for those who lack the will and patience to hear him out in his own terms. The difference between the disciples (including eventually Nicodemus) and most teachers of the Law in the New Testament is that the disciples want above all to *know* Jesus and eventually, through him, to know the Father (John 14:6–11). They want to know who God *is*, not just what the Law says.

It wasn't easy for the disciples to enter into the register of Jesus' poetic voice. John's Gospel records Jesus patiently giving them figural means for grasping something of his divine nature: "I am the bread of life," he says (John 6:35,

48–51); "I am the door of the sheep" (10:7–9), "the good shepherd" (10:11), "the way, the truth, and the life" (14:6), "the true vine" (15:1–8). These passages, prototypes for the metaphysical conceits of poets such as John Donne and George Herbert, are tropes in which the comparisons between spiritual entities and ordinary objects are naturally incongruous, but their ingenious and sustained development provides striking, memorable, breakthrough insight into spiritual reality. In the last example cited, the poetic conceit serves to show that without being grafted right into the being of Christ, our own spiritual life, not just our fruitfulness, would perish. In the first, the Bread of Life discourse, its metaphysical character takes us to the heart of what we now know as the eucharistic mystery, so grotesque an imagination for Jesus' early followers that many of them said, "This is an hard saying; who can hear it?" and turned back (John 6:60). But Jesus does not deter them from leaving by making his saying more prosaic and user-friendly; his purpose is to teach a deeper truth, one that perhaps cannot be perceived without the poetry.

Nevertheless, near the end of his earthly ministry, just before his betrayal, Jesus says to the faithful,

> "I have said these things to you in figures of speech [*paroimiais*]. The hour is coming when I will no longer speak to you in figures, but will tell you plainly of the Father." (John 16:25 NRSV)

In great relief the disciples reply, "Yes, now you are speaking plainly, not in any figure of speech!" (16:29 NRSV). Their faith has been tested—and exercised—by his indirect "figurative" method; the divine poetry has winnowed out good wheat from the chaff in their intentions.

As a final example, when the triumphant Christ returns in glory, as envisioned in the Revelation to John, everything pertaining to ultimate meaning is given in highly figurative, symbolic discourse:

> And I turned to see the voice that spake with me.
> And being turned, I saw seven golden candlesticks;
> And in the midst of the seven candlesticks
> one like unto the Son of man,
> clothed with a garment down to the foot,
> and girt about the paps with a golden girdle.
> His head and his hairs were white like wool, as white as snow;
> and his eyes were as a flame of fire;
> And his feet like unto fine brass, as if they burned in a furnace;
> and his voice as the sound of many waters.
> And he had in his right hand seven stars:

and out of his mouth went a sharp two-edged sword:
and his countenance was as the sun shineth in his strength.
And when I saw him, I fell at his feet as dead.
And he laid his right hand upon me, saying unto me,
"Fear not; I am the first and the last:
I am he that liveth, and was dead;
and, behold, I am alive for evermore, Amen;
and have the keys of hell and of death." (Rev. 1:12–18)

What are we to make of this very Hebraic pattern, a rhetorical device marked by the *vav* consecutive (the string of "ands"), and the persistence of Hebrew poetic speech in the mouth of the Lord even here, at the end of the Greek New Testament? At the least, we are obligated to see that one of the many ways in which God's thoughts are above our own, his ways "higher" than our ways, is his preference for a mode of discourse that is the very opposite of simple indicative prose or reductive proposition: it is exalted, not casual. Though some much prefer plain speech in a series of commandments that could be mastered in a system, the God whose voice booms through the prophets, in Job, and in the vision of John, as in the teaching of Jesus in the Gospels, does not so limit himself. Figural speech, irony, riddling aphorisms, paradoxes, melismatic Hebrew parallelism, metaphor, and story upon story are what we get instead. *Caveat lector*—it turns out that in neither Testament, when he is disclosing his nature and purpose, does the Lord of heaven and earth always talk like we do. In our own culture's terms, God does not talk like a lawyer, a philosopher, or even a theologian, let alone a TV talk-show host. Very often, however, he speaks like a poet. We might wish it otherwise, or be lulled into imagining that the Word of God should be coming to us in the lingo of the coffee shop or the faux-authoritative patter of the newscast, but we would be hard-pressed to find much warrant for that in Scripture. The fact that God speaks poetry when the issues are most weighty suggests that appreciating his poetry might be an essential element in our knowledge of God; that is, we should understand him as a poet—the originary Poet—the One who writes the world.

The Nature of Poetry

To think of poetry in the Bible is inevitably to think about the Psalms and the author of so many of them, David, the "man after God's own heart" (1 Sam. 13:14; Acts 13:22). Whether in the Coverdale translation from the Book of Common Prayer or the later KJV, these intensely human poems have shaped conversation between God and those who worship him in English since the Reformation. In these English versions, many of the basic features of Hebrew poetry can readily be identified; parallelism, envelope structure, binary opposition, and various tropes of intensification all come across remarkably well.[3] The Hebrew title of this collection of one hundred and fifty poems, the backbone of both Jewish and Christian liturgies for three millennia, is *tehellim*, praises (cf. *hallel*, "praise," from which we get *hallelujah*, "praise God"); and most are just that, at least by their concluding lines. Yet they are also *tefillim*, prayers, and they have anchored thanksgiving and supplication to God in a wide range of languages all over the world. Among those languages is Latin, the worship language in Western Christendom from the third to the fifteenth century—until the Reformation. Latin translation of the Hebrew—namely, in the Vulgate of St. Jerome—blurred some of the Hebraic features of the verse, but compensated by intruding features of Latin poetics that began to shift the translated psalms toward the later introduction of meter and rhyme. This feature was amplified in the early hymns of the church in such a way that the Bible was echoed in song and high poetry of a Latin character.[4] In other languages similar coloration occurred; the Old Germanic poetics of stress, alliteration, and rhythm is characteristic of the Anglo-Saxon psalters, as are Celtic language oral poetic features in Welsh and Gaelic translations of the Psalms. In none of these environments was anyone in doubt that the proper way to praise God, even to pray to him, was in poetry.

Beginning in the twentieth century, biblical translations have tended toward more prosaic rendering, and the fashionable imposition of culturally chic paraphrases has deadened many an ear to the actual rhetorical manner of divine self-disclosure, which is seldom colloquial. The tendency to make it so is not exclusively a modern presumption; in our time, however, it has been the poets more often than the preachers who have heard the divine Voice in something more akin to its original register, and have responded in a spirit of admiration and respect. One of the goals of this study is to consider how poets have frequently been in this sense better translators, not least in that so many have understood intuitively that the *manner* of divine speech in Holy Scripture is not incidental to the *matter* of it. Certain Christian poets in particular have discovered that understanding something of the poetry of divine speech in the Bible gives us knowledge of the Holy that we can ill afford to be without if we truly wish to understand, as the writer to the Hebrews puts

---

3. See Robert Alter, *The Art of Biblical Poetry* (New York: Basic Books, 1985), 62–84, for a useful elaboration.

4. F. J. Raby, *A History of Christian-Latin Poetry: From the Beginnings to the Close of the Middle Ages* (Oxford: Clarendon, 1927), offers a thorough review.

it, "him with whom we have to do" (Heb. 4:13). In short, if the witness of Scripture as it comes down to us is to be heeded, one of the most appropriate routes to a competent biblical theology may require us to get out of our prosy habits of mind and, at least occasionally, rise up and into the poetry of God.

To some readers it may seem an infelicity that I have just used the figurations "down" and "up" to suggest a distinction between our usual way of speaking and the dominant way Scripture represents God speaking—awkward because today we resist hierarchies, even in genre, and typically see "leveling down" as a virtuous activity and elevated speech of any kind as something of an affront to our democratic sensibilities. This is among the reasons that poetry in our culture has fallen into neglect in comparison to a century or so ago. Sometimes poetry is now seen as a kind of elitism; in yet other contexts, it is sometimes seen as childish. Ironically, both forms of denigration capture something true about poetry, but in a way that misses the point as we need to address it here—namely, that God seems disposed to use poetry in communicating with us concerning *who he is.*

As far as the extant records of all cultures can tell us, poetry is the first literature in any language. Typically, in cultures of which we have knowledge, poetry, whether epic or lyric, was sung, a characteristic of primeval as well as of children's verse.[5] Most children love rhymes, sung especially, and if not discouraged will make little poems of their own and present them to parents and friends as gifts. Songs, especially love songs, are still the staple poetry of popular cultures, and a majority of people will identify with favorites: "That's our song they're singing," we say. When a young man falls in love, he may wish to write love poems as gifts to his beloved. If he has not been entirely deprived of the pleasures of poetry, he may well attempt to write one, and work hard to make his poem worthy of his beloved. In turn, the beloved (whether the writer is a gifted poet or an amateur one) is likely to recognize his poem as a special kind of tribute, better than a Hallmark card.

What, then, is a poem, as distinct from prose? Succinctly, a poem is a certain form of words, sometimes rhythmic or musical in character, in which meaning arises indirectly, not only from the lexical denotation of its constituent words but also from a synthesis of rearrangement such that new insight or fresh appreciation results. For ancient writers it is essentially *alieniloquium,* saying things in an unexpected or strange way. Almost everyone recognizes, even if deprived by poor education of familiarity with poetry, that poetic speech is not merely different from normal speech, but that socially it is often

---

5. Alfred B. Lord's *The Singer of Tales,* ed. Stephen Arthur Mitchell and Gregory Nagy (Cambridge, MA: Harvard University Press, 1960; 2000), is the classic study.

intended as a "higher" way of communicating. There are analogues in other spheres of life. At festival seasons our tables may be furnished with tableware (such as fine china) that we don't use every day. Guests at such times, even if they have no personal liking for a beautifully set table or are intimidated by the challenge of which fork to pick up for the salad, will understand at once that this tableware has been "set apart" for special occasions, the best that the family's hospitality can offer. Things "set apart" (the literal meaning of Hebrew *qodesh*, "holy," is just that, "set apart") have the potential to elevate us all when we learn to understand and enjoy them as special gifts.

Most of us are unavoidably aware that there are unholy songs as well as holy ones, and, more innocuously, that there are lower and higher degrees of excellence in just about anything literary. Hardly anyone will fail to see that while "Roses are red, violets are blue, angels in heaven know I love you" and John Donne's "Valediction Forbidding Mourning" are both "valentines," so to speak, there is more poetic elegance and a higher pitch of feeling in Donne's declaration. So too in the matter of hymns; the 1950s Sunday school chorus "I'm so happy, and here's the reason why, Jesus took my burdens all away" expresses much the same gratitude for personal redemption as Charles Wesley's "And Can It Be" ("My chains fell off, my heart was free, I rose, went forth, and followed thee"), but few can fail to see that Wesley has written a better poem and, with it, attracted a finer musical setting.[6] The spirit in which these two hymns are sung may be equally authentic, certainly, but in elegance of expression and richness of theological understanding they are not interchangeable just because their sentiment is similar. Wesley's poem has attuned itself much more closely to the poetics of Scripture.

Wesley and Donne are excellent representatives of the biblically formed poetic imagination at work. But they are far from singular; the poets we will consider in this volume include many whose poetry is attuned to the way in which God speaks in Scripture, as well as to what Scripture represents him as saying. This has been true even when the poets have known the Bible not in Hebrew or English, but only in the Latin translation of Jerome in the medieval period (e.g., Dante). Others since the seventeenth century, having "heard" the poetry of divine speech through the unusually sensitive capturing of Hebrew parallelism and other poetic devices by the translators of the KJV, have probably had a clearer sense of it.[7] The influence of the KJV, as

6. Wesley's poem was set to the hymn tune "Sagina" (the Latin name of the flower dianthus) by Thomas Campbell, whose collection of twenty-three musical settings for hymns all have floral names—thus, *The Bouquet* (London, 1825).

7. David Lyle Jeffrey, ed., *The King James Bible and the World It Made* (Waco: Baylor University Press, 2011), introduction; also chap. 7 below.

we shall see, has been profound among poets both Jewish and Christian, as well as among many who were only nominally religious. This has enabled the best of our poets to offer a response to Scripture in many species, drawing on divine poetry to enrich English poetry in myriad ways. The chapters in this volume are intended to provide examples of this ongoing antiphonal, a selected brief anthology of English-speaking poets responding to the music of divine speech in Holy Writ. A subsequent volume will consider the divine poetry itself more closely, a task that will be more explicitly theological even though the methods will be, as here, those of literary analysis. We shall come to see, I think, that literary analysis ought properly to be part of a theological reading of Scripture, since *how* God chooses to speak is surely in itself a very important part of *what* he wishes to reveal to us about himself.

PART 1

MEDIEVAL POETRY
and the BIBLE

The first English poem of any kind to have come down to us is Caedmon's creation hymn, written in the late seventh century. Certainly among the very first instances of English being phonetically transcribed as a living literary language, its composition is notable for being recorded as a miraculous event by the Venerable Bede, the overnight creation by a previously unpoetic cowherd of an Old English poem in praise of the Creator and first Maker.

Nu sculon herigan *heofonrices Weard*
Now ought we to praise heavenly kingdom's Lord
Meotodes meahte *and his modgeþanc*
the Creator's power and his thought
wearc Wuldor-Fæder *swa he wundra gehwæs*
the work of the Glory-Father when he of wonders, every one
ece Drihten *or onstealde*
eternal Sovereign in the beginning established
He ærest sceop *ielda bearnum*
he first created for the sons of men
heofon to hrofe *halig Scyppend*
heaven as a roof; the holy Creator
ða middangeaerd *moncynnes Weard*
then Middle-earth, mankind's Guardian
ece Drihten *æftere teode*
eternal Sovereign afterwards made

| *firum foldan* | *Frea ælmihtig* |
| for humankind, | Master almighty.[1] |

The miracle, a sudden overnight gift of poetic inspiration to one who had long been embarrassed by being hitherto unable to take his turn at the harp in the mead hall (when the Anglo-Saxon Benedictine community after the evening meal still sang their ancient pagan poetry), is doubtless part of the reason Bede records it in his *Ecclesiastical History.*[2] We may imagine the astonishment the next morning when lowly Caedmon, his boots likely still carrying organic evidence of his occupation, was brought to the august and formidable Abbess Hilda. I imagine her rather skeptically folding her arms and saying something like, "Well, out with it," then melting like a judge at a talent show when something completely exceeds expectations—maybe not tearing up, but saying, "This is clearly of the Lord. One of you write this down." (I can also imagine her telling Caedmon, "Next time scrape your boots!")

Caedmon's experience is hardly the only reason for this homely but touching account of the Word from the beginning (*bereshit / en archē / in principium*) coming down to someone in a stable, though surely the parallel with Christ was noticed in retrospect. Bede and his fellow monks, fully able to sing hymns and psalms in Latin, had heretofore clearly associated divine poetry with the liturgy, and Anglo-Saxon poetry with the mead hall. Suddenly they experienced a kind of Pentecostal moment, a complete transformation of their expectations in which now their own mother tongue had become the vehicle for a poem, clearly admirable in its native Anglo-Saxon style, not celebrating pagan feats of death-dealing war but praising God as Creator and Sustainer of life. As in biblical Hebrew, in Caedmon's Old English there are many names for God; in only a few lines he is *Weard* (guardian or warden, from which is derived *hlaf-weard*, "loaf-warden," later contracted to *hlaford*, then to our word "Lord"), but also Creator, Glory-Father, Sovereign, Holy Designer (*halig Scyppend*), and Master Almighty. Notably, as Creator (the verb in Old English is *sceop*, from the noun *scop*, or "poet"), God is credited here with being the original Artist, the originator of everything, and said to have created all things for the "sons of men." Not only is this a sound compression

1. Text taken from *Medieval English: An Old English and Middle English Anthology*, ed. Rolf Kaiser (Berlin: Berlin-Wilmersdorf, 1954; 1961), 44; the translation is mine.

2. See David Lyle Jeffrey, *People of the Book: Christian Identity and Literary Culture* (Grand Rapids: Eerdmans, 1996), chap. 3; Bede, *Ecclesiastical History of the English People* 4.24, trans. Thomas Stapleton (London: Burns, Oates, and Washburne, 1935), 239–43; James H. Wilson, *Christian Theology and Old English Poetry* (The Hague: Mouton, 1974), 100–140.

of biblical theology; it reflects an understanding of God in which his divine "making" is the prompt for human making. *Sceop* is fully analogous here to Greek *poiitis* (from *poesis*) and Latin *poeta*.

Poetic paraphrase becomes a foundation stone in the building up of the English poetic tradition. One of the ways it manifests itself is in the rapid growth in Anglo-Saxon verse of various forms of biblical paraphrase, such as the so-called Caedmonian *Genesis A* and *Genesis B* poems, *Exodus* from the same Junius manuscript, and such slightly later works as the more personal and lyrical poem attributed to Cynewulf, *Christ and Satan*, a paraphrase retelling of Christ's temptation in the wilderness (Luke 4:1–14). Though a lyrical mode, influenced by the Psalms in Latin, begins to gather strength in compositions such as *The Advent Lyrics of the Exeter Book* and elegiac poems such as "The Wanderer" and "The Seafarer," the dominant works are, as is Caedmon's hymn, in characteristic four-stress line with alliteration and a mid-line caesura. Their subject matter is biblical or apostolic history. This vigorous tradition of poetic paraphrase extends into the late medieval retellings of the basic biblical narratives, which collectively were understood as the history of human salvation (*historia humanae salvationis*) from creation to doomsday, or the last judgment. Later works, such as the Middle English *Cursor Mundi* (fourteenth century), offer rhymed paraphrases of a large percentage of the Bible and were clearly used for vernacular instruction at a time when not all who wanted knowledge of the biblical grand narrative could be expected to read it in Latin.[3] The rhymed Middle English couplets of the *Cursor Mundi* made memorization of passages much easier.

Late in the fourteenth century there arose a more general concern regarding basic biblical instruction for those whose literacy in any language was marginal or nonexistent. This is where the present study begins in earnest, with a type of biblical paraphrase that is looser still, but that imaginatively transforms highlight stories from the history of salvation into theater, entertaining folk dramas of considerable sophistication, yet fully accessible to everyone. The Corpus Christi (or biblical cycle) plays survive in a rich array of regional examples, and while their attempts to render the biblical story accessible have varying degrees of success, to be sure, no account of the history of biblical poetry in English would be complete without a foray into this territory. In these plays biblical knowledge is communicated, and something of its poetry too, even though in some cases at considerable risk to theological precision. Despite that, as influential a scholastic theologian

---

3. Richard Morris, ed., *Cursor Mundi: Four Versions*, 3 vols., Early English Text Society Original Series 57, 59, 61 (London, 1874–76; repr., London: Oxford University Press, 1961–68).

as St. Bonaventure could affirm such plays as a light, a source of insight and understanding leading to theological truth.

Quotation from the Bible is, of course, found everywhere in the annals of English poetry, and with it what I have called here "inflection," by which I mean a digestion and incorporation of biblical text and teaching into a work of narrative poetry of wide-ranging complexity. In comparing the way in which Chaucer's *Canterbury Tales* and Dante's *Purgatorio* draw on the Sermon on the Mount (Matthew's and Luke's versions respectively), I intend to offer luminous examples of this mode of relation between Scripture and the poetic imagination from two of the greatest exemplars of the poetic imagination in all of Western culture. An effect of this comparison will be to reveal something of how thoroughly the Bible has become not just a source of religious conviction but a force shaping the overall poetic imagination of the English poet in particular.

The extent to which the Christian Scriptures are an intertextual presence in a poetry like Chaucer's is not fully measured, however, until we recognize the degree to which the Bible becomes a lens through which other texts, including classical pagan texts, are read and then themselves woven into the opus of the medieval Christian poet. St. Augustine's famous invitation in his *On Christian Doctrine* (2.40.60) to see that all truth is under the sovereignty of God and, accordingly, that true and worthy insights of the pagan poets and philosophers could rightly be incorporated into Christian interpretation was widely influential among medieval poets. What the great bishop referred to as taking "Egyptian gold" and employing it for the liberation of the Christian spirit on its journey toward God became a prompt to remarkably creative biblical allegorization of pagan works, even by authors such as Ovid, whose works in themselves contained much that was far from an encouragement to sanctification.

Chaucer was keenly aware of the propensity of an unrepentant heart to self-serving misreadings of the Bible; his *Canterbury Tales* is a masterful excursus into the way in which "every way of a man is right in his own eyes, but the LORD pondereth the hearts" (Prov. 21:2). But deliberate misreadings of Scripture, and an incapacity finally to comprehend irony and indirection as a pedagogy leading to truth and righteous life, are seldom illustrated so well as in the life of King Henry VIII. Henry was an avid reader of poetry and something of a would-be theologian, recognized as such by Pope Leo X for writing against Martin Luther's view of the sacraments (*Assertio Septem Sacramentis*). For this he was given the title "Defender of the Faith" by the pope, who was surely not the only one to regret that honor later. For his willfulness and serial adulteries Henry remains infamous; less well known are his attempts to edit the Bible in such a way as to remove such passages as might convict him of his sin. There is no sense, as we shall see, of the divine poetry and its majesty sufficient to temper this monarch's self-promoting tyranny; his story is one of those to which many a biblically informed poetic imagination has been a sorrowful witness.

two

PARAPHRASE AND THEATER

Bonaventure's Retracing the Arts
to Theology *and Literary Evangelism*

Anyone who has ever thought about the hazards of theatricality for presentation of the Gospel narratives will realize that it takes a very special sort of daring to face up to the challenge.[1] Too nice a liturgical conscience—or too rigid a sense of decorum—will shrink from embracing an uninhibited theatrical imagination in such a context.

A performance of an annual Christmas pageant in a West Coast Canadian evangelical church some years ago illustrates the point. One feature of the elaborate staging called for a man playing the part of an angel to be swung on a wire out above the singing choir, from whence he would proclaim a redoubtable "Fear not . . ." (etc.) to the shepherds below, just before the choir broke into some version or other of the *Gloria*.

Now it so happened that one Christmastide the traditional angel fell desperately ill with the flu at the last moment, and the company were hard put upon to discover a replacement. They lighted upon a newcomer to the church, a small man just about the size of the sick angel. Despite his protests that he had never done anything of the sort before and was a bit nervous of heights—indeed, that he was fairly new to churchgoing itself—they soon persuaded him that his brief

---

1. Part of this material is adapted from a longer, more technical study: David Lyle Jeffrey, "St. Francis and Medieval Theatre," *Franciscan Studies* 43, no. 21 (1983/1988): 321–46, used by permission.

lines would constitute little difficulty, and recruited him just in time for the first performance. Up in a high balcony, the substitute angel fastened his harness to the wire and, when his time came, let off on cue and came swooping down over the choir, gently flapping his artificial wings and saying, "Fear not" (etc.).

But it appears something was forgotten. His colleagues neglected to tell him that he was supposed to fasten the loop of a second wire to his ankle—not only to permit his being pulled back, but to keep from spinning at the end of the wire. It seems he did spin, and quite rapidly, even as he flapped his wings and spoke his lines. And, though the choir below him carried on with "Hark! the Herald Angels Sing," he continued to spin. After a stanza or two, his vertigo turned to nausea. He began to lose his appetite—all over the choir below him, or at least that portion of it within his involuntary, circling trajectory. Even so, the choir endeavored to keep singing, though some members were seen to clutch and brush at their hair and robes. The attention of the shepherds on the sight above was rapt. Finally the substitute angel could take it no longer (it is to be remembered that he was relatively new to churchy business), and he erupted into a series of expressions one does not normally associate with angels. This effusion was coupled with a repeated demand that he be gotten "out of" there. At this unfortunate moment, the pastor of the church staggered up, called for the lights, and pleaded with everyone to please go home and come back for the next night's performance.

This story may not at first seem to have very much to do with choirs of medieval monks solemnly intoning the *Iubilemus regi nostro* for the Latin *Play of Daniel*. Yet it suggests precisely the sort of imagination we must temporarily acquire if we are to understand the dominant, popular spirituality of the Franciscan movement and thus appreciate the legacy of St. Francis for popular culture—especially the theatrical arts. We must not think of the medieval Franciscan approach to proclaiming the gospel as conventional or "high church," but rather as if the friars were a kind of medieval combination of charismatic enthusiasm and the street wisdom of the Salvation Army. In such an imagination we may begin to appreciate how theater, with all of its risky business, may have appealed to the evangelical imagination of Francis of Assisi and his medieval followers.

There used to be an old evolutionary hypothesis about medieval vernacular drama whereby it was thought to have developed from Latin liturgical tropes in the Mass. That view has now been more or less put to rest.[2] Instead, scholars

2. O. B. Hardison, *Christian Rite and Christian Drama in the Middle Ages* (Baltimore: Johns Hopkins Press, 1965); V. A. Kolve, *The Play Called Corpus Christi* (London: Edward Arnold, 1966).

have come to believe that historical and textual records describe *two* distinct traditions for medieval drama, developing, from about 1140 on, concurrently with each other for approximately three hundred years.[3] We know of two notable early examples from vernacular tradition in the early Middle Ages. They are the Anglo-Norman *Jeu d'Adam* (between 1140 and 1175)[4] and the play of the nativity for which St. Francis requested permission for performance from the pope (1223).[5] Of these two, the *Jeu d'Adam* seems initially more useful to historians of medieval theater, not only because it is earlier but also because a substantial portion of its text survives. Yet, although the *Jeu d'Adam* models much of the technique and scope of the vernacular cycle drama that follows it, it stands almost alone in time, earlier by at least one hundred and fifty years than any comparable example in vernacular cycle history.[6] Moreover, it would seem to be a response to conditions fundamentally analogous to those which later produced an explosion of vernacular religious drama, first in Italy, then in Western Europe and England, from the second half of the thirteenth and especially through the fourteenth century.

At the beginning of this tradition it is possible to see the nativity play of St. Francis. For a number of reasons, the performance record of St. Francis's nativity play offers an equally useful point of departure in our quest to understand the tradition and development of later medieval theater. First, we know that at this time the Franciscans in Italy were already employing scriptural plays in their evangelical efforts.[7] Second, we know that, just as in their use of vernacular lyric,[8] Franciscans soon obtained the extensive involvement of laymen through the development of confraternities. The earliest annals of Italian *teatro religioso* are replete with Franciscan confraternity plays.[9] A third invitation to consider the rise of vernacular English drama in light

---

3. Kolve, *Play Called Corpus Christi*, 41.

4. *Le Mystère d'Adam*, ed. Paul Aebischer (Paris: Minard, 1964).

5. St. Bonaventure recounts the occasion: "Contigit autem anno tertio ante obitum suum, ut memoriam nativitatis pueri Jesu ad devotionem excitandam apud castrum Graecii disponeret ager, cum quanta maiori solemnitate valeret. *Ne vero hoc novitati posset ascribi*, a Summo Pontifice petita et obtenta licentia, fecit praeparari praesepium, apportari foenum, bovem et asinum ad locum adduci. Advocantur fratres, adveniunt populi, personat silva voces, et venerabilis illa nox luminibus copiosis et calris laudibusque sonoris et consonis et splendens afficitur et solemnis" (*Legenda Maior* [*Opera Omnia* 8:535, Quaracchi edition]).

6. David M. Parry, "The Play of Adam: Drama, Art, and Society in the Twelfth Century" (MA thesis, University of Victoria, 1974), esp. 1–5, 50–74.

7. See Arnaldo Fortini, *La Lauda in Assisi e le origini del teatro italiano* (Assisi: Edizioni Assisi, 1961).

8. See my *The Early English Lyric and Franciscan Spirituality* (Lincoln: University of Nebraska Press, 1975), 121–28.

9. Natalino Sapegno, ed., *Poeti Minori del Trecento* (Milan: Ricciardi, 1953), 1014ff. His examples are largely Franciscan and Franciscan confraternity pieces.

of Italian Franciscan models is provided by another discovery: in the field of the vernacular lyric, which so often lent itself to dramatic performance in the Middle Ages,[10] medieval Italian and English literary history are not only parallel but demonstrably connected.[11]

Franciscan Spirituality and Popular Culture

In all their early cultural activities the Franciscans are distinguished among their contemporaries for their attention to popular culture and to vernacular language as a means of transmitting biblical narratives.[12] St. Francis himself, proto-poet of the order, wrote hymns and songs in Provençal and in Umbrian rather than in Latin.[13] And following Francis's famous invitation to his followers to transform popular song into sacred melody, in Umbria and elsewhere in Italy lay brotherhoods of *laudesi* soon sprang up, providing employment for *jongleurs* and poets who, it has been said, "with more devotion than art, framed rude songs or dramatic pieces on the chief events of the Gospel story."[14] These pieces, often familiar secular tunes with new words, were sung by friars to attract crowds for a sermon, by the fraternal groups in session, and ultimately for the entertainment and devotion of middle-class households.

The Franciscans carried with them a passionate determination to harness popular culture as a medium for communicating the gospel. Examples in the field of vernacular verse extend to Germany and Hungary, where Franciscan Berthold von Regensburg by 1250 actively sought out vernacular composers

10. Cf. P. H. Lang, *Music in Western Civilization* (New York: W. W. Norton, 1941), 113–14. The greatest Franciscan "stabat" poem is the *Donna del Paradiso* of Jacopone da Todi. In about one-half of its extant copies it was incorporated into a Franciscan sermon, usually by a Franciscan. Several of these inclusions have directions for dramatic performance (see Vincenzo de Bartholomaeis, *Le origini della poesia drammatica italiana* [Bologna: Zanichelli, 1924], 249, 374, 375). R. W. Ingram has demonstrated that songs and musical accompaniment were grafted into the drama in the Shepherds' play and elsewhere ("The English Planctus Mariae," *Modern Philology* 4 [1907]: 15): "It is hardly going too far when we say that about one-fourth of the great body of material found in the York and Towneley cycles is, in the broad sense of the word, lyrical."

11. See Jeffrey, *Early English Lyric*; Jeffrey, "Forms of Spirituality in the Middle English Lyric," in *Imagination and the Spirit*, ed. Charles A. Huttar (Grand Rapids: Eerdmans, 1971), 55–85; and Jeffrey, "Franciscan Spirituality and the Elevation of Popular Culture," *Canadian Journal of History* 9 (1976): 1–18.

12. Jeffrey, *Early English Lyric*, chap. 1, "Forms of Spirituality."

13. J. R. H. Moorman, *The Sources for the Life of St. Francis* (Manchester, UK: Gregg Publishing, 1967), 17.

14. F. J. E. Raby, *A History of Christian-Latin Poetry from the Beginnings to the Close of the Middle Ages*, 2nd ed. (Oxford: Oxford University Press, 1953), 430.

for spiritual songs, asking that the songs be short (lyric) and accessible to learning by a child.[15] The Franciscans' instinct for preserving secular vernacular songs is persistent and results in a healthy admixture in many a medieval manuscript, including the major manuscripts of Middle English and Anglo-Norman lyric verse, for example, of which a large number are of Franciscan provenance.[16] Even the work of a poet such as Jacopone da Todi, who wrote in both Latin and the vernacular, is characterized in both languages by an affection for popular idiom and emotional affect. These qualities shape both style and content, so that in all the arts influenced by Franciscan spirituality, the ordinary, physical elements of common culture get portrayed as seldom before in Christian art. The justification for this emphasis on mundane reality arises not only from the middle-class roots of the poets, or from the Franciscans' desire to speak in the language of the common culture to which they ministered, but also from the spiritual and theological principles that defined the Franciscans' origin and calling. The two most important of these principles are those of spiritual *identification* with Christ and *redemption* of the ordinary world.

The most striking illustration of Francis's conviction that each Christian is called to a life of identification with Christ is not his detailed imitation of the *vita apostolica* and the poverty of Christ but, of course, the mimetic stigmata he is reported to have received on Monte Verna. For Francis, this ultimate identification with Christ's Passion was the acknowledgment of his response, already made, to a previous identification—that which God made with the world in sending Christ. That Christ was not only a man, but a poor working man, was the ground of many an ordinary layperson's identification. In Christ's becoming human, ordinary people, donkeys, sheep, straw, shepherds, and carpenters were elevated, recognized as being as worthy of the presence of the Son of God as any noble. When Francis runs to embrace the leper's sores, when he preaches to the birds, or when he gives his last rags to a beggar, he is on one level merely acknowledging an identification that Christ had already made with humble folk, even outcasts and the terminally ill.

Apart from the *Fioretti* and the *Speculum Perfectionis*, the Franciscan text that makes this double action of the spiritual principle of identification most clear is not a theological treatise, but a popular paraphrase of the Gospels, the

15. Franz Pfeiffer, ed., *Berthold von Regensburg: Vollständige Ausgabe seiner Predigten*, 2 vols. (1862–80; repr., Berlin: Dunker und Humbolt, 1965), 405–6.

16. See chap. 5, "*Ioculatores Dei* in England," in Jeffrey, *Early English Lyric*; also David Lyle Jeffrey and Brian J. Levy, eds., *The Anglo-Norman Lyric* (Toronto: Pontifical Institute of Mediaeval Studies, 1990; rev. 2nd ed. 2006).

Meditations on the Life of Christ.[17] It is also the Franciscan text of greatest influence on the arts. In addition to the partial translation of Robert Manning of Brunne, Richard Rolle used this work as the basis of his *Meditations on the Passion*; *The Privity of the Passion* is also an abridged prose translation (chaps. 74–92);[18] Nicholas Love translated it in 1400; and it was a substantial influence on the "Passion" of MS Jesus College Oxford 29.[19]

The most notable feature of the *Meditations*, in any of its versions, is its fusion of the affective, pious ideals of Franciscan spirituality with an attempt to transmit the essential gospel more realistically. A spirituality that encourages imaginative contact with the life of the Lord extends itself in this work to a more intimate affection for the ordinary things of life surrounding him. Besides noting a cast of cows, sheep, and chickens, the Franciscan author, John of the Cabbages, refers to such items as the actual table of the Last Supper, which he says he saw and measured at the Lateran Church in Rome (*Med.* 277). One Middle English translator faithfully transcribes the description of the table and the seating arrangements so as to show how it was physically possible for the whole company to eat from one dish on the night of Jesus' betrayal. Other examples of this sort of concretizing abound, and in illustrated versions of several manuscripts the drawings are characteristically concerned with common physical details and rendered with a high degree of verisimilitude. In the *Meditations*, as elsewhere in Franciscan popular literature, and explicitly in the Christology of its theologians,[20] a fuller identification with the human life of Christ thus intimates a higher estimation—indeed glorification—of everyday life and unprivileged human experience.

The theological connection between the principle of identification and the goal of the redemption of the ordinary world is thus direct, and really a matter of emphasis. The atonement is typically seen by the Franciscans as key to the possibility of salvation, but with a special emphasis on the reality of the incarnation, which made salvation possible. That is, in Franciscan

17. *Meditations on the Life of Christ: An Illustrated Manuscript of the Fourteenth Century*, ed. and trans. Isa Ragusa and Rosalie B. Green (Princeton: Princeton University Press, 1961).

18. John Edwin Wells, A Manual of the Writings in Middle English, 1050–1400 (New Haven: Connecticut Academy of Arts and Sciences, 1916), 358, 456; Robert Manning, Medytacyuns of þe soþer of pure lord theus, and also of hys passyun, ed. J. M. Cowper, Early English Text Society Original Series 84 (London, 1875).

19. Jeffrey, *Early English Lyric*, 210.

20. See, e.g., D. J. Unger, "Robert Grosseteste, on the Reasons for the Incarnation," *Franciscan Studies* 16 (1956): 1–37; also St. Bonaventure in *Tractatus de Praeparatione ad Missam* 1:10 (*Opera Omnia* 8:1026 [Quaracchi]); *Feria Sexta in parasc.*, Sermo I (9:259a); and *Dom. II post Pascha*, Sermo I (9:293a). See also Jean Bonnefoy, "La Question hypothèque: Utrum si Adam non peccasset [. . .] au XIII siècle," *Revista española de teologia* 14 (1954): 327–68, esp. 334–35.

theology and spirituality there is taken up a twelfth-century idea, formulated by St. Anselm, in which the fall, our fallen condition, is almost to be praised.[21] If Adam and Eve had not sinned, so the argument goes, there would have been no need for the greatest of human glories, the virgin birth. Christ's human nature, necessarily central if his sacrifice for humanity is to be substitutionary, thus came to be a primary emphasis in the imitative life of Francis and the spiritual style of his followers.

The dramatic narrative paraphrase of the gospel in the *Meditations* strongly resembles the unique presentation of the gospel story that occurs in medieval religious drama.[22] For example, the *Meditations* appears to be the direct source for most of the *Passion Play* of Arnoul Greban.[23] And the *Meditations* had a marked influence on English cycle drama, for the elements of the Gospel story covered in the *Meditations* find corresponding treatment in the Corpus Christi plays. The English cycles, in 75 (Chester) to 85 (Hegge) percent of their material, correspond to the balance and arrangement of these episodes in the *Meditations*. The general correspondence between the *Meditations* and the Hegge (*Ludus Coventriae*) cycle includes the favored Franciscan rewriting of Scripture (John 20:11–18), which has the resurrected Christ appear first to the Virgin Mary. But the influence of the *Meditations* is not limited to such examples; it has been shown, in fact, that several passages and whole plays depend—often line for line—on Nicholas Love's 1400 translation.[24] Just as the author of the *Meditations* sees biblical history in naturalized human terms, so every dramatic work he influenced seems to follow suit as a form of biblical paraphrase, conceiving the narrative of the Gospels especially by imagining its physical and emotional events. This in turn led to a high degree of vernacularity and attempted verisimilitude in theatrical enactments.

Bonaventure's *Retracing the Arts to Theology*

These apparently haphazard experiments in paraphrase had a remarkable theorizing in their favor. St. Bonaventure's *Retracing the Arts to Theology* is

21. St. Anselm, *Cur Deus Homo*; a modern translation is in *Trinity, Incarnation, and Redemption: Theological Treatises*, ed. J. Hopkins and H. Richardson (New York: Harper Torchbooks, 1970).

22. One might wish to include also the *Northern* and *Southern Passions* and the *Cursor Mundi*, for which mendicant authorship has been occasionally suggested.

23. See Eduard Wechssler, *Die romanische Marienklagen* (Halle, 1893), 66–74; also Ubald d'Alençon, "Le Jeu de la Passion par Arnoul Greban," *Études Franciscaines* 39 (1927): 286.

24. *Ludus Coventriae*, ed. K. S. Block, Early English Text Society Extra Series 120 (Oxford: Oxford University Press, 1922), xxiii–xxiv, lviii ff.

a theological treatise and short educational textbook that sets out to integrate all recognized forms of liberal and mechanical learning with the knowledge of God mediated through and revealed in the Bible. In detailing how his four lights to knowledge lead to the light of Sacred Scripture, Bonaventure, significantly, first considers the one that is most basic, the illumination of sense perception. This process, he says, concerns itself exclusively with the cognition of sensible objects and occurs in three phases: "cognoscendi *medium*, cognoscendi *exercitium*, cognoscendi *oblectamentum*."[25] If we consider the *medium* of perception, he says, we shall see therein the Word begotten from all eternity and articulated—made flesh, in time—because of generic, specific, or symbolic likeness to the Creator. Words inhere in the Word: in language and in vision the processes of creativity are analogous to the formulations of the Creator. When the contact between organ or faculty and object is established, there results a new perception, an image by means of which the mind reverts to the object. The *exercise* (*exercitium*) of sense perception reveals, accordingly, the normal patterns of human life. But the *delight* (*oblectamentum*) we have at such a moment opens us up to the union of the soul with God:

> Indeed, every sense seeks its proper sensible with longing, finds it with delight, and seeks it again without ceasing, because "the eye is not filled with seeing, neither is the ear filled with hearing" (Eccles. 1:8). In the same way, our spiritual senses must seek lovingly, find joyfully, and seek again without ceasing the beautiful, the harmonious, the fragrant, the sweet, or the delightful to the touch. Behold how the Divine Wisdom lies hidden in sense perception and how wonderful is the contemplation of the five spiritual senses in the light of their conformity to the senses of the body.[26]

The regard for sense perception expressed here is highly unusual, especially for the thirteenth century. It says that the spiritual senses not only may but *must* "seek longingly, find joyfully" the divine wisdom hidden therein. Sense perception begins in tactile delight and ends in transcendent delight, as language and desire retranslate, in tangible expression, the metaphor of the body. Bonaventure concludes by calling on all works of art and artifice— not only music and poetry, but such diverse human enterprises as medicine, navigation, and pharmacy—to illustrate the necessary harmony of creation and human creativity. Yet among all the arts that contribute to the "welfare of man," he says, "*theatrica, autem, est unica*" ("dramatic art, however, is

25. St. Bonaventure, *De Reductione Artium ad Theologiam*, ed. and trans. Emma Thérèse Healy, 2nd ed. (St. Bonaventure, NY: Franciscan Institute, 1955), 28, 30.
26. Bonaventure, *De Reductione Artium*, 50–51.

distinctive").[27] Notably, his view of the relationship of the arts to the needs of humanity helps to suggest what, for Bonaventure, leads to their evangelical virtue when they are practiced in the light of gospel imperatives:

> That these [arts] *suffice* is to be accepted [in this way]: every mechanical art is intended for man's *consolation* or his *comfort*; its purpose, therefore, is to banish either sorrow or want; it either *benefits* or *delights*, according to the words of Horace: "Either to profit or to delight is the wish of poets."

And again:

> "He has gained universal applause who has combined the profitable with the pleasing."
>   If its aim is to afford consolation and amusement, it is *dramatic art*, or the art of putting on plays, which embraces every form of entertainment, whether song, music, fiction, or pantomime.[28]

The quotations of Horace are far from disingenuous. While Bonaventure says that every (*omnis*) mechanical art is intended for human consolation or comfort, their purpose is to banish *either* sorrow or want—that is, to afford consolation—and they either benefit or delight "*secundum illud Horatii*." Dramatic art, he says, has the double aim of both consolation and amusement (*solatium et delectationem*). Dramatic art is unique in its ability to combine the two properties, and this is the true source of its special value, "to profit and to delight." It is clear that by *theatrica* Bonaventure means the art of exhibiting plays, and that this art embraces every form of entertainment (*omnem modum ludendi continens*)—song, music, fiction, and pantomime. And he explicitly states that the *delight* to be achieved in sense perception (whether of art or nature) leads to the union of the soul with God.[29] We may, then, reasonably draw two conclusions from Bonaventure's

27. Bonaventure, *De Reductione Artium*, 38.
28. "Quarum *sufficientia* sic accipitur. Quoniam omnis ars mechanica aut est ad *solatium*, aut ad *commodum*; sive aut est ad excludendam *tristitiam*, aut *indigentiam*; sive aut *prodest*, aut *delectat*, secundum illud Horatii:
     Aut prodesse volunt, aut delectare poetae.
     Et iterum:
     Omne tulit punctum qui miscuit utile dulci.
     Si est ad *solatium* et delectationem, sic est *theatrica*, quae est ars ludorem omnem modum ludendi continens, sive in cantibus, sive in organis, sive in figmentis, sive in gesticulationibus corporis." (*De Reductione Artium*, 38–40)
29. *De Reductione Artium*, 31: "By the same process of reasoning is Divine Wisdom to be found in the illumination of the mechanical arts, the sole purpose of which is the *production of works of art*. In this illumination we can see the *eternal generation*, and *Incarnation of the*

statements about art, and particularly about what he calls *theatrica*. The first is that the arts identified may act as a *speculum* (mirror) of the divine revelation in the same manner as Scripture or nature, and in such a case are subject to similar exegetical study. Second, drama, music, and lyric (*cantus*) legitimately function according to the threefold purpose of scriptural and natural revelation: to demonstrate the "eternal Incarnation of the Son of God," to illustrate the "pattern of human life," and to orient us toward the ultimate evangelical objective of "union of the soul with God." Bonaventure gives us, in short, a pedagogical theory of dramatic art entirely consistent with everything we know about the Franciscans' commitment to vernacular paraphrase of the Scriptures, especially as it appeared in English biblical plays of the fourteenth century.

Sermons Dramatized

In reaching the world of common folk, the more normative instrument of Franciscan pedagogy was naturally the sermon. In a spirit encouraged by the Fourth Lateran Council of 1215 and subsequently reconfirmed by proclamations such as Franciscan Archbishop of Canterbury John Pecham's *Lambeth Constitutiones* in 1273,[30] friars and other preachers built into their sermon notes vernacular lyrics to heighten the effect of their preaching.[31] The point of these vernacular pieces was to provide memorable instruction for layfolk in the articles of the faith such as the Apostles' Creed, the Pater Noster, the Seven Vices and Seven Virtues, and the Works of Mercy.[32] Yet these vernacular insertions, it appears, were not only catchy verses to be sung or read. Some were longer, more complex, and clearly theatrical.

When poetic dialogue could be adapted to some form of enactment, it seems to have developed into a subspecies of homily. The *sermone semidrammatico*, as it came to be called in Italian, was often an extended vernacular lyric in which dialogue—for example, between Christ on the cross, Mary, and John—was supported by representation and characterization. In most

---

Word, the *pattern of human life*; and the *union of the soul with God*. And this is true if we consider the *production*, the *effect*, and the *advantage* of the work, or if we consider the *skill of the artist*, the *quality of the effect produced*, and the *utility of the advantage to be derived therefrom*."

30. Jeffrey, *Early English Lyric*, 188.

31. See Étienne de Bourbon, *Anecdotes historiques, légends, et apologues*, ed. A. Lecoy de la Marche, Société de l'histoire de France (Paris, 1877), 479–80.

32. *Speculum Christiani*, ed. Gustaf Holmstedt, Early English Text Society Original Series 182 (London: Oxford University Press, 1933), 6.

instances the parts were likely mimed, with a narrator-preacher reading all the parts while the action was portrayed below him and before the audience.[33] In Italy there are records of situations in which such activity is incorporated into a friar's sermon as a kind of living Gospel, with intermittent retirements by the actors and a return to homiletical exposition by the narrator-friar.[34]

Among a substantial number of Italian examples of the more highly articulated dramatic sermon-poems, two or three models emerge for illuminating comparison with examples from the rising English vernacular drama. For example, in Franciscan Codex 36-IV di S. Stefano, a confraternity manuscript, there occurs a set of sermon notes that contain a typical "trialogue" poem—Christ, a sinner, and Mary—which, though sketched incompletely, nevertheless has rubrics indicating impersonation and performance.[35] The poem resembles the common variety in which Christ debates with his sorrowful mother from the cross, but here the repentant sinner also enters the conversation to invoke the aid of Mary as mediatrix in his plea for mercy.[36] Interjected between some of the stanzas and fragments are directions for "voicing," such as "*Qui parla Christo a la sua madre*" or "*Qui parla Christo e alloca peccatori.*"

Another poem, from the Assisian Codex 656, is a long dramatic piece in which the directional rubrics and general internal flow seem to indicate that the friar who was preaching probably played the role of Christ himself, addressing the specific weaknesses of various kinds of *peccatori*.[37] In the Assisian poem the narrative line changes from third person at the opening to the first-person singular, exactly in the manner of a similar, Middle English poem from MS Harley 913, the Kildare book.[38] One soon sees how effective the addition of such dramatization to the homiletical enterprise might be. The Assisian poem, much longer, concludes in the manner of English Lazarus and Judgment plays, with those who represent the damned being led off into hell by the devil in a snake dance called "the devil's dance."[39] This spectacle conjures up a scene reminiscent of the Franciscan wall painting at St. John's,

33. De Bartholomaeis, *Le origini della poesia drammatica italiana*, 382.

34. See de Bartholomaeis, *Le origini della poesia drammatica italiana*, 373.

35. Fortini, *La Lauda in Assisi*, 279.

36. A good Italian example is edited by de Bartholomaeis, *Laude drammatiche e rappresentazioni sacre* (Florence, 1943), I:7ff.; cf. Grimestone's poem in *Religious Lyrics of the XIVth Century*, ed. Carleton Brown, 2nd ed., revised by G. V. Smithers (Oxford: Oxford University Press, 1957), 85.

37. Fortini, *La Lauda in Assisi*, 280ff. This is in the six-line stanza, which is the most popular following the four-line *a a a X*.

38. W. Henser, ed., "Die Kildare Gedichte," *Bonner Beiträge zur Anglistik* 14 (1904): 128ff.

39. Fortini, *La Lauda in Assisi*, 290.

Winchester,[40] and it is interesting that a similar dance highlights the morality play *Wisdom*, from the Digby and Macro manuscripts.[41]

Another such sermon, for Holy Thursday, survives in three copies. It takes for its theme the *amore langueo* ("I am sick with love") theme of the Canticles (Song of Songs). At a certain point the preacher is instructed to cease his discursive exposition and to intone the *lauda*, "*Venete tucte, o creature grate*" ("Come ye thankful people, come"). At the conclusion of his song comes the following instruction: "*Qui se vol fare un poco de pietoso exordio, dirigendo li dire, recorrendo alla Croce, colle seguenti stantie*" ("Here, if you wish to exhort them to piety, direct them to follow the Cross according to the following steps"). After four stanzas more of the song are sung by the *oratore*, the preaching resumes, only to be interrupted a little later at the point where Christ "*era menato alla Croce in colla*," where again the *oratore* sings (or speaks) several more stanzas taken from the *Donna del Paradiso* (of Jacopone da Todi). Here the manuscript adds an instruction: the stanzas should be spoken "*pietosamente et con cordiali lacreme*" (literally, "piteously and with heartfelt tears"), and it is clear that the intonations involve further dialogue. In many of these "sermons" the specific directions make it impossible to mistake the representational nature of the performance, and in several cases

40. See plate no. VI in A. G. Little, *Franciscan History and Legend in English Medieval Art* (Manchester, UK: Manchester University Press, 1939), chap. 1.

41. In *Wisdom*, the seven sins, pseudo-named for the traditional Seven Deadly Sins, are called in by the degenerate Mind to dance an inverted dance, the portent of which Mind is at that moment not fully aware:

> let se, com In, Indignacion and sturdynesse,
> Malyce also and hastynesse,
> wreche and discorde expresse,
> And the vijth am I, mayntenaunce.
> Vij is a nombyr of discorde and imperfightnesse,
> lo, her' is a yomanry with loveday to dresse,
> And the deuyll had swore it, their wold bere vp falsnesse,
> And mayntyn it at the best; this is the develys daunce;
> and here menstrellys be conuenyent,
> ffor trompys shulld blowe to the Iugement;
> of batayle also it is one instrument,
> yevyng comfort to fight;
> therfor thei be expedient
> to these meny of mayntement,
> blow sett, se madame regent,
> and daunce, ye laddes, your hertes ben light!

The Digby Plays, ed. F. J. Furnival, Early English Text Society Extra Series 70 (London, 1896), 164. Apparently in the same tradition is the powerful poem by the Scottish observant Franciscan friar William Dunbar, called simply "The Dance of the Sevin Deidly Synnis" (*The Poems of William Dunbar*, ed. W. Makay Mackenzie [London, 1932; repr., Edinburgh: The Mercat Press, 1990], 120–23).

it appears as though parts were actually spoken or sung by designated players. In the semidramatic sermon, however, the preacher typically retained the prominent role as narrator and acted as a control on the action.[42] Nonetheless, in such cases regular preaching seems to have assumed a secondary role to that of the performance, a performance which consisted of a succession of static scenes controlled and perhaps unified by the intermittent commentary of the preacher.

The dialogue poems that in Italy are most often preserved with "staging directions" are versions of Jacopone da Todi's *Donna del Paradiso* and "*De compassione Filii ad Matrem tempore Passionis sue.*"[43] The latter poem survives in a representative text in a manuscript from the Franciscan confraternity at Santa Croce, Urbino. It is of the late thirteenth century, though probably composed in its original form much earlier, and in the Umbrian dialect. The dialogue alternates between Christ and the Virgin:

> *Mamma, come dolore de morte,*
> *me pare forte lo planto che fait*
> (Mamma, with the sadness of death,
> it seems the plan has been strongly made)
> . . . .
> *Le plage che lo mio corpo ha de fore*
> *tu l'hai in core, o Mamma pietosa. . . .*
> (The pain I have in my body
> you have in your heart, holy Mother. . . .)
> *O figlio mio*
> *Iesu, tu se crucifisso*
> *por l'omo salvare. . . .*
> (O my son
> Jesus, you are crucified
> for the salvation of mankind. . . .)[44]

Not all the Italian preaching manuscripts containing *sermoni semidrammatici* preserve explicit directions or even complete poems. But both those manuscripts that are relatively complete in text and rich in directions and those that are fragmentary bear a great deal of resemblance to the English

42. Quoted in de Bartholomaeis, *Le origini della poesia drammatica italiana*, 378.
43. See n. 10 above.
44. De Bartholomaeis, *Laude drammatiche*, I:7–9 (my translation). Copies of this poem occur in *laudari* of Siena and Pisa, and there are direct similarities in about twelve poems of the Jacopone school. De Bartholomaeis claims to perceive in the Urbino manuscript the direct influence of St. Bonaventure (p. 4).

homiletical collections in which we find the majority of the Middle English lyrics of the dramatic type.[45] Among them is the "Stond, wel, moder" from Franciscan manuscript Digby 86,[46] a poem clearly influenced by Jacopone's poems. One of the Franciscan friar John Grimestone's poems, also a dialogue between Christ and the Virgin at the cross, goes so far as to separate its stanzas according to the person speaking, and to indicate that person with a "Ihesu" or "Maria" in exactly the manner of a careful dramatic text.[47] If the poems' ascriptions of voice are assumed to be functional, then Grimestone's cross poem, also found in a collection of sermon materials, could well have been performed dramatically in the same manner as several Italian poems from *semidrammatico* sermons.

There are other elaborate examples in English texts of the genre *sermone semidrammatico*.[48] One occurs in Sloane MS 2478, from the early fourteenth century. The sermon was preached in a Palm Sunday procession at Wells Cathedral, perhaps as early as 1300,[49] and is remarkably similar to Italian prototypes. It is clearly meant to be a dramatic performance, though a mono-logue, and begins with the performer on a platform or some raised object:
He says:

Alle hayle and wel y-met	All hail and well met!
Alle ȝee shulleþ beo þe bet	You'll all be better off
Nou icham y-come	Now that *I* am here!
Blysful and blyþe ȝee mowe boe	Blissful and cheery you ought to be
Such a prelat her y-soe	When you see such a fine prelate
I-tolled to þis trone	As me called to this diocese.
ȝe boeþ wel wery aboute y-go	You must be getting weary of this parade

45. E.g., the various manuscripts of the *Fasciculus Morum* (MS Laud Misc. 111, MS Bodleian 416, etc.), the Kildare MS (MS Harley 913), the *Speculum Christiani* (MS Harley 7322), and John Grimestone's Commonplace Book (MS Avocates 18.7.21).

46. Carleton Brown, ed., *English Lyrics of the XIIIth Century* (Oxford: Oxford University Press, 1962), 86.

47. Brown, *Religious Lyrics of the XIVth Century*, 85. The first eight lines in the text from MS Sloane 2593 (T. Wright, *Songs and Carols* [London: Percy Society, 1856], 13, 38–39) are assigned to John Grimestone.

48. It has been printed, in another context, by Carleton Brown, ed., *Anniversary Papers by Colleagues and Pupils of George Lyman Kittredge: Presented on the Completion of His Twenty-Fifth Year of Teaching in Harvard University, June, MCMXIII* (Boston: Harvard University Press, 1913; repr., 2012), 105–17. A deficient edition is in Thomas Wright and J. O. Halliwell, *Reliquae Antiquae* (London, 1841), 241–45.

49. Brown, *Anniversary Papers*, 110, 113–17. Brown adduces evidence for a southwest dialect, though there are mixed forms to indicate transmission.

So icham my sulf al so	(I'm a little pooped myself).
Ich bysschop Cayface	I am bishop Caiphas.
Ich moste her sone synge	I must sing pretty soon now
þe prophecye of heuen kynge	the prophecy of heaven's King
þat whyle ich seyde by grace	which I may say by grace. . . .
þy stondeþ a stounde and bloweþ breþ	Hey! you that stand a minute and catch your breath . . .
And ȝif icham as ȝee soeþ	if I am as you see
Ichulle bere me bolde	I'll be bold about it
And synge ȝou sone a lytel song	And sing you soon a little song
Ha schal boe schort and no þyng long	—It'll be short and no way long—
þat raþer ichadd y-tolde	Let me tell you:
Ich was bysschop of þe lawe	I was the "bishop" of the law
þat ȝer þat crist for ȝou was slae	who arranged it that Christ was slain for you.
ȝe mowe boe glade perfore	You ought to be glad therefore!
Hit com to slþe þat ich þo sayde	Remember what I said?
Betere hit were þat o man deyde	It were better that one man died
þan al molk were y-lore expedit et cetera.[50]	than all the people were lost etc. etc.

A portion of the poem in Caiphas's voice seems to be omitted in this text, but it is abundantly clear that the speaker has deliberately assumed the *role* of Caiphas the high priest, and that the things he says about himself in that role correspond to the claims of Caiphas in English cycle plays. The impersonation has been but a prelude to something else that the speaker has in mind. He continues:

Ichot ȝe mowe nouȝt longe dwelle	I know you can't stay long at this spot
þy are ȝe go ichow wol telle	but before you go I want to tell you
of crist ane litel tale	one little tale of Christ
And of ȝour palm þe bereþ an honde	and of the palms you bear in hand.
Ich schal habbe leue ich onder stonde	I would have you understand
of grete men & smale	something, whatever your status.
A welsooþ so lich ys seyd	There is an apt saying we have:
Ech god game ys god y-pleyd	*Each good game is well played.*
Louelych ant lyȝt ys leue	*Lovely and light is love.*

50. Brown, *Anniversary Papers*, 105–6 (my translation).

þe Denes lette and alle manne	I have the Dean's permission
To rede and synge ar ich go hanne	to counsel you and sing before I go,
Ich bydde þat ȝon ne grene	I ask you! Please don't groan.

He then launches into his homily. It is noteworthy that the preacher has acknowledged permission from the dean of the cathedral—a requisite for mendicant preachers who wished to address a local congregation, and something that would have been unnecessary for secular clergy. Suddenly the Latin sermon notes break off again (possibly in anticipation of restlessness in the crowd), and "Cayface" resumes his role:

Welcome boe ȝee: þat stondeþ aboute	Welcome to you that stand about
þat happeþ y-siwed þis grete route	who have followed this long trek—
Sone ychulle ȝou synge	now soon I'll sing.
ȝou alle today ic mot y-mete	I must meet you all today
Ichabbe leue of þe grete	for I have special leave
Wysdom for to wrynge	to wring out a bit of wisdom.
A bysschop ich was in cristes tyme [. . .]	A bishop I was in the time of Christ [. . .]

(37–48)

The role continues for twenty-one six-line stanzas, with four more interruptions for exposition indicated in the text. In the course of his performance the preacher is able to work in a sermonette on the three foes of man—world, flesh, and devil—from whom the audience is finally urged to flee, along with the Seven Deadlies. He then goes on to explain to the "lewede þat bereþ palm an honde / þat nuteþ what palm ys tonderstonde" ("people that carry palm branches in their hands / but don't understand the significance of it"), and when at last he is done he favors the congregation with another song, unrecorded (a small note reads "*Cantat expedit*"), which he apparently sings from a book.[51]

Ich moste synge & þa go
Schewe me þe bok þat ic hadde þo
   þe song schal wel an hey
Ich may noȝt synge hym al bi rote
Vorto tele eche note
   Ny boeþ y-nome wel ney. (lines 145–50)

51. Jeffrey, *Early English Lyric*, chaps. 5 and 6.

After finishing the song, the preacher urges his contrite congregation to confess to Simon, his companion, swiftly, before the bell rings. At last he invites his audience to join in singing again the burden or chorus of his final song.

The resemblance of this performance to some of the Italian Franciscan dramatized homiletical pieces is obvious. Moreover, there are a number of reasons for believing this particular Middle English dramatic sermon to have been, like most of its Italian cousins, of Franciscan provenance. They are as follows: first, the preacher was one of a pair, of which one "cumpayngnoun" had the duty of confession, the other of preaching; second, they obtained permission from the dean to preach and hear confession; third, the educational nature of the sermon entirely accords with Franciscan homiletical programs and hermeneutical values;[52] fourth, this dramatic sermon as a whole is of a kind with the Italian Franciscan examples I have here (and more fully elsewhere)[53] surveyed; and finally, the theological miscellany that precedes the *Caiphas* sermon in MS Sloane 2478 contains several specifically Franciscan tales.[54]

It is interesting in this context that the Friars Minor had come to England in 1224, before the vernacular drama had really gotten under way in Italy, and at a time when most of the clerical response to the theatrical arts was still traditionally negative. For example, in 1244, Robert Grosseteste, spiritual father to the English Franciscans, was having difficulties with parish priests who allowed "inordinate and lascivious" celebration in connection with the performance of pageants for May Day and autumn festivals.[55] Robert Manning was harsh in

52. Jeffrey, *Early English Lyric*, chap. 2.

53. See my "English Saints' Plays," in *Medieval Drama*, ed. Neville Denny, Stratford-upon-Avon Series (London: Arnold, 1973), 69–90.

54. E.g., fol. 14b, in which the dying Count of Rimini, unable to swallow, receives the viaticum through his side, said by "sancte memorie frater Petrus de Suynesfold"—seventh Minister of the Franciscans in England—to have occurred when he and "frater Adam de Maddol" were passing through Rimini about 1268; fol. 17b, St. Anthony and the archer; fol. 30, St. Anthony is saved from tormenting fiends by a light from heaven; fol. 35b, a demoniac is questioned at Corinth by two Franciscans on St. Mary Magdalene's Day, about 1266; etc. Most of the other stories are from the *Vitae Patrum*; also included is a life of St. Alexis (fols. 39–42b). No Dominican or Dominican legend is mentioned in this collection.

It is also interesting to note in a sermon of St. Bernardino for Holy Week, "*Primae Partis Principalis Passionis Christi,*" the extensive treatment of the Caiaphas story, in which Bernardino has the high priest ranting, raving, stamping, crying "Blasphemy!," appealing to the Old Law, and wishing to strike Christ—all probably supported by energetic gestures and mimicry in the usual Bernardino manner, as in the Caiaphas sermon and role in the cycles—e.g., the Towneley cycle (lines 204–8 [Quaracchi]).

55. In a circular to the archdeacons of the Diocese of Lincoln, p. 311 of *Epistolae Roberti Grosseteste*, ed. H. R. Luard (Rolls Series, 1861). Harold Goad (*Greyfriars: The Story of St. Francis and His Followers* [London: Westhouse, 1947], 168ff.) suggests that Grosseteste urged the Franciscans to take charge of the plays as early as 1224. I can find no adequate support for this statement.

his criticism in his *Handlyng Synne*.[56] But if we examine Manning's statement, we find that it is primarily secular amusements in the form of tournaments, dances, carols, and general summer ribaldry that he denounces, and those miracle plays that represent the nativity and the Passion only when not acted in the church. That is, his condemnation, like his warnings against *ioculatores* (comedians, jugglers, and wandering players), is qualified; he accepts drama whose licensed religious purpose is assured. Similarly, the Franciscan author of the *Liber exemplorum* vigorously condemns, not all plays, but *ludi inordinati*;[57] to be sure, his description makes it quite clear that some medieval *ludi* (carnival plays) could with propriety be considered quite "inordinate." He too accepts drama whose motive is religious instruction of the laity.

There are, of course, risks attendant upon any effort to instruct the laity by means of biblical paraphrase interspersed with elements of commentary, even when not offered on stage in a context where the temptations of entertainment may prove too much to resist. One of these performance temptations is unintended burlesque, which in many of the biblical plays was in fact a staple element of the entertainment. In the *Second Shepherds' Play* (there are two in the Wakefield cycle), we see an example in which the meaning of Jesus' nativity for the shepherds, especially as imagined by contemporary equivalents in the Christian community seeking to hold their audience by means of humor, seems almost to eclipse the basic Lukan narrative. This happens because of a subplot in which a sheep stealer named Mak, despite the attempted vigilance of the true shepherds he befriends, escapes with a lamb and gets his rough-and-ready wife, Gill, to hide it under swaddling clothes in a cradle when the shepherds come looking for it. Mak and Gill pretend the lamb is their newborn, and Gill protests their innocence by saying,

> I pray to God so mylde,
> If euer I you begyld,
> That I ete this chylde
> That legys in this credyll.[58]

—precisely, of course, her intention. But when the neighborly and charitable affections of the shepherds cause them to look closely at the "baby" in the crib, they are comically aghast:

56. Edited by F. J. Furnivall, Early English Text Society Original Series 119, 123 (London: Oxford University Press, 1903).
57. A. G. Little, *Liber exemplorum ad usum praedicantium*, British Society of Franciscan Studies I (Aberdeen, 1908), 109–11.
58. *The Wakefield Pageants in the Towneley Cycle*, ed. A. C. Cawley (Manchester, UK: Manchester University Press, 1958), 57.

> 3 Pastor. Gyf me leve hym to kys, and lift up the clowt. *(peeps)*
>   What the dewill is this? He has a long snowte!
>   Saugh I neuer in a creydyll
>   A hornyd lad or [before] now. (58–59)

The shepherds threaten to have Mak hanged, but mercifully settle for tossing him in a blanket while he shrieks and howls—uproariously entertaining in a carnivalesque manner. They then go on their way with the recovered lamb, and almost immediately look up to see and hear the angel's joyful annunciation "to men with whom God is pleased" of the Savior who is also the chosen Lamb of God; this they are called upon to go and check out for themselves. The intent of the playwright is clear enough; the juxtaposition of the false lamb/child with the true Lamb/Child not only retells the Lukan narrative in paraphrase but simultaneously warns about false shepherds and injurious substitutes for God's gift to the world. The play ends with the shepherds going their way and worshiping the newborn Savior, singing in three-part harmony the praises of God's glory in imitation of the angel's *Gloria in excelsis Deo*.

There was plenty here for a biblical purist not to like. It has been noted that categorical opposition to the plays "came not from the heads of the Church, but from its heretics."[59] Heretics or not, the most vocal of the opponents seem to have been the Wycliffites, who appear to have been responsible for *A Tretise of Miraclis Pleyinge* and *On the Minorite Friars*, both of which appeared before 1400.[60] These two utterly negative Wycliffite accounts indicate both that the Franciscans were deeply involved in drama and that the pedagogical principles of the Franciscans were directly served in the functions claimed for vernacular drama.

The Wycliffite author of *A Tretise of Miraclis Pleyinge* clearly identifies six claims of value set forth by proponents for the plays, each of which he wishes to counter. The first claim is "that they pleyen these myraclis in the worschip of God"; second, "ofte sithis by siche myraclis pleyinge ben men convertid to gode lyvynge"; third, "ofte sythis by siche myraclis pleyinge men and wymmen, seynge the passioun of Crist and of hise seyntis, ben movyd to compassion and devociun, wepynge bitere teris"; fourth, "also, prophitable to men and to the worschipe of God it is to fulfille and sechen alle the menes by the whiche men mowen seene synne and drawen hem to vertues; and sythen

59. E. K. Chambers, *The Medieval Stage* (Oxford: Clarendon, 1903), 2:102.
60. The first is edited in Thomas Wright and J. O. Halliwell, *Reliquae Antiquae*, lines 42–57; the second appears in *Monumenta Franciscana*, ed. J. S. Brewer (Rolls Series, 1858), line 606ff. Other editions are listed by Laurence Craddock, OFM, "Franciscan Influences on Early English Drama," *Franciscan Studies* 10 (1950): 398–99.

as ther ben men that only be ernestful doynge wylen be convertid to God, so ther been othere men that wylen be convertid to God but by *gamen and play*";[61] fifth, "summe recreatioun men moten han, and *bettere it is* or lesse yvele *that thei han theyre recreacoun by pleyinge of myraclis* than *bi pleyinge of other japis*"; and finally, "sithen it is leveful to han the myraclis of God peyntid, why is not as wel leveful to han the myraclis of God pleyed, sythen man mowen bettere reden the wille of God and his mervelous werkis in the pleyinge of hem than in the peyntynge, and betere thei ben holden in mennus mynde and oftere rehersid by the pleyinge of hem than by the pentynge, for this is a deed bok the tother a quick."[62] These claims, however disputed in this text, accord with the Franciscans' evangelical ideal of affective piety as illustrated vividly in the *Meditations on the Life of Christ*.

The other notable fourteenth-century attack on drama specifically links it with the Friars Minor.[63] *On the Minorite Friars* begins with this refrain:

> Of thes frer mynours me thenkes moch wonder,
> That waxen are thus hauteyn that som tyme weren under,
> Amonge men of holy chirch thai maken mochel blonder
> Nou he that sytes vs aboue make ham sone to sonder.[64]

The Wycliffite poet then begins to list his specific charges against the "frer mynours," most of which relate to dramatic performances conducted under their auspices. The first stanzas indicate that a Passion play or crucifixion scene from a cycle drama might be involved:

> First thai gabben [mock] on God that alle men may se
> When thai hangen hom on hegh on a grene tre,
> With leues and wit blossomes that bright are of ble,
> That was neuer Goddes Son by my leute.
> With an O and an I, men wenen that thai wede
> To carpe so of clergy, thai can not thair crede.

The balance of the stanza describes wings that appear on the Crucified. If we remember the Franciscan penchant for adding apocalyptic prefiguration to the details of the Passion, this scene represents another example of built-in commentary. In Franciscan lyric poems, details of Jesus' crucifixion could be

---

61. Cf. John Mirk and the *Dives et Pauper*, quoted in Kolve, *Play Called Corpus Christi*, 5 (italics added).

62. *Reliquae Antiquae*, lines 45–46.

63. See n. 58 above.

64. *Monumenta Franciscana*, line 606.

neatly woven into passages from the Apocalypse; in a related example, the drawing made by Brother William for the illustrated Apocalypse so prized by Matthew Paris depicts a Christ who has the apocalyptic wings of Isaiah's seraph.[65] In fact, the association of the Apocalypse and last judgment with the scene of the Passion is a commonplace in medieval English Franciscan poetry.[66] For the Wycliffite author, the problem is simply that the symbolism and iconography are not present in the biblical text itself.

Finally, in another performance on the same occasion, the poet has apparently observed a saint's play (not now extant):

> Went I forther on my way in that same tyde,
> Ther I sawe a frere blede in mydds of his syde,
> Bothe in hondes and in fete had he woundes wyde.
> To serve to that same frere the Pope mot abyde,
> With an O and an I, I wonder of thes dedes
> To se a Pope holde a dishe whyl the frer bledes.
> A cart was made al of fyre as it shuld be,
> A Gray frere I saw ther inne that best lyked me.
> Wele I wote thai shal be brent by my leaute,
> God graunte me that grace that I may it se.

The play involved here would not have been in any sense a paraphrase of Scripture such as was normative to the biblical cycle plays. Rather, it appears to have portrayed the stigmatization of St. Francis, and the pope who holds the dish recalls Pope Gregory IX's vision of the stigmatized saint after Francis's death.[67] The only scene that appealed to the Wycliffite—the sight of a Grey Friar in a burning chariot—indicates his ignorance, willful or actual, of another feature of Franciscan hagiography: the fiery assumption of the saint's spirit in the manner of the story of Elijah and Elisha—also recorded by Bonaventure[68]—and Francis's mystical appearance in a fiery chariot to his brethren at Rivo Torto. What the Wycliffites propose, in effect, is a standard by which the Bible itself must be represented more or less literally, and saints' legenda accordingly excluded. This would become a position of the Reformers in the sixteenth century as well, and it would extend to the Puritan closing of all theaters in the seventeenth century.

65. A. G. Little, *Franciscan Papers, Lists, and Documents* (Manchester, UK: University of Manchester Press, 1943), 19. Bonaventure refers to Francis as the "angel of the sixth seal" in the Apocalypse.
66. Jeffrey, *Early English Lyric*, chaps. 5 and 6.
67. See St. Bonaventure, *Legenda Maior* (*Opera Omnia* 8:550 [Quaracchi]).
68. St. Bonaventure, *Legenda Maior* (*Opera Omnia* 8:513–14 [Quaracchi]).

Conclusion

The legacy of Franciscan attempts at biblical paraphrase in the medieval English biblical plays and sermons is undeniably characterized by a hyperbolic, folksy style and sometimes overzealous appeal to popular audiences. But by all accounts, these plays and sermons were effective. If theatricality seems to us to be a risky way to preach the gospel (and it surely must have seemed that way to many among the Dominican preachers and regular clergy), for Francis and his followers it was consistent with other risks they were wont to take. We should not lightly equate this risk-taking with naïveté. Rather, we should more wisely see that it proceeds from confidence in the sovereignty of God and in the power of grace released in the incarnation—grace sufficient to redeem all our most homely mischief and ineptitude, witting and unwitting.

three

QUOTATION AND INFLECTION

Dante and Chaucer on the Sermon on the Mount

While biblical knowledge among the less literate continued through-out the medieval centuries to be acquired largely through various forms of paraphrase and visual imagery, among more literate layfolk the text of the Bible became gradually more accessible, especially in Latin but also through vernacular translations. One effect of this shift was to make the Bible familiar to Christian poets in a fashion comparable to the textual familiarity they enjoyed with classical Roman texts. Just as the poetry of Virgil, Statius, Ovid, and Horace was part of the literary legacy of learned poets, so too, by degrees, the texts of Scripture became more precisely part of late medieval literary experience and intellectual furniture, acquired to different degrees and divergent effects, in different parts of Europe. Poets familiar with Roman grand narrative as found in the *Aeneid* and with Christian *historia humanae salvationis* as sketched out in the Bible—and commentary on them, such as Augustine's *City of God*—found ample reason to borrow as well as contrast and compare in their own attempts at culturally specific grand narrative. In Italy, unsurprisingly, Virgilian narrative had a more abiding magnitude than in England, and the role of Scripture in poetry was more formative at the level of allusive enrichment and moral formation. In England, where the biblical story effectively created the vernacular tradition, the structure of biblical grand narrative, mediated by Augustinian exegesis, was dominant. Accordingly, to compare the greatest Italian poet, Dante, at the end of the thirteenth century, and the most eminent English poet, Chaucer, at the end of the fourteenth, is to begin to understand how the Christian Scriptures had already become so much more formative for literary imaginations in England than elsewhere in Europe.

A specific example may suffice to indicate one aspect of this general reality. As readers of a core text such as the Sermon on the Mount, Dante Alighieri and Geoffrey Chaucer drew upon it to heighten their visions of spiritual progress. To compare them closely in this particular is to sample perhaps the most overt sensibility shift with regard to the place of Scripture in Christian pedagogy to occur between late antiquity and the Reformation. If this seems too immodest a claim, I pray you bear with me as we strive to catch up with Dante and Virgil, mid-*Purgatorio*, twelfth canto, on the first cornice:

> Noi volgendo ivi le nostre persone,
> *Beati pauperes spiritu*, voci
> Cantaron sì, che nol diria sermone.
>
> Ahi quanto son diverse quelle foci
> Da l'infernali! ché quivi per canti
> S'entra, a la` giu per lamenti feroci.
>
> [As we turned thither, voices in our ear
> Sang out "Blessed are the poor in spirit;"
> No tongue could tell how sweet they were to hear.
>
> What different phrases these from those we knew
> In Hell! For there with hideous howl of pain,
> But here with singing, we are ushered through.][1]

So Dante, still with Virgil, "step by step, like oxen in the yoke" (*Purg.* 12.1), remembers where he has but lately been. Now his feet are gliding over mosaics on the floor, like funerary *memento mori* in a mausoleum. He looks down on fleeting images of those who, since Lucifer, have fallen prey to Pride and fallen far, then up to see, by contrast, "a beauteous creature, clothed in white . . . a star of dawn all tremulous with light" (12.88–90). It is the angel of humility, mentor of the first cornice. As Dante mounts the proffered stair, his burden seems suddenly lighter, and as he climbs from cornice to cornice, the weight and the stain of sin lift slowly, stage by stage, through six of the

---

1. Dante's Italian text is taken from *Dante Alighieri: The Divine Comedy*, trans. with commentary by Charles S. Singleton, 6 vols. (Princeton: Princeton University Press, 1973), 3:128; the English translation is from Dorothy Sayers, *The Comedy of Dante Alighieri the Florentine*, 3 vols. (New York: Basic Books, 1962).

Matthean Beatitudes. At the summit of Mount Purgatory a mediate *summum bonum* will be his: to become "blessed as those whose sins are covered" (Ps. 32:1; *Purg.* 29.3). Correspondingly, he will have here at last a renewed vision of beatitude in the person of Beatrice.

Beata / *Beatitudo* / Beatrice

That Dante thus employs the Matthean Beatitudes in his pilgrim's purgatorial education is widely known. Although this rich text contains but a small fraction of Dante's alleged 570 allusions to Holy Scripture (principally in the *Commedia*), it is for many moderns easily the best-known instance of his use of the Bible. Perhaps partly as a consequence, much has been made of the mere fact of it. Yet with but two exceptions, these six citations are the only portions of the Sermon on the Mount to be integrated into his poetic theology.

It has long been apparent to readers of the *Commedia* that Dante's primary intellectual sources are classical poetry and philosophy, on the one hand, and scholastic theology and the liturgy of the church, on the other. It may be the case, as Peter Hawkins has seemed to suggest, that Dante more or less habitually read the Bible directly.[2] But if so, it was surely in a context laden with exegetical and theological reflection, perhaps as in the glossed Bible (the *Glossa Ordinaria* commonly was inscribed in the margins of medieval Bibles) or in a compendium commentary such as the *Catena Aurea* of Thomas Aquinas. Further, since his biblical allusions are cryptic, disconnected, and even in the case of the Beatitudes textured with associated liturgical psalms, hymns, and allusions to poetry and the visual arts, it seems wiser to me to be cautious about attributing to Dante any sustained textual reflection on the Sermon on the Mount in and for itself. John Freccero has rightly observed that "major revelations come to the pilgrim subjectively, in a landscape suffused with mist," fragments in a cortex of nostalgic reminiscence or reverie.[3]

Analysis of Dante's biblical allusions suggests that liturgy provides the dominant formation. Biblical quotations thus come chiefly from the Psalms, Song of Songs, Isaiah, Jeremiah, the Gospels, the Pauline Epistles, and Revelation in more or less that order of frequency. Unsurprisingly, the *Inferno*

2. Peter S. Hawkins, *Dante's Testaments: Essays in Scriptural Imagination* (Stanford, CA: Stanford University Press, 1999), e.g., 14, 37–38. Elsewhere, Hawkins says that the "absorption of the Vulgate into the poet's vernacular shows on a minutely linguistic level the larger effort of the *Commedia* to rewrite the Bible." See his "Dante and the Bible," in *The Cambridge Companion to Dante*, ed. Rachel Jacoff (Cambridge: Cambridge University Press, 1993), 128.

3. John Freccero, *Dante: The Poetics of Conversion*, ed. Rachel Jacoff (Cambridge, MA: Harvard University Press, 1986), 210.

offers the fewest. But it may surprise us that, in the *Commedia*, the *Purgatorio* alludes to the Bible most profusely, with thirty direct citations and about forty allusions.[4]

What makes Dante's citations from the Beatitudes in the *Purgatorio* somewhat unusual for him is that they are quoted in a sequence at least evocative of their biblical context, and they are systematically integrated into an ordered spiritual pilgrimage, even a kind of Bonaventuran *itinerarium mentis in deum* (mind's road to God). Thus, they can be said to contribute to structure or form in the poem itself.[5] The structure, however, remains more Bonaventuran than biblical. Bonaventure's *Itinerarium* begins as a mediation on the vision St. Francis experienced on Mount Alverna; in Bonaventure there are not, as in Dante, seven angels to symbolize stages and elements of the required askesis, but the one seraph with six wings that Francis saw, whose biblical source was the vision of Isaiah (Isa. 6:1ff.). Yet in Bonaventure, quite precisely as in Dante,

> he who wishes to ascend to God must, avoiding sin which deforms nature, exercise [knowledge of the truth according to the symbolic, literal, and mystical modes of theology, and] . . . strive toward the reflection of truth [so that] . . . by striving he mounts step by step to the summit of that high mountain where we shall see the God of gods in Zion (Ps. 83:8). (*Itinerarium* 1.7–8, my translation)

Bonaventure's goal, like Dante's, is a state of beatific vision. It is to be obtained by an experience of grace that follows upon a practice of the seven virtues (the four cardinal and three theological) and is marked by the addition, *gratia gratis data*, of seven gifts of the Holy Spirit that had been thought of as their analogues at least since the time of St. Augustine (Bonaventure, *Breviloquium* 5.5). Here, if not also from the "five senses" of Hugh of St. Victor, is a prototype for Dante's *scala* of seven pedagogical ministrations.[6]

---

4. John A. Scott, *Understanding Dante* (Notre Dame, IN: University of Notre Dame Press, 2004), 299; cf. Hawkins, *Dante's Testaments*, 36, 42–43.

5. See Anne Maria Chiavacci Leonardi, "Le beatitudini e la struttura poetica del 'Purgatorio,'" *Giornale storico della letteratura italiana* 141 (1984), fasc. 513, 1–29, esp. 7–8, 24. See also Christopher Kleinhenz, "Dante and the Bible: Biblical Citation in the Divine Comedy," in *Dante: Contemporary Perspectives*, ed. Amilcare A. Iannucci (Toronto: University of Toronto Press, 1997), 74–93; and, though less usefully for present purposes, *Dante e la Biblia: Atti del convegno internazionale promosso da "Biblia,"* ed. Giovanni Barblan (Firenze: Leo S. Olshki Editore, 1988).

6. Bonaventure, *Breviloquium*, trans. Erwin Esser Nemmers (London: Herder, 1946), chap. 6. Hugh of St. Victor's *De Quinque Septenis* relates five sets of seven topoi in a pattern of doctrinal correspondence. In this work the Beatitudes are prescribed as antidotes to the Seven Deadly Sins. For a good discussion see Erich Loos, "Die Ordnung der Seligspreisungen der Bergpredigt in Dantes Purgatorio," in *Literatur und Spiritualität: Hans Sckommodau zum siebzigsten Geburtstag*, ed. Hans Rheinfelder, Pierre Christophorov, and Eberhard Müller-Bochat (München:

But their ordering is not parallel to the order of the Matthean Beatitudes, and it is thus difficult to construe Dante's handling of the Beatitudes as, in any normative sense, either a commentary or a direct engagement with the biblical text.

From Dante this is, quite precisely, what we should expect. Here, as is usual for him, he is responding far more to *sacra dottrina* than to the Scriptures themselves, and he is in this respect typically scholastic (cf. Thomas Aquinas, *Summa Theologiae* 1.1). For example, in Aquinas, as with Bonaventure, treatment of the Beatitudes is situated in a formative discussion of the habits and virtues. It follows immediately upon the distinction Thomas makes between moral and intellectual virtues, and his discussion of the cardinal and theological virtues as a subset of these. (Immediately precedent to the four articles on the Beatitudes is Thomas's account of the gifts of the Holy Spirit.)[7] As it happens, this type of virtue "schematic" actually arises quite early in the exegetical literature itself. Dante would have been familiar with some of it, perhaps even from an encyclopedic compendium of biblical commentary such as the *Catena Aurea*. If so, he could hardly have escaped connecting Augustine's remarks in *The City of God* (19.1) relating the supreme good of philosophical inquiry and biblical "blessedness," or noting that John Chrysostom allegorized the mount from which Jesus addressed his followers as signifying that "he who teaches, as he who hears the righteousness of God should stand on a high ground of spiritual virtues,"[8] or that Augustine in his commentary on the text in Matthew connected the "seven degrees of blessedness" to the "seven-form Holy Spirit" as he finds it proleptically present in Isaiah (*De Sermo Domine in Monte*). It may be that Augustine's teacher, Ambrose, and Lactantius are those most formative for the tradition in framing evaluations of the Beatitudes in this way. In these early fourth-century writers, the virtue ethics of Jesus are seen not so much as a perfection, but rather as a contrary of Roman, especially Stoic, accounts of virtue—not least because the Christian

───────────────────────────

Wilhelm Fink Verlag, 1978), 153–64. Hugh's system is generated from Isa. 11:1–3 and New Testament passages (esp. 1 Cor. 12) on the sevenfold gifts of the Holy Spirit. See here also Étienne Gilson, *Dante and Philosophy* (New York: Harper, 1949), 2–16.

7. This relates to the work of Hugh of St. Victor just cited. See here Thomas Aquinas, *Summa Theologiae* 1–2, article 69.1–4. The Latin text I have used is the Dominican edition by Nicolai, Franciscus Sylvius, Charles Billuart, and C.-J. Drioux, *S. Thomae Aquinaatis Summa Theologica, edito septima*, 8 vols. (Roma: Barri, 1856; 1873), but supplemented by the Blackfriars edition published in London by Eyre and Spottiswoode, concluded in 1980. (Translations are checked against this edition.)

8. As cited in Thomas Aquinas, *Catena Aurea: Commentary on the Four Gospels, Collected out of the Works of the Fathers*, translation edited by John Henry (Cardinal) Newman, 4 vols. (London: Parker, 1841; repr., The Saint Austin Press, 1997), 1:1146; regarding Augustine on Isaiah, see p. 157 (on Matt. 5:10).

virtues of the Beatitudes can be practiced, as Lactantius famously insisted, by women and children.[9]

Little in this exegetical genealogy need detain us. Yet we should acknowledge Dante's debt to the patristic and medieval tendency to situate the Beatitudes (and the Sermon on the Mount more generally) in a context of a comparative study of virtue ethics whose purpose was generally Christian apologetic. Such a contextualization had become formative for medieval readings of both the Matthew and Luke accounts of Jesus' discourse. In such accounts the Beatitudes are the farthest things from "Be Happy Attitudes"; rather, they are disciplines, cultivated habits of the heart, at their most rigorous an askesis or purgation essential to the process of Christian perfection. Five of the Beatitudes from the Matthew Sermon are employed so as to provoke a practice of the virtue they embody in redressing a dominant vice. Thus, "Blessed are the poor in spirit" counters Pride, as the angel of humility makes clear. So also the "merciful" oppose Envy (*Purg.* 15.38), the "peacemakers," Anger (17.68–69), the "pure in heart," Lust (27.8), and so on. Yet in Dante the commandment ultimately enjoined is evidently (though tacitly) the most intimidating of all: "Be ye therefore perfect, even as your Father which is in heaven is perfect" (Matt. 5:48). He does not undertake to show how such perfection is possible in this mortal life.[10]

Though the doctrine of purgatory Dante inherited draws little from the Sermon on the Mount (Matt. 5:25–26 is marginal, even extrinsic to the main tradition), it had long been established in relation to a forensic understanding of the Pauline doctrine of grace (e.g., 1 Cor. 3:11–15) and certain other sayings of Jesus (notably Matt. 12:32).[11] Moreover, the doctrine of purgatory developed in such a way that the Beatitudes, understood in terms of the expurgation

9. This point contrasting the Beatitudes with Roman accounts of virtue has been made frequently—e.g., Lactantius, *Divine Institutes* 5.9.1; 5.15.1. (A good translation is by Anthony Bowen and Peter Garnsey [Liverpool, UK: Liverpool University Press, 2003], 297ff.) It was then taken up by Ambrose. See his *Exposition of the Holy Gospel according to St. Luke*, trans. Theodosia Tomkinson (Etna, CA: Center for Traditionalist Orthodox Studies, 2003), 5.49–63, 76 (pp. 174–82). The point about women and children receives modern attention in Leonardi, "Le beatitudini e la struttura poetica del 'Purgatorio,'" 7–8, and in Patrick Boyde, *Human Vices and Human Worth in Dante's* Comedy (Cambridge: Cambridge University Press, 2000), 110, though Boyde comments on the Matthew text directly.

10. Aquinas offers no comment on Matt. 5:48.

11. Among the sources typically adduced were Isidore of Seville, *De Ordine Creaturae* 14.6; Augustine, *De Civitate Dei* 21.24; and Gregory the Great, *Dialogues* 4.39, all on Matt. 12:32. 1 Cor. 3:11–15 attracts similar connections to the idea of purgation in the afterlife—e.g., by Ambrose in the fourth chapter of his *Commentarium in Amos*, Augustine (on Ps. 37), Gregory again (as cited), and Thomas Aquinas in his *Contra Gentiles* 4.91. For a modern overview, see Jacques Le Goff, *The Birth of Purgatory*, trans. Arthur Goldhammer (Chicago: University of Chicago Press, 1984).

of contrary vices, could be seen as anagogy, a meditatively internalized process of completion in ultimate virtue. When infused by sacramental grace, their practice becomes mystically propaedeutic to an absolute fulfillment of beatitude possible only in the world to come. That the one beatitude Dante omits (the second in the Vulgate: "Blessed are the meek: for they shall inherit the earth" [Matt. 5:5]) has unambiguously to do with this world rather than eternal reward may well explain his omission of it and, for his purpose, his dividing the fourth, "Blessed are they which do hunger and thirst after righteousness" (5:6), into two parts (*Purg.* 22.6; 24.151–54).

Accordingly, it is important to stress at this point the subordination of biblical allusion to Dante's elaboration of an *anagogicus mos*, or "upward leading way." As every reader has seen, his focus, as in all mystical literature, is intensely (even if representatively) personal.[12] It is in his own individual consciousness, Dante the poet suggests, that the great poetic and theological synthesis both occurs and is rendered explicit. As with much mystical literature, we who are readers are overhearers and bear witness not so much to a repentance and conversion as to a word of prophecy. In Dante this is a powerful word, and the *Purgatorio* in particular is, as Dorothy Sayers insists, for theologically attuned readers the most powerful of the *Commedia*'s three books. But it makes little or no contribution of substance to our understanding of the Sermon on the Mount. Indeed, even though *Purgatorio* 12 may be regarded as Dante's most extended meditation on a pericope in Scripture, the comment of Karl Vossler applies: "Whoever runs through the biblical references, reminiscences and allusions in Dante's writings will be amazed to see how great are the poet's debts in number, and how small in artistic importance."[13] Yet perhaps that does not so much matter in a realm where it is poetic imagination itself that makes us "*puro e disposto a salire a le stelle* [pure and prepared to leap up to the stars]" (*Purg.* 33.145).

Blessedness and Social Virtue

Geoffrey Chaucer admired Dante but had a lower view of poetry. Chaucer's pilgrim guide in *The Canterbury Tales* is not Virgil or any other of the honorable classic Roman poets, but rather a boisterous, inept, ale-mongering

12. Cf. Sayers, *Comedy of Dante*, who describes the *Commedia* as "at the same time intensely personal and magnificently public" (2:42). My point is that in a comparison with Chaucer, there is overwhelmingly a greater sense of the poet/persona's personal consciousness in Dante.
13. Karl Vossler, *Medieval Culture: An Introduction to Dante and His Times*, 2 vols. (New York: Frederick Ungar, 1929; repr. 1966), 2:100.

innkeeper with a tin ear for both poetry and theology. The voice of Chaucer's narrative persona, meanwhile—though, as with Dante, deliberately identified with the actual author—appears far less univocal, much more tentative, willing to let a wide array of fictive narrators speak as if for themselves, even obtrusively so, to the point of disruption. "Diverse folk diversely they seyde" (e.g., Reeve's Prologue, 3587; Man of Law's Tale, 211; Merchant's Tale, 1469; cf. Tale of Melibee Prologue, 2131) is a recurrent motif, often appearing precisely at those moments in which, were it Dante's *Commedia*, Dante, Virgil, Beatrice, or St. Bernard would be speaking somberly and authoritatively about a lesson to be drawn, so that the pilgrims' progress could move forward in something like tranquility and good order. But on Chaucer's road to Canterbury, good order proves exceedingly difficult to maintain.

Structurally, several features invite comparison rather than contrast between the two great works. Both poems are presented as Lenten or Eastertide exercises; each is overtly penitential in presupposition and thematic development.[14] The basic linear structure of medieval pilgrimage narrative, figuratively from a *civitas terrena* (city of the world) to the *civitas aeterna*, is drawn from scriptural commentary and in such conceptual terms as were famously formalized by Augustine in his *City of God*. There is a profound sense, moreover, in which the goal of each work is a restoration of "communion," not merely as a matter of theme but as an aspiration in the poet himself.

Yet even as we consider these plausible analogies, at each point we are confronted with a deliberate *différence* in Chaucer that bears directly on his considerably more prominent use of biblical text. Space permits noting only a few of the most obvious points. First, Chaucer's more explicit invocation of the two-cities motif (London/Southwark as a point of worldly departure is succeeded by Canterbury as a "City of God" symbolically)[15] is plainly in evidence at the "literal" level of his fiction. Dante's spectral pilgrimage is from shadow (albeit the shadow of Florence and Rome) to light (that of

14. The overt Eastertide setting in Dante is much discussed. See Hawkins, *Dante's Testaments*, 247–64; Guiseppe Mazotta, *Dante: Poet of the Desert* (Princeton: Princeton University Press, 1979); Dunstan J. Tucker, "'*In Exitu Israel de Aegypto*': The Divine Comedy in the Light of the Easter Liturgy," *American Benedictine Review* 11 (1960): 43–61; and Charles Singleton, "*In exitu Israel de Aegypto*," in *Dante: A Collection of Critical Essays*, ed. John Freccero (Englewood Cliffs, NJ: Prentice-Hall, 1965), 102–21. Comparatively less notice has been made of the Lenten setting for *The Canterbury Tales*, but see Chauncey Wood, "The April Date as Structuring Device in *The Canterbury Tales*," *Modern Language Quarterly* 25 (1964): 259–71.

15. Much is made in the General Prologue of the pilgrimage origin and destination, yet only in the Parson's Prologue does the analogy of the English Eastertide pilgrimage to Canterbury with the voyage of the *civitas aeterna* become explicit (Parson's Prologue, 48–51). See here Russell A. Peck, "Number Symbolism in the Prologue to Chaucer's Parson's Tale," *English Studies* 48 (1967): 205–15.

the Celestial City), and his poetic form evokes a distinctive genre—namely, individual dream-vision allegory and its topos of mystical ascent. Chaucer's pilgrims, by contrast, travel in a much more workaday world, as in "a compagne of folke . . . and pilgrims were they all." They ride to a place of evident temporal as well as spiritual reconciliation—with one another as well as with God—and toward an Eastertide celebration of Holy Communion at a literal English cathedral in Canterbury. That is to say, Chaucer's pilgrimage foregrounds a more mundane realism textured with allegory and tropology (the moral sense), in contrast to Dante's mysteries of dream vision, transfigured by anagogy (reference to life after death).[16] In elaborating by means of fictive narrators a wide diversity of voices and potential perspectives—shaped (or distorted) as these must be by divergent motives in the human heart—Chaucer's poem becomes notoriously polyvocal. Though much of it was presented in person orally in the court as a species of court counsel (something Dante's work could not be), the poem as a seriatim social performance conveys, among other things, a sense of practical political urgency for reformation in the active life, a feature that contrasts sharply with the studied inwardness of Dante's imaginative *via contemplativa*.[17]

Perhaps it is Chaucer's choice of polyvocity, rather than reliance on polysemeity alone,[18] that makes his appeal to Scripture itself as authority so apparently inevitable. Though riskier, there are certain advantages in such a strategy: when a diversity of voices eventually converge in meaning, their "collective witness" gains in strength. But one can discern something more: Chaucer's characters, adroit or inept, effective or, for our ironic instruction, most laughably misguided, seem natively far more naturally engaged in a conversation with the texts of Scripture directly. There is little scholastic context or embedding, nor, for Chaucer's purposes, does there need to be. Indeed, one can easily trace in *The Canterbury Tales* a deep hermeneutic suspicion of commentary, which often is dismissed as a "gloss" meant to gild the lily or even, when assigned to more malign characters, is revealed as a means of deception concerning the actual teaching of Holy Scripture. (Chaucer's sensibility, when compared with Dante's, seems almost Protestant.)

16. Dante, as is evident from both his *Convivio* and *Letter to Can Grande della Scala*, was intimately familiar with the typical four-level schemata of medieval exegesis. So was Chaucer, and not only because it was included in, e.g., the preface to the Wycliffite Bible. But in *The Canterbury Tales* there is little anagogy suggested, and certainly nothing to support readings on that level of the sort proposed by Dante's son Pietro and later commentators for the *Commedia*.

17. See here Gilson, *Dante and Philosophy*, 129–42.

18. Dante's seminal discussion of the polysemous character of poetic language is found in the *Letter to Can Grande* (7), in *Literary Criticism of Dante Alighieri*, trans. and ed. Robert S. Haller (Lincoln: University of Nebraska Press, 1973), 99.

The Summoner's false friar offers a representative example of Chaucer's rhetorical strategy, arousing suspicion because he preaches "after his symple wit, / Nat al [entirely] after the text of hooly writ"—offering as his reason that he reckons the text of Scripture would be too difficult for his hearers. Therefore he will teach rather the "glose" (ostensibly *scolia* on the text), since, after all,

> "Glosynge is a glorious thyng, certeyn,
> For lettre sleeth, so as we clerkes seyn." (Summoner's Tale, 1793–94)

The implication here is plainly that, in the friar's eyes, commentary is in some sense both more appealing and of more spiritual value than the text itself. Similar views—always from characters of dubious integrity—are sprinkled throughout *The Canterbury Tales*.[19] Scripture and its institutional apparatus of interpretation are thus set in tension in Chaucer, and the cumulative effect of many "stagey" misreadings by his fictive narrators early on heightens the actual reader's suspicions about slanted and repackaged citation of the Bible in such a way as to create a desire for a clarifying, more direct encounter with the Holy Scriptures in and for themselves.[20]

Nowhere is this tactic of *sensus interruptus* more evident than in Chaucer's extensive use of the Sermon on the Mount. The Sermon first makes obvious entrance into Chaucer's text in the Prologue to the Reeve's Tale. The Reeve, as a carpenter, is angered by the Miller's Tale just ended, which he perceives as a slight to his guild, if not outright slander, and so he sets out to get even through a pillory of the Miller's Tale in the same low terms he sees have been used by his enemy.

> "I pray to God his nekke mote to-breke [might break];
> He kan wel in myn eye seen a stalke,
> But in his owene he kan nat seen a balke [big board]."
> (Reeve's Prologue, 3918–20)

Two characteristic features of Chaucer's use of the Sermon are here immediately apparent. First, the text of Matthew 7:1–4 (cf. Luke 6:41–42), "Judge not, that ye be not judged," is transliterated fully enough that the reader sees it as evidence that the Reeve thinks he "knows" and has to some

19. For a full account, see Lawrence Besserman, "Glosynge Is a Glorious Thyng: Chaucer's Biblical Exegesis," in *Chaucer and Scriptural Tradition*, ed. David Lyle Jeffrey (Ottawa: University of Ottawa Press, 1984), 65–73.

20. I have discussed this matter at length in a chapter titled "Authorial Intent and the Willful Reader," in my *People of the Book: Christian Identity and Literary Culture* (Grand Rapids: Eerdmans, 1996), 167–207.

degree appropriated a familiar biblical text to his purpose. But then, the Reeve's selfish purpose is actually to replicate the *fault* to which the biblical text is diagnostic, whereas the intent of our actual author, Chaucer, clearly in control of the wider context of this verse in Matthew, is to allow the Reeve's perverse reading of Scripture to function as a kind of dramatic irony that prepares us for a better resolution from another quarter. Presently, the actual "readers" or "hearers" of Chaucer's text are able—whether such dullards as the Miller or Host Harry Bailly can manage it or not—to refer the "spirit" of the Reeve's use of the text back to that legalistic disposition which Jesus has already condemned earlier in his mountain discourse. Thus, when the agent of the Reeve's revenge, the carnal Cambridge divinity student Aleyn, gets to planning a comeuppance for the mischief done to him and his fellow student by the Miller's thievery (their plot is to cuckold the Miller), he says:

> "For, John, ther is a lawe that says thus:
> That gif [if] a man in a point be agreved,
> That in another he sal be releved." (Reeve's Tale, 4180–82)

The biblically literate reader, remembering Chaucer's initial direct evocation of the Sermon on the Mount, will be on guard at this point, or to put it in our terms, will be inclined to a hermeneutic of suspicion where these Cambridge divinity students' "eye for an eye" sense of "the Law" is concerned.

There were actually many biblically literate readers in the court of Richard II—not only the so-called Lollard Knights but also the Bohemian courtiers of Queen Anne, many of whom were simultaneously students of John Wyclif at Oxford. Nor should we forget the queen herself, who kept a copy of the Wycliffite translation of the Gospels by her bedside and read from it daily.[21] Such readers would readily remember here Matthew 5:38, the evocation by Jesus of the familiar *lex talionis*. But what follows from that verse in Jesus' Sermon, and famously so, of course, is a corrective: rather than take revenge in the manner of the Old Law, the disciple of Jesus is admonished to turn the other cheek (Matt. 5:38–44). One might expect a divinity student to know that (though perhaps not a Cambridge divinity student, Chaucer seems to suggest!). The force of the allusion is to reinforce the first citation from Matthew 7:3–4 in the Reeve's Prologue, so highlighting the Reeve, with his well-advertised tale-telling motives, as a "measure for measure" judge of the

21. David Lyle Jeffrey, *The Law of Love: English Spirituality in the Age of Wyclif* (Grand Rapids: Eerdmans, 1988), 40–43 and notes. Reprinted as *English Spirituality in the Age of Wyclif* (Vancouver: Regent College Publishing, 2000).

stamp we meet later on in Shakespeare's play of that title—in which play, of course, the Sermon on the Mount likewise prominently figures.[22]

Chaucer seldom introduces a text from the Bible without subsequent allusion or citation of such a fashion as to make of the quotation a motif or theme. Thus, it is characteristic of him that in the prologue of the next full tale (in the normative sequence), that of the Man of Law, Matthew 5:38 returns once more via the lips of this officious yet obtuse lawyer as he announces the theme of his own tale as he imagines it.

> "For swiche [such] lawe as a man yeveth [gives] another wight [person]
> He sholde hymselven usen it, by right;
> Thus wole [this is the intention of] oure text."
> (Prologue to the Man of Law's Tale, 43–45)

But we soon learn that here again we have been misled: this is not at all the Man of Law's actual text. Rather, the tale he remembers turns out to be about a saintly woman (Custance, whose name suggests "perseverance" or "constancy") who seems the very embodiment of the Beatitudes, one who never descends to the letter of the law or seeks revenge, but takes in patience all the harm done to her. By creating such deliberate frisson between actual intention ("entente") in a text itself and that which may be merely strategic for one who uses that work for a self-interested purpose, Chaucer shows us that the intention driving the use of any text, in any tale, requires almost as much interpretation as the text itself. Further, he frames and corrects his fictive storytellers in such a way as to show that when a governing authorial intention is independently declared, it can correct misunderstandings—or, indeed, legalistic precisionism—authoritatively.[23] That, of course, would seem to be what Jesus himself was doing in his Sermon on the Mount. And it is apparent that both Wyclif and his favorite predecessor, Nicholas of Lyra, understood the Sermon on the Mount in this way—that is, as a divine declaration of Authorial intent.[24]

<hr/>

22. See Paul A. Olson, "The *Reeve's Tale*: Chaucer's *Measure for Measure*," *Studies in Philology* 59 (1962): 1–17; and G. Wilson Knight, "*Measure for Measure* and the Gospels," in his *Wheel of Fire* (New York: Meridian, 1949), 73ff. *Measure for Measure* is still referred to conventionally in such terms: a *Guardian* (May 3, 2003) review of the production in London's West End by the Royal Shakespeare Theatre Company refers to the "complexity of Shakespeare's version of the Sermon on the Mount."

23. Jeffrey, *People of the Book*, 194–204. See also Chauncey Wood, "Chaucer's Man of Law as Interpreter," *Traditio* 23 (1967): 149–90.

24. Nicholas Lyra, *Postilla super Totam Bibliam* (printed in Strassburg, 1492; repr., Frankfurt am Main: Minerva, 1971), is followed closely by Wyclif in his own *postilla* on Matt. 5–7. See

Chaucer, like Wyclif his contemporary, worked simultaneously under the patronage of John of Gaunt. It may safely be said that Chaucer and Wyclif shared at least one concern: each was almost as preoccupied with drawing attention to a plague of faulty or perverted interpretations of Scripture as with presenting a "right reading" correctly. Even before he gets to the anti-fraternal satire of the Friar's and Summoner's Tales, Chaucer offers, in the Wife of Bath's supersized Prologue, an unmistakable burlesque of biblical exegesis. By it we are prepared in ways we do not yet realize for more conclusive satisfactions to come. For instance, the Wife of Bath cites the Bible more than any other pilgrim except the Parson, yet every text she adduces she chops out of context, radically misconstrues, or knowingly deconstructs to hilarious effect in a fashion transparent to a literate medieval audience. Yet her overt misreading—of New Testament as well as Old Testament texts—has about it a still more insidious character. When her ardent ecclesiastical suitors (especially the Friar and the Summoner) appear no more reliably acquainted with Scripture than she is, we begin to see just how self-serving "glossing" (rather than taking the text on its own terms) can become a problem for religious authority. Here is the Summoner's friar's ploy:

> "But herkne [listen] now, Thomas, what I shal seyn.
> I ne have no text of it, as I suppose,
> But I shall fynde it in a maner glose,
> That specially oure sweete Lord Jhesus
> Spak this by freres, when he seyde thus:
> '*Blessed be they that povere in spirit been.*'"
> (Summoner's Tale, 1918–23 [italics added])

After this apparently accurate citation of the first beatitude, the Summoner's false friar makes a claim regarding the divine *intentio auctoris*—namely, that his "profession" or order (doubtless, he insists, the friars are those to whom Jesus was referring) lives more in conformity with the gospel than other people. Therefore, layfolk, like his next victim, Thomas, should not be reluctant to cough up money to support the friars' increasingly opulent lifestyle (cf. Summoner's Tale, 1836–53). Perforce, Thomas must yield to the shameless religious fraud that supports the friar, whether he can afford to or not (1854–84). No angel of humility appears on this "cornice," but rather a chubby little bundle of greed and prideful vices, entirely alien to the first condition of beatitude (cf. 1935–36). Fittingly, when, in the Summoner's friar's

---

Douglas Wurtele, "Chaucer's Canterbury Tales and Nicholas of Lyre's *Postillae litteralis et moralis super totam Bibliam*," in Jeffrey, *Chaucer and Scriptural Tradition*, 89–107.

groping attempt to recover gold from the breeches of his host, he gets instead a gargantuan *bumbulum* (fart) in the face, everyone feels he has had his just deserts. Even the lord to whom he is confessor (and who is likely his biggest donor) cannot resist a humorous allusion to the Sermon on the Mount in precisely such terms as the friar has been misappropriating it:

> "Distempre yow noght; ye be my confessour;
> Ye been the salt of the erthe and the savour."
> (Summoner's Tale, 2195–96)

Lest any reader think this allusion to Matthew 5:13 to be approbatory, Chaucer has this same lord, completely doubled up in laughter, take up the literal-minded friar's "problem"—namely, finding an "ars-metrike" by which to divide the odious booty into twelve parts, so that each member of his conventicle (as per the Franciscan rule) gets an equal share: "Who sholde make a demonstracion," he asks in his hilarity, "That every man sholde have yliche his part / As of the soun or savour of a fart?" (Summoner's Tale, 2224–26). Both audiences for this ribaldry have more than enough occasion at this point to recall the *rest* of the sentence in Matthew's text ("But if the salt have lost his savour, wherewith shall it be salted?" [Matt. 5:13]), and to realize that this point is the precedent and, for the friar's lost spiritual authority, really the determinative question. The repeated use of one word, "savour," performs the necessary mnemonic trick. Of these sorry interpreters it may be concluded that their "savour" is thoroughly degraded. Here again, like Wyclif, Chaucer regards the friars as destructive of the authority of Scripture and betrayers of their own rule.[25]

There are far more allusions to the Sermon on the Mount in Chaucer than can be discussed here.[26] It is meet, however, that we give special attention to those that occur in the homiletic Tale of Melibee, the tale Chaucer allots to his fictive pilgrim persona, as well as in the Parson's Tale, which concludes *The Canterbury Tales* and is, after all, itself a sermon calling for repentance. The theme of the Tale of Melibee is drawn from Matthew 5:9:

25. Antifraternal literature abounds in the fourteenth century, and when texts from the Sermon on the Mount figure in Dante's ringing denunciation of friar preachers (in *Par.* 29.85–126, no less), they follow upon St. Peter's invective (*Par.* 27.55–56) against corrupt clergy of all kinds as "rapacious wolves clothed in the garb of shepherds" (cf. Matt. 7:15), Dante's only other significant use of our text (also occurring in his *Convivio* 4.16). Chaucer's antifraternal attack is, if anything, more intense (and certainly more sustained) than Dante's, especially in his treatment of the Friar, the friar in the Summoner's Tale, and the Pardoner.

26. See Lawrence Besserman, *Chaucer and the Bible: A Critical Review of Research, Indexes, and Bibliography* (New York: Garland, 1988), 352–53, for a basic list.

"Blessed are the peacemakers." This was a theme of some importance to Chaucer. There is evidence that he, like at least two of the knights close to Wyclif, belonged to a confraternal association that called itself the Order of the Passion of Our Lord. The objectives of this group included ending warfare between Christian nations (especially England and France), ending the papal schism whereby there were rival popes in Rome and Avignon, and reestablishing European courtly values and virtues.[27] By 1391, in the political contretemps at court over these issues, Chaucer and his colleagues had come out on the short end, and for his part Chaucer lost his job as Clerk of the King's Works.[28] (Would-be peacemakers are not always well regarded by those of a more bellicose nature, and John of Gaunt was bellicose.) In addition, by this time Wyclif had lost his teaching chair at Oxford and been sent down to Lutterworth parish, where in 1384 he died of a stroke during Holy Communion. By the 1390s, storm clouds were swiftly gathering for Wyclif's sympathizers.

We generally date Chaucer's version of the Tale of Melibee to just after the death of Wyclif and before the death of Queen Anne in 1394.[29]

Beatitude and Political Wisdom

As a kind of intensifying frame for the tale he gives to himself, Chaucer the pilgrim commences his turn at bat with an abortive swing at low-grade, soap opera–like romance in hideous doggerel rhyme. This deliberately lame effort at mindless entertainment is cut off by the Host's exasperated roar in midsentence, who demands something in which there is either "murthe" or "doctryne." Chaucer the pilgrim then agrees to tell a "moral tale vertuous / Al be it told somtyme in sondry wyse / Of sondry folk [in various times in various ways by various people]" (Sir Thopas, 2130–32), invoking again the principle of polyvocity, yet which he surprisingly illustrates not by indulging the perverse and ribald misuse of Scripture to which his hearers have already

27. Still useful here is W. T. Waugh, "The Lollard Knights," *Scottish Historical Review* 11 (1914): 55–92. Cf. N. Jorgu, "Phillippe de Mezières et la Croisade au XIVième siècle," *Bibliothèque de l'École des Hautes Études* 110 (1896; repr., London, 1973).

28. Martin M. Crow and Clair C. Olson, eds., *Chaucer Life-Records* (Oxford: Oxford University Press, 1966), 402–76. When one of Chaucer's Wyclif-sympathizing friends, Phillipe de la Vache, suffered a similar fate, he took it rather badly, prompting Chaucer to send de la Vache as exhortation his well-known short poem "Truth."

29. The Tale of Melibee is a free translation of the French *Le Livre de Melibee et de Dame Prudence*, which in turn was based on the thirteenth-century *Liber Consolationis et Consilii* by Albertanus of Brescia. The Tale was most probably reworked by Chaucer and inserted in its present position in *The Canterbury Tales* in the final stages of assembly.

been much exposed, but by sober reference to the apparent polyvocity of the four Gospels. While of Matthew, Mark, Luke, and John, he says, "al be ther in hir telling difference," "natheless hir sentence is al sooth [entirely true]," and there is evident concord as to meaning: "Douteless, hir sentence [meaning] is al oon [in agreement]" (Tale of Melibee, 2130–42). So also with my tale here, he says. Though he intends to recount somewhat more "proverbs" than his audience has yet heard, we are to understand that the meaning of his own signature story diverges as to meaning not at all from the overall meaning of *The Canterbury Tales*.[30]

Once again the presenting social issue in Melibee is injury and revenge. But here a solution is not to be found except through the offices of a wisdom personified as Dame Prudence, who patiently reviews both biblical and classical authorities to argue that the restoration of health in such circumstances can come only by forgiveness and a practice of justice that is tempered with mercy. In this critical part of *The Canterbury Tales*, Chaucer alludes to the Sermon on the Mount intermittently (e.g., Matt. 7:1, "Judge not, that ye be not judged") (1458, 1865ff.), but more significantly, the whole Matthean narrative is built into his narrative in such a way that a concordance of both biblical and classical texts is made to resolve on two key themes from the Sermon on the Mount—namely, the blessedness of peacemaking and the necessity of forgiveness rather than *lex talionis* judgment. "Ye knowen wel," says Prudence to her vengefully minded husband, Melibee,

> "that oon of the gretteste and moost sovereyn
> thyng [stabilizing forces] that is in this world is unytee and pees.
> And therfore seyde oure Lord Jhesu Crist to
> his apostles in this wise: '*Wel happy and
> blessed been they that loven and purchacen
> pees, for they been called children of God.*'"
> (Tale of Melibee, 2867–70 [italics added])

As Chaucer's exemplary peacemaker, Dame Prudence here takes on a quality of beatitude at once more dialogic and, in its extensive development, of greater political immediacy than is the case even for Dante's Beatrice. The direct citation of Matthew 5:9 here recapitulates the discourse of Prudence to this point; it declares "authoritatively" her intent as a narrator within Chaucer's tale and, as we know from the beginning and see again at the conclusion of the tale, it signals Chaucer's authorial intention representatively as well. The "entente" of Prudence is made explicit in her last speech:

30. For a fuller discussion, see Jeffrey, *People of the Book*, 198–202.

> "Wherfore I pray yow, lat mercy been
> in youre herte, to th'effect and entente [purpose]
> that God Almighty have mercy on yow
> in his laste juggement."

She then adds, as often in this tale, confirmation from the earliest canonical commentary on the Sermon on the Mount:

> "For Seint Jame seith in his Epistle:
> 'Juggement withouten mercy shal be
> doon to hym that hath no mercy of another
> wight [person].'" (Tale of Melibee, 1867–69)

Chaucer's narratorial voice then comments that, in light of her faithful teaching, the "herte" of Melibee "gan enclyne to the wil of his wif, considerynge hir trewe entente [purpose]"—that is, her intention to be faithful to Christ's teaching—and he "conformed hym anon," forgiving his enemies and reconciling them to himself. The last words of the tale still more deliberately recall the conditional clause of the Lord's Prayer (Matt. 6:14–15) as application, as well as the "comfortable words" following absolution in the Sarum rite—namely, 1 John 1:9:

> "For doutelees, if we be sory and repentant
> of the synnes and giltes [faults] which we han trespassed
> in the sighte of oure Lord God, he is so free
> and so merciable that he wole foryeven us
> our giltes and bryngen us to the blisse that
> nevere hath ende." Amen. (Tale of Melibee, 1883–86)

We see, then, that Chaucer has put in the mouth of his own pilgrim persona a sermon—indeed, a sermon whose thesis and key texts come openly from the Sermon on the Mount. Moreover, the form of his exposition of the text in this tale is not by means of a "gloss" in the conventional sense, but rather by a concordance of many related Scriptures, supplemented in Augustinian fashion by a few apt citations from Cicero and Seneca, yet interwoven in such a way that the Matthew text provides not merely the theme but also authoritative closure to a reflection on the wisdom of peacemaking. In this concordance of wisdom authorities, internal commentary on the Matthew text from elsewhere in Scripture (e.g., the Letter of James) is granted the next highest level of authority after the words of Jesus. James's apostolic emphasis on the enactment of virtue—here the highlighted virtue of peacemaking—gets

correlative and dramatic embodiment in the Knight's counterintuitive, genuinely shocking insistence that the sexually ambiguous, loathsome Pardoner
and his enraged would-be victim, Harry Bailly, literally kiss and make up
so that the fellowship of pilgrims en route to Communion be not destroyed
(Pardoner's Tale, 946–68). This gesture would have been more countercultural
in Chaucer's time than in our own.

It may to some degree reflect a modernist bias that available translations
of Chaucer typically omit both the Tale of Melibee and the Parson's Tale, the
tale with which Chaucer concludes his great work. For similar reasons, perhaps, these two texts are seldom taught now, however incongruous that must
appear for any structural consideration of *The Canterbury Tales*. In respect
of structure, however, to some degree analogously with Dante's *Purgatorio*,
Chaucer's Parson's sermon is not merely a "knitting up"—as the Host, on the
outskirts of Canterbury, asks that it be—of all the "greet mateere" (Prologue
to the Parson's Tale, 28–29) of the collected tales. It is a prompt to an examination of conscience in both the fictive and the actual readers (or hearers) of
the tales and an orthodox catechism in true repentance. Chaucer's Parson is
highly conscious of the social nature of sin and the healing social function
of repentance. After all, the pilgrims are about to end their voyage by being
restored to Holy Communion. Because repentance is notoriously easier to
talk about than to perform (whatever the original intention, a pilgrimage to
Canterbury could be about as unpenitential as the average Cook's tour to the
Holy Land), the Parson is appropriately concerned at this point to distin-
guish between true and feigned repentance. Hence, he takes up the matter
of genuine contrition at the outset. "And therfore our Lord Jhesu Crist seith
thus," he quotes Matthew 7:20, "*by the fruyt of hem [them] shall ye knowen
hem*" (Parson's Tale, 116).

As is typical of late medieval penitential manuals,[31] the requisite examination of conscience follows a diagnostic schema ordered by the seven "chief-
taynes of synnes," as Chaucer's Parson calls the Seven Deadly Sins (Parson's
Tale, 385). In respect of the second of these, Envy (*Invidia*), and in particular
as to its remedy, the Gospel of Matthew becomes critical to the Parson's

---

31. One such, frequently but unconvincingly associated with the Parson's Tale, is the *Summa
Virtutum de Remediis Anime*, ed. Siegfried Wenzel (Athens: University of Georgia Press, 1984);
another is the *Summa de Vitiis* of Raymond Pennaforte. I agree with Siegfried Wenzel that
Chaucer worked quite independently with the biblical sources—probably from both the Vulgate
and a French translation. Wycliffite work came late and, given Chaucer's situation, was possibly
too politically charged after 1384 for him to quote overtly. At least since Dudley R. Johnson's
1941 Yale dissertation, "Chaucer and the Bible," there has been consensus that Chaucer seems
to have been using an unglossed version of the Bible in most instances of citation. But cf. T. P.
Dolan's review of Wenzel in *Studies in the Age of Chaucer* 8 (1986): 260–63.

purpose. He begins with the Great Commandment, or Law of Love, from Matthew 22:37–40, translating and elaborating it in such a way that the hearer is given to understand that by the term "neighbor" we are to understand not only "brother" but "enemy."

> Certes, man shal louen [love] his enemy, by the
> commandement of God; and smoothly [truly] thy freend
> shaltow love in God . . .

He then moves seamlessly into exposition dependent on citations from the Sermon on the Mount, each carefully paraphrased and expounded. One citation must suffice:

> Agayns hate and rancour of herte, he shal love hymn in herte. Agayns chidyng and wikkede wordes, he shal preye for his enemy. Agayns the wikked dede of his enemy, he shal doon hym bountee [be generous toward him]. For Crist seith: *Loveth your enemys, and preyeth for hem that speke yow harm, and eek for hem that yow chacen and pursewen, and dooth bountee to hem that yow haten* [hate you]. Loo, thus comaundeth us oure Lord Jhesu Crist to do to oure enemys. . . .
> For right as the devel is disconfited by humylitee, right so is he wounded to the deeth by love of our enemy. Certes, thanne is love the medicine that casteth out the venym of Envye fro mannes herte. (Parson's Tale, 520–30 [italics added])

Curiously enough, then, for those who, like Chaucer himself, are familiar with Dante,[32] the counterbalance to Envy in this equivalent to Dante's second cornice of the *Purgatorio* is neither the angel of mercy nor the fifth beatitude, "Blessed are the merciful" (Matt. 5:7). Rather, it is the *last* of the Beatitudes, "Blessed are you when they revile and persecute you" (cf. Matt. 5:10–11). This was (no surprise) a portion of the Sermon on the Mount dear to the hearts of many who sympathized with John Wyclif.[33] They knew about having evil said of them falsely, and that much of it was born of *invidia*. A good deal of it took the form of a hair-trigger prejudice against what might appear to some to be excessive piety. That is, serious piety itself could seem to be Wycliffite.

32. Chaucer names Dante specifically in many places, and in *House of Fame* 1.499ff., he may be borrowing directly from *Purgatorio* 9.19–20 and 2.17–24. Chaucer spent time in Italy between 1372 and 1376. The Wife of Bath's old loathly lady also quotes extensively from the *Convivio* in her account of *gentilesse* (true nobility of character), beginning at 3.d.1125–65.

33. Wycliffite writers and others conventionally refer to the Lollard preachers as "povre men," and the language of the Beatitudes permeates their work. Thus, in the Wycliffite exposition of the Lord's Prayer, this language figures richly in respect of the holiness in which those who pray "halwid be thi name" ought to pray. See F. D. Matthew, *The English Works of Wyclif*, Early English Text Society Original Series 74 (1880; repr., Millwood, NY: Krauss, 1975), 197–202.

In the first abortive attempt by the Host to get the Parson to address the pilgrims, following the Man of Law's Tale, Harry Bailly dismissively refers to the Parson twice as a "Lollere" (Lollard). In Chaucer's time, such an epithet had the force of calling someone a "fundamentalist" today. Harry employs this dismissive term simply because the Parson has expressed concern about Harry's penchant for profanity (Man of Law's Tale, 1170–83). The Shipman, notably one of the most profane of the pilgrims, then angrily intervenes to prevent the Parson from accepting the Host's invitation.

Under *Ira*, Anger, in the Parson's sermon comes the problem of spiritual "homicide," or "spiritual manslaughtere," which on the Parson's account is akin to profanity. The text recollected here, Matthew 5:21–22 (also 6:23ff.), has analogues in John's Gospel, and the resulting analysis is synthetic. Nevertheless, as Chaucer's Parson develops the point, our Matthew text is central:

> Also oure Lord Jhesu Crist seith, by the word of Seint Mathew, *"Ne wol ye nat swere in alle manere* [you ought not to swear in any fashion]; *neither by hevene, for it is Goddes trone; ne by erthe, for it is the bench of his feet; ne by Jerusalem, for it is the citee of a greet kyng; ne by thyn heed, for thou mayst nat make an heer* [hair] *whit ne blak. But seyeth by youre word 'ye, ye,' and 'nay, nay'; and what that is moore, it is of yvel* [evil],*"*—thus seith Crist. (Parson's Tale, 587–90 [italics added])

The development through Matthew 5:33–37 is here again by way of direct quotation: the Parson is determined to adduce irrefragable authority—namely, the words of Jesus himself, "for Crist is verray trouthe [true truth]" (Parson's Tale, 592). Because "true truth" is a matter of Christ's example, and not his words only, the remedy for Anger is not then, as with Dante, *beati pacifici* (Matt. 5:9) imagined as a verbal intervention; rather, it is the virtue of patience "that maketh a man lyk to God, and makyth hym Goddes owene deere child, as seith Crist" (Parson's Tale, 600–601). Here Matthew 5:9 is clearly conflated with James 1:2–4 in such a way as to let us see how Chaucer regards the Letter of James as the best of commentaries on the Sermon on the Mount.[34] Scripture upon Scripture is the Parson's general exegetical *regula*; though Ambrose, Augustine, Jerome, Gregory, Isidore of Seville, and Bernard of Clairvaux all are adduced at some point in his sermon, the place of the magisterial tradition is distinctly secondary to that of the text of Scripture

---

34. This has been noticed with respect to other tales. See especially here John McNamara, "Chaucer's Use of the Epistle of St. James in the *Clerk's Tale*," *Chaucer Review* 7 (1972–73): 184–93.

itself, and the concordance of Scripture as *lex Dei, lex Christi* invariably forms the main channel of his exposition.

Always in the background, as in Wycliffite sermons, are "wolves in sheep's clothing" (here in Chaucer, e.g., the Friar, the Summoner, and the Pardoner) and those secular authorities who, like the Man of Law and the Reeve, "devouren the possessiouns or the catel of povre folk wrongfully, withouten mercy or mesure." Yet part of what enables patience in the face of such adversaries is confidence in the ultimate sovereignty of God, and knowledge that "they shul receyven [receive], by the same measure than they han mesured to povre folk [Matt. 7:2], the mercy of Jhesu Crist, but if it be amended" (Parson's Tale, 774–75).

The Parson's sermon systematically (in a fullness that can only be hinted at here) provides Chaucer's audience a measure by which the full range of sinful miscreance exhibited in the intentions and actions of the pilgrims, as well as of the overt hijinks of the characters in their tales, can be instructively assessed. And that sinful deeds need not actually be performed to occasion real sin—even in a reader of inordinate affections—is made clear in the Parson's treatment of *luxuria* (lechery). What Dante thought of as *"l'adulterio del cuore"* (adultery of the heart; cf. Matt. 5:28) can rather easily become a reader's problem too: witness Paolo and Francesca, it can also lead to a damnable performance (*Inf. 5*). Augustine's *De Sermo Domine in Monte* is cited by the Parson in support:

> "In this heeste [commandment]," seith Seint Augustyn, "is forboden [forbidden] alle manere coveitise [imaginative desire] to doon lecherie." Lo, what seith Seint Mathew in the gospel, that *"whoso seeth a womman to coveitise of his lust, he hath doon lecherie with hire in his herte."* Heere may ye seen that nat oonly the dede of this synne is forboden, but eek the desir to doon that synne. (Parson's Tale, 844–46 [italics added])

Already we can anticipate in the self-deprecating Chaucer, actual author of this entire work, an acknowledgment that in an attempt to deal candidly with sin, a poet—or poetic confessor—can occasion by his narrative that form of voyeurism that may lead its practitioner along a path to perdition. Indeed, once the tales are ended, he confesses as much in his very last words, by way of his Retraction.[35]

---

35. "Wherefore I beseke yow mekely, for the mercy of God, that ye preye for me that Crist have mercy on me and foryeve me my giltes; and namely of my translecions and enditynges of wordly vanitees, the which I revoke in my retracciouns. . . . And many a song, and many a leccherous lay; that Crist for his grete mercy foryeve me the synne" (Retraction, 10.1084–86).

But these are not his last words as to meaning, or to *intentio autoris*, in his concluding tale, the Parson's sermon. His words have to do no longer with contrition (he is most brief about this) or even with auricular confession, but rather with the traditional third part of the traditional process of repentance, what the apostle Paul calls "works meet for repentance" (Acts 26:20), or "satisfaction," as traditional doctrine refers to it. For Chaucer's Parson these works are to be done, if possible, unostentatiously—or if not out of view, then in a spirit of self-displacement and gratitude to Christ for the grace that is our means of redemption. But the portion of the Sermon on the Mount adduced here, as we draw toward the conclusion of the Parson's sermon and, thus, the tales, is explicitly such as to cause us to think of the corporate character of our accountability to bear a faithful witness to our salvation:

> For, as witnesseth Seint Mathew, capitulo quinto [chap. 5], "A citee may nat been hyd that is set on a montayne, ne men lighte nat a lanterne and put it under a busshel, but men sette it on a candle-stikke to yeve light to the men in the hous. Right so shal youre light lighten before men, that they may seen youre goode werkes, and glorifie your fader that is in hevene." (Parson's Tale, 1035–38)

Among these good works in Matthew 5:14–16 is prayer, which the Parson defines as a "pitous wyl of herte, that redresseth it in God [a self-effacing desire of the heart that seeks its completion in God]." In the exemplar,

> the orison [prayer] of the *Pater noster* hath Jhesu Crist enclosed moost thynges. Certes, it is privyleged of thre thynges in his dignytee, for which it is moore digne [more worthy] than any oother preyere; for that Jhesu Crist hymself maked it; and it is short, for it sholde be koud [memorized] the moore lightly [easily], and for to withholden [retained] it the moore esily in herte, and helpen hymself the ofter [more often] with the orisoun; and for a man sholde be the lasse wery [less weary] to seyen it, and for a man may nat excusen hym to lerne it, it is so short and so esy; and for it comprehendeth in it self alle goode preyers. (Parson's Tale, 1039–43)

As he expounds the significance of the Lord's Prayer (Matt. 6:7–15) as a model for all prayer in the Christian life, the Parson acknowledges that while deeper exposition is to be had from "this maistres [masters] of theologie," for him (as for Augustine) a key point is

> that whan thow prayest that God sholde foryeve [forgive] thee thy giltes [wrong-doings] as thou foryevest hem that agilten to thee, be ful wel war that thow ne be nat out of charitee. (Parson's Tale, 1043–44)

It is crucial, he says, that this prayer and all prayer should be prayed "ordinately, discreetly and devoutly," and that "alwey a man shal putten his wyl to be subget to the wille of God" (Parson's Tale, 1045). Yet prayer is to be continued not with mere words but "with the werkes of charitee."

This declaration summarizes the entire force—as penitential doctrine and social criticism both—of Chaucer's *Canterbury Tales*. It shows us how the Sermon on the Mount has not only been present all along the pilgrim ride from London to Canterbury, but in a crafted, deliberate way has served to declare the intention of "oure auctor," as Chaucer calls him—the ultimate Author, making plain his will for those who would seek to align their will with it.

Accordingly, the goal of Chaucer's journey is not, as in Dante's ethereal voyage, a mystical vision. Rather, it is a moment in the pilgrimage of this ordinary life where, in the grateful recognition of sins forgiven, we are prepared once again to become "one with the body of Christ" even as, by means of that Host more real, we become one with his body in an act of obedience, participation in the eucharistic meal. That this state of grace, this experience of Communion, is a foretaste of divine glory (or *paradiso*) the Parson grants. But in Chaucer it is not an experience of solitary mystical vision but the worship of a gathered church that occasions our understanding of future hope:

> Thanne shal men understonde what is the fruyt of penaunce [repentance]; and, afer the word of Jhesu Crist, it is the endelees blisse of hevene, ther joye hath no contrariousteee of wo [sorrow] ne grevaunce [nor aggravation]; ther alle harmes been passed of this present lyf; ther as is the sikernesse [preservation] fro the peyne of helle; ther as is the bisful compaignye that rejoysen hem everemo, everich [each person] of otheres joye; there as the body of man, that whilom [beforehand] was foul and derk, is moore cleer than the sonne; ther as the body, that whilom was syk, freele, and fieble, and mortal, is inmortal, and so strong and so hool that ther may no thyng apeyren [injure] it; ther as ne is neither hunger, thurst, ne coold, but every soule replenyssed [restored to wholeness] with the sighte of the parfit knowynge of God. (Parson's Tale, 1076–79)

And the very last word in *The Canterbury Tales*? Well that, most fittingly, alludes to the first words of the Sermon on the Mount and, indeed, of the Beatitudes:

> This blisful regne may mene purchace by poverte espirituel, and the glorie by lowenesse, the plentee of joye by hunger and thurst, and the reste by travaille [disciplined labor], and the lyf by deeth and mortificacion of synne. (Parson's Tale, 1975–80)

Following Chaucer the poet's confession to the reader concerning his own inevitable failure to realize his better intentions, he appeals for the prayers of his readers and hearers that he shall be granted the "grace of verray [true] repentance, confessioun and satisfaccioun to doon in this present lyf." Chaucer's focus is not on the prospect of purgatory. It is on repentance and perseverance—grace for obedience in the here and now.

Conclusion

Dante makes minimal use of the Sermon on the Mount, and more narrowly the Beatitudes, as the traditions of *sacra dottrina* make it possible for him to incorporate them into a mystical askesis in which the purgation of sins for which penitential satisfaction remains incomplete in the world may be imagined as being satisfied *post mortem*. Chaucer, by contrast, finds in the Sermon on the Mount primarily a key to the moral appropriation of Scripture for personal and social action—to works meet for repentance in this present life. This luminous portion of Jesus' teaching is for him a kind of exegetical cornerstone in terms of which all of Scripture finds its focus, and its resolution, in Christ. In the words of Jesus he finds a declaration of the divine Author's authorial intent—gathering in and ordering to meaning all those divergent, unruly narratives from Genesis, Judges, and Job as well as the occasional befuddlement of Jesus' disciples, and so declaring the finally unified meaning of "oure Auctor" for us: *lex Dei, lex Christi*. But in the law as Jesus lives and teaches it, the question of "our Author's" intention, the alignment of our diverse wills with his own singular will in purity of heart, is distilled for the sake of action—what is to be done *now*. For Chaucer that obedience must begin in true contrition, proceed through confession of mouth, then move toward restorative deeds done in gratitude, works meet for repentance, which in their grateful doing might just transform the world. The biblical text has inspired the poetic imagination of both great medieval poets, but in different ways, to similar ends. In Dante that end is a teleology of political as well as moral understanding; in Chaucer the end is a practicum for political and moral reformation.

four

EGYPTIAN GOLD

Biblical Transformations of Ovid in The Canterbury Tales

I n the second book of his highly influential treatise on literary interpretation, *On Christian Doctrine*, St. Augustine makes the case for Christian
literary formation that both honors and makes use of great texts of pagan
literature, beginning with Plato and the Platonists:

> For, as the Egyptians had not only the idols and heavy burdens which the people
> of Israel hated and fled from, but also vessels and ornaments of gold and silver,
> and garments, which the same people when going out of Egypt appropriated to
> themselves, designing them for a better use, not doing this on their own author-
> ity, but by the command of God . . . in the same way all branches of heathen
> learning have not only false and superstitious fancies and heavy burdens of un-
> necessary toil . . . they contain also liberal instruction which is better adapted
> to the use of the truth, and some most excellent precepts of morality; and some
> truths in regard even to the worship of the One God are found among them.[1]

Augustine's suggestion, applied immediately in his own work to the formation of readers of the Scriptures, was so influential upon successive generations
of Christian thinkers that "Egyptian gold" became a principle for appropriat-
ing nonbiblical texts by reading through the lens afforded by biblical analogue
or allegory. Among the many works of classical Greek and Roman culture so

---

1. Augustine, *On Christian Doctrine* 2.40, trans. J. F. Shaw, Nicene and Post-Nicene Fathers,
first series, ed. Philip Schaff (Peabody, MA: Hendrickson, 2004), 2:554.

seconded to biblical exegesis, theology, and imaginative writing were Virgil's *Aeneid* and the *Thebaid* of Statius, as well as those of Ovid, moralized both in Latin and medieval French versions, especially the *Metamorphoses*.

Ovidian Gold

It is evident that Chaucer was familiar with these "Christianized" versions of Ovid, probably both in the Latin *Ovidus Moralizatus* and the medieval French *Ovide Moralisé*. We may trace his Ovidian borrowings in many parts of *The Canterbury Tales* as well as in his other works, but in one curiously incomplete tale at the penultimate stage of the larger unfinished poem, we get a particularly good example of how Chaucer transmutes the Egyptian gold of an Ovidian tale by means of Christian metanarrative and allegory. Notably, he does this in such a way as to occasion our appreciation of the greater transformation made possible in Christ, illustrating thereby how a biblically mediated use of Ovidian story might effectively transpose it to a new key, putting it to "better use." A good illustration of this principle comes in the Manciple's Tale, which appears nearly at the end of the pilgrimage to Canterbury. Chaucer's Manciple is presented as a garrulous person; his tale is of a pet crow who has the same problem, and who occasions thereby not merely the death of someone dear to his master, but also his own demise. Traditional studies of this oddly unconcluded tale have concentrated on its relationship to its prologue and, attending to the vulnerable Manciple's immoderate dialogue with the Cook, have convincingly established the appropriateness to him of a tale that seemingly warns against a loose tongue.[2] But there is more.

One of the most interesting aspects of the Manciple's moral reading of his tale is the way in which it measures up to a reading of the original story in the *Ovide Moralisé*.[3] In its recasting of Ovid, the *Moralisé* equates Phebus with any young prince, and the white pet crow with a false courtier who would seduce his master's confidence by revealing his lady's infidelity, and concludes:

2. See J. Burke Severs, "Is the Manciple's Tale a Success?," *Journal of English and Germanic Philology* 51 (1952): 1–16; J. D. Elliott, "The Moral of the Manciple's Tale," *Notes and Queries* 1 (1954): 511–12; R. M. Lumiansky, "Chaucer's Cook-Host Relationship," *Medieval Studies* 17 (1955): 208–9.

3. C. de Boer, ed., *Ovide Moralisé*, 5 vols. (Amsterdam: de N.V. Noord-Hollandische Uitgeversmattschappij, 1936), 1:217ff.; see Severs, "Is the Manciple's Tale a Success?," 2n. Cf. A. J. Minnis, "A Note on Chaucer and the *Ovide Moralisé*," *Medium Aevum* 48 (1979): 254–57. A new edition and translation is in preparation by Sarah Jane Murray.

Nulz homs, por plere a son seignor,
Ne doit de sa dame mesdire,
Et s'ele veult faire avoultire,
Il ne s'i doit pas consentir
N'encuser la. Mieux doit mentir,
Ou taire soi, pour pais avoir,
Que mal souffrir pour dire voir.[4]

[No man, to please his lord,
Ought to speak ill of his lady,
And if she should wish to commit adultery
He ought neither to consent
Nor accuse her. Less ought he to reveal
Where mischief may be, to maintain peace.
Such evil to suffer, just to say what one sees!]

Chaucer, of course, considerably expands the "moral," having the Manciple remember advice from his "old dame" and sputter well-intentioned but incautiously realized proverbial Scripture to the ostensible point of the crow's and his own confounding. Most of the biblical references come, as indeed the Manciple himself suggests, from the book of Proverbs (or "Salomon," Manciple's Tale, 314), though some of them, as befits "a man nought textueel," are quoted out of context and incomplete (318–62).[5] This biblical addition to the *Moralisé* version appears actually to heighten the "moral" reading, and so confirms that Chaucer intended his tale to be understood in the way the Manciple himself argues it should be. But before consigning the tale to the Manciple's own belabored interpretation, a glance at some of the other changes Chaucer makes in his sources may help us intuit a plausible reason for his offering a mundane and apparently not integral tale at the penultimate stage of the Canterbury journey.[6] Why would so expert a craftsman, after a

4. *Ovide Moralisé* 2.2542–48, from W. F. Bryan and Germaine Dempster, *Sources and Analogues of Chaucer's Canterbury Tales* (Chicago: West Richard, 1941), 709. While it is possible still to use the edition, blending four manuscripts, by de Boer, a modern edition is needed. See Marc-René Jung, "Les Éditions Manuscrites de l'*Ovide Moralisé*," *Romantische Zeitschrift für Literaturgeschichte / Cahiers d'histoire des littératures romanes* 20, nos. 3–4 (1996): 251–74; Jung, "Ovide, texte, translateur et gloses dans les manuscrites de l'*Ovide Moralisé*," in *The Medieval Opus: Imitation, Rewriting, and Transmission in the French Tradition*, ed. Douglas Kelly (Amsterdam: Rodopi, 1996), 75–98. See also John Lowden, *The Making of the Bibles Moralisées*, 2 vols. (University Park: Pennsylvania State University Press, 2000).

5. F. N. Robinson, ed., *The Works of Geoffrey Chaucer* (Oxford: Oxford University Press, 1968), 235; cf. Severs, "Is the Manciple's Tale a Success?," 12–13.

6. I am accepting here the weight of traditional textual arguments for the placing of the Manciple's Tale, as in Robinson, *Works of Geoffrey Chaucer*, 762–63.

successful string of tales with complex and interlocking significance, and just before his weighty conclusion, insert a tale whose only structural justification seems to be the "self-exposure" of the Manciple with a moral about heedless loquacity? While such a moral ironically suits the teller, it doesn't really seem to integrate the tale itself with the major thematic lines of the Canterbury poem.

Among the changes Chaucer makes in his story is to give it to an obtuse narrator. Not only is the Manciple's excessive and anticlimactic moralizing of his tale without precedent in known analogues of the story (surely he is one of Chaucer's least witting raconteurs), but Chaucer has altered the balance of character development in the story. As Earle Birney has demonstrated, "it is only in the Manciple's telling that Phebus' 'wyf' and her lover are portrayed with complete lack of sympathy, and only here that the actual murder of the wife is passed over in a single casual line."[7] Departing from the *Ovide Moralisé* and Guillaume de Machaut's version in *Le Livre du Voir Dit*, and differing also from Gower, Chaucer highlights moral turpitude and apparently tasteless judgment in the "wyf." Unlike other retellings, here her lover is not a "youth" or a "knight" but rather "a man of litel reputacioun" (Manciple's Tale, 199) whose character is unambiguously denigrated by Chaucer's rather unromantic analogy of the lecherous she-wolf from the *Roman de la Rose*.[8] Further, Chaucer carefully develops a special relationship between Phebus and his white crow. Not only is it (like Phebus himself) a singer of marvelous melody, but Phebus has it

> fostred many a day,
> And taughte it speken, as men teche a jay. (Manciple's Tale, 131–32)

To heighten our sense of the kinship between Phebus and his wonderful bird, Chaucer poignantly recalls the pair's history at the moment of the crow's unhappy revelation:

> "What, bryd!" quod Phebus. "What song syngestow?
> Ne were thow wont so myrily to synge
> That to myn herte it was a rejoysynge
> To heere thy voys? Allas, what song is this?" (Manciple's Tale, 244–47)

7. Earle Birney, "Chaucer's 'Gentil' Manciple and His 'Gentil' Tale," *Neue phililogische Mitteilungen* 61 (1960): 267.

8. Bryan and Dempster, *Sources and Analogues of Chaucer's Canterbury Tales*, 720–21. This follows a convention in medieval French courtly literature in which the condemnation of such women is largely for the insult of their tastelessness—e.g., in *Le Pescheor* ("De la pucelle qui abevra le polain"); *La Bible Guiot de Provins*, 146ff.; *Le Livre de Manières*, MS Angers 295, ccil, ccxi.

In the same vein, and deliberately unlike his sources, Chaucer does not have the crow fly over a great distance to tell Phebus what has happened. He omits the long intervening dialogue between raven and crow, found in Ovid, Machaut, and the *Ovide Moralisé*, in which the pet of Phebus is strongly, though vainly, counseled by the other bird to eschew tale-telling. In the Manciple's story the crow doesn't fly anywhere or take counsel from anyone; it is merely caged, can't help what it sees, and without hesitation blurts out the unhappy report. In the new structure, Phebus's tender fostering of the crow in his house serves to add virtuous context to the generous description of his noble character, which occupies the first twenty-odd lines of the tale. Save in his descriptions of Theseus and the Knight, Chaucer is not so lavish in his attribution of qualities with the weight of "gentilesse," "honour," "worthynesse," "as wel in fredom as in chivalrie."[9] Again in a departure from other versions, Chaucer's crow is given a longer revelation speech that focuses not on the "wyf" but on Phebus:

> "By God," quod he, "I synge nat amys.
> Phebus," quod he, "for al thy worthynesse,
> For al thy beautee and thy gentilesse,
> For al thy song and al thy mynstralcye,
> For al thy waityng, blered is thyn ye
> With oon of litel reputacioun,
> Noght worth to thee, as in comparisoun,
> The montance of a gnat, so moote I thryve!"
>   (Manciple's Tale, 248–55)

All of this hardly serves to achieve what the older versions manage—sympathy for the girl, disdain for the bird, and resentment for Phebus as the perpetrator of vengeful judgment. By crafting a more sympathetic relationship between the crow and Phebus, while at the same time allowing a much more distinctly negative portrayal of the wife's behavior, Chaucer has completely altered the balance of sympathies in his version of the story.

In the earlier versions, Phebus's "wyf" is not his wife, but rather "pucelle" or "acointa," and her attributes are those of a mistress.[10] Chaucer not only gives her a matrimonial commitment to Phebus, but, in the denigration of her lover and the replacement of her attractive characterization with the analogue of

---

9. Robinson, *Works of Geoffrey Chaucer*, 123–26.

10. R. Hoffman, *Ovid and the Canterbury Tales* (Philadelphia: University of Pennsylvania Press, 1966), 194, seems, in citing the reverse, inadvertently to have slipped here; see *Metamorphoses* 2.542ff.; *Ovide Moralisé*, 2143; Guillaume de Machaut, *Le Livre du Voir Dit*, 7785 (in Bryan and Dempster, *Sources and Analogues of Chaucer's Canterbury Tales*, 711).

the she-wolf, allows her to be seen in a much darker light. On the other hand, the genial relationship between Phebus and the crow, as in the lines selected above, seems to make Phebus's own role in the narrative structure of the tale more positive, even to mitigating somewhat, perhaps, our distress at his angry response to the crow's discovery. For how can we have much more sympathy in Chaucer's version for the "wyf" than for Phebus himself? Chaucer has nearly reversed his audience's identification with the principals by interchanging the prominence of their characterization. Moreover, the interchange seems to be consistent with other transformations that work toward redressing the balance of our affections—for example, the reduction of the murder scene to just one line.

Even so, most would agree that in Chaucer's version we are likely to be disturbed by the slaying of Phebus's unnamed wife, more concerned by his devastating reaction to her than by the plight and lesson of the jangling crow. In fact, were it not for the Manciple's own lengthy, pretentious, and anticlimactic moral exegesis, our attention would not likely attach to the "janglyng" moral at all. For Chaucer nowhere prepares us for this moralizing of the Manciple in the tale itself. Indeed, his longest and most obvious omission from the original story is the one passage in Ovid, the *Ovide Moralisé*, and Machaut that was basic to their "moral" reading: the central and lengthy counsel of crow (*la cornille*) to raven (*li corbiaus*) on the ill-advisedness of jangling. The list of characters in the Manciple's Tale has been cut to one bird, and, in Chaucer, the tale concludes not with the Manciple's moral but rather with a lamenting by Phebus of "rakel ire" (rash anger). It is with good reason, as we shall see, that Chaucer has allowed the Manciple to interchange the two *corbiaux* of the *Moralisé*, keeping for his own reporter the singular white crow. The advisory voice of the other bird, Ovid's *garrula cornix*, seems to become in Chaucer the peremptory croaking of the Manciple himself, outside his tale, preaching.

To be sure, the Manciple tries to get as much advice into his tale as he can. After a curiously inverted conclusion to his examples of bird in cage, cat and mouse, and the lecherous she-wolf with vulgar taste, his next sententious utterance is offered to justify a titillated use of the word "lemman" to describe Phebus's rival.[11] Given what he has already said without apparent qualm, we should immediately suspect him of affectation. There is, however, a ring of familiarity in his excuse:

> The wise Plato seith, as ye may rede,
> The word moot nede accorde with the dede.

11. Robinson, *Works of Geoffrey Chaucer*, 187ff.

> If men shal telle proprely a thyng,
> The word moot cosyn be to the werkyng. (Manciple's Tale, 207–10)

Medieval writers, Chaucer not least among them, are typically careful about the beginnings and endings of their work.[12] At this final stage of Chaucer's great work, an attentive reader ought to pay careful attention to the fact that the first enunciation of the principle of plainspokenness came in the General Prologue. After concluding his description of the Canterbury pilgrims, Chaucer there continues his posture as a reporter of their tales by asking his audience leave to speak the tales "pleynly":[13]

> For this ye knowen al so wel as I:
> Whoso shal telle a tale after a man,
> He moot reherce as ny as evere he kan
> Everich a word, if it be in his charge,
> Al speke he never so rudeliche and large,
> Or ellis he moot telle his tale untrewe,
> Or feyne thyng, or fynde wordes newe.
> He may nat spare, althogh he were his brother;
> He moot as wel seye o word as another.
> Crist spak hymself ful brode in hooly writ,
> And wel ye woot no vileynye is it.
> Eek Plato seith, whoso kan hym rede,
> The wordes moote be cosyn to the dede. (General Prologue, 730–42)

Truthful speech is here accorded both biblical and classical warrant; euphemism can deceive. These lines, spoken by Chaucer's own narrator persona, are usually taken to be an advance apology for colorful language. But they are also a statement of conviction about the court poet's conciliar obligation; that is, in his own voice, so to speak, Chaucer asks us to acknowledge with him that fidelity to one's "auctor" demands "that nothing be extenuate," that the fair truth is the whole truth. To the authority of Plato in this case, the authority of Christ is added. A faithful counselor should tell it like it is.

This is not, however, quite what the Manciple has in mind. His pretended recollection of Chaucer's principle is something of a ruse. Indeed, there is nothing very risqué in his language at all; the Nun's Priest would have had more reason to make apology, and thought it unnecessary. Rather, the

---

12. See Russell A. Peck, "Number Symbolism in the Prologue to Chaucer's Parson's Tale," *English Studies* 48 (1967): 205–15.

13. Robinson, *Works of Geoffrey Chaucer*, 727.

Manciple is facetiously calling for license to identify the miscreance in cruder terms, whatever the social class:

> I am a boystous man, right thus seye I:
> Ther nys no difference, trewely,
> Bitwixe a wyf that is of heigh degree,
> If of hir body dishonest she bee,
> And a povre wenche. (Manciple's Tale, 211–15)

The Manciple's curious social and literary hesitancy vindicates William Wordsworth's judgment that his case is one in which we can discern in Chaucer's artistry a built-in distance between the poet and his narrator, and to which there is adequate warning.[14] Given to us as a man of careless speech and twice "nought textueel," the Manciple can perhaps make his part in the tale a "feyne thyng" by failing to "reherce as ny as evere he can, / Everich a word"—that is, by thoughtless omission. Yet if we continue in our attentiveness to Chaucer's warning to his audience about the conflict of motives at play in offering counsel to the powerful, we may well imagine that even the Manciple's verbal carelessness, so effectively revealed in the moral he tries to draw in the circumstances, is in the larger context integral to a larger purpose: highlighting the difference between faithful and self-serving court counsel.

Both structurally and in relation to sources, there appears to be a flat contradiction between the Chaucerian version of the Ovidian tale and the traditional moral of the original, drawn at such lugubrious length by the tedious Manciple. That the Manciple sees the "janglyng" theme to the exclusion of anything else is obviously to recall the clichéd reading. But in its Chaucerian transformation I doubt that we can consider the story of Phebus, "wyf," and crow to be any longer primarily about jangling. For if that were so, why would Chaucer have allowed the Manciple to wreak so many fundamental changes in the original narrative, all of whose effect is to undermine that convention?

Scriptural Refinement

Our answer begins, I think, with Chaucer's biblically mediated reading of Ovid. The *Ovide Moralisé* is the most explicit source for the Manciple's moral as well as his tale. Typically, however, it includes an *"autre sentence"*

---

14. E. De Selincourt and Helen Darbishire, eds., *The Poetical Works of William Wordsworth* (Oxford: Oxford University Press, 1947), 4:471. One might still wish to disagree, however, with Wordsworth's own reading of the tale.

for its version of the story. This second "sentence" (meaning or interpretation) is allegorical. In the *Ovide Moralisé*, Phebus is envisioned as "*devine sapience*" greatly in love with "*nostre humanité*"; that is, the relationship between Phebus and Coronis calls to mind that between the deity and mankind, between God and his people, between Christ and his bride.[15] The lover in the *Moralisé* is likened to the temptation of mortal vices that corrupt our proper love, earning us in consequence the "*mortal floiche*" of death. The "*corbiaux*," respectively, are compared to "*le dyable*" and "*l'accuseor, le decevable*," whose ignominious eagerness to accuse in the *Moralisé* causes its author to see the principal bird's punishment as just, whose warning might be phrased "Judge not that ye be not judged."[16] The "Phitoun" slain by Phebus, though twice mentioned by Chaucer, is not part of this particular Ovidian story, but is given a compatible identification when it occurs elsewhere in the *Moralisé*: "*le serpent orible et redoutable . . . [le] dyable*" (that horrible and dreadful serpent . . . the devil). Its double inclusion in the Manciple's Tale suggests that other mythological qualities of the Phebus-Coronis story did not entirely escape Chaucer in giving it to the Manciple.[17] The Accuser would seem to be a particularly gifted fallen angel.

Measured against the portion of the Ovidian tale that we, following the Manciple, have examined, the Christian allegorical "sentence" given in the French version may seem slightly tendentious. The colorless Phebus of the *Moralisé*, for example, hardly seems equal to "*devine sapience*." In fact, the allegory begins to appear plausible only in the light of the balance of the story that the Manciple does *not* tell. In that conclusion, the dying Coronis acknowledges her guilt, repents, and laments that Phebus has unwittingly condemned their unborn son to death as well. Sorrowing, Phebus then takes the infant from her womb and causes him to be nourished. He is "Escupalius" (Aesculapius), the mythological sometime-discoverer of medicine and surgery, whose supernatural healing powers "*pot faire les mors revivre*" (are able to revive the dead).[18] But for Coronis, alas, Phebus cannot obtain the art of Aesculapius in time:

> Puis qu'il n'i puet conseil metre
> Il n'a fors de l'entremetre
> Coment el soit en terre mise. (*Ovide Moralisé*, 2437–39)

15. De Boer, *Ovide Moralisé*, line 2549ff.
16. De Boer, *Ovide Moralisé*, lines 2616–22.
17. Robinson, *Works of Geoffrey Chaucer*, 109, 128; de Boer, *Ovide Moralisé*, lines 2652, 2675.
18. De Boer, *Ovide Moralisé*, line 2432.

At that point he was unable to offer more;
He had no power to intercede
That she might be restored to the world.

Aesculapius is made to be *"l'âme,"* the eternal soul that *"ne souffre Dieus en li morir"* (God does not allow to die), and though beyond the suggestive language of his account the writer did not go on to further allegorization, in the birth of a miraculous son, despite the death of Coronis, he at least held out some hope for the future.[19]

By contrast, what is absolutely clear about the version Chaucer permits the Manciple is that, in his telling, it emphatically denies any redemptive hope offered by the original tale, with or without an *"autre sentence* [another meaning].*"* And there are other signposts to draw this harsh omission to our attention. First, Chaucer has implanted manifold warnings about the Manciple's reliability. Second, he has achieved a modification of protagonist sympathy by exalting Phebus and adding the Phiton incident, so that the allegorical values given in the Manciple's Tale (*"nostre humanité"* and *"devine sapience"*) seem in some respects more reasonable than in the *Moralisé*. Even, as we shall see, by the interchange of the raven for the crow, Chaucer suggests that the peculiarities of the Manciple's version may be expected to capture his reader's attention. All of this should suggest that we are not unjustified in looking beyond the Manciple's "moral" for the presumed conclusion of the tale—which is not given by the Manciple.

We might ask: Were the changes Chaucer allows his Manciple meant to lead us to appreciate that the crow did the wrong thing, or to be all the more disturbed by Phebus's "rakel ire"? The story itself suggests the latter. There are altogether ample grounds for feeling that Phebus's own bitter condemnation of his "rakel ire" is more appropriate to the action as we have seen it than the Manciple's moral. Our narrator gives us little reason to doubt that the "wyf" is guilty (here he follows Ovid very closely), and there is much less motive in Chaucer's version for pouring blame on the crow.[20] The bird's misfortune is an unavoidable witness to calamity, and his report a compulsive reaction predicated upon established affection for Phebus, not on an expressed love of jangling or hope of reward. Because of this palpable innocence and the special relationship of master and bird, the reader may be nearly as disturbed by Phebus's treatment of the crow as of his wife, for in the case of the bird

19. De Boer, *Ovide Moralisé*, lines 2587–90. On Aesculapius as a figure for divine redeemer, cf. Arnobius, *Adversus Gentes*, in *Patrologia Latina* 5:1279; cf. Isidore of Seville, *Etymologiae* 4.12.3.

20. *Metamorphoses* 1.543–46.

there seems to be no justice at all.[21] What the Manciple says about jangling is true enough, but in mismanaging the characterization given to the crow, it falls aside from the effective center of his story.

Nevertheless, the "moral" appears on the page, and I think it is important to try to see how Chaucer uses the Manciple's autobiographical criticism to help create a more comprehensive frame for the tale than the Manciple himself suspects. To begin where Phebus left off: if we can now ask why Chaucer might introduce a story about rash anger and precipitous judgment at the penultimate stage of the Canterbury journey, it will surely cause us to reflect that this subject relates to a carefully developed theme of *The Canterbury Tales* as a whole. Beginning in the Knight's and the Reeve's Tales and moving through the Tale of Melibee toward resolution in the Parson's sermon, the theme of advice and consent has been subordinate to the Chaucerian courtly theme of justice and mercy. The relevance of this theme to courtly poetry (especially Christian courtly poetry) is obvious, and Chaucer demonstrates his concern with this aspect of human social behavior by making it paramount at the beginning, middle, and end of his overall poem. Much as early on, when the pilgrims were making their way out of London, reckoning with the irate vengefulness of the Reeve's Tale helped heighten retrospectively an appreciation of the restrained and merciful judgment of Theseus, so here, prospectively, the "rakel ire" and condemnation of the Manciple's Phebus prepare our appreciation for the Parson's tempering of justice by mercy in specific biblical terms. However much we dislike the effects of Phebus's wrath, we see that, if nothing else, the crow's report is true, and that what ensues is in strictest Ovidian terms justice.[22] But we hope for more.

Classical justice is not the justice modeled for us by Theseus, explained by Prudence, and fulfilled in the Parson. Unlike Ovid's Phebus, Theseus (like the educated Melibee) has learned to control his ire with wisdom and mercy. Such judgment is an imaginative foreshadowing of the quality of mercy extended to the penitent among whom and of whom the Parson is about to speak. And the Parson, skillfully connected to the Manciple in many ways, will effectively supply again the redemptive hope that the Manciple has ignored in his foreshortening of the story, giving in God's mercy the ultimate model for princely judgment. The Parson's Tale forms the "answer," as it were, to the Manciple's perspective: a remorseless naming of sin, but with news of a remedy as well. The problem of the Manciple's Tale is that, though the crow's

---

21. E.g., William Cadbury, "Manipulation of Sources and the Meaning of the *Manciple's Tale*," *Philological Quarterly* 43 (1964): 541, finds the crow more a scapegoat than a villain.
22. *Metamorphoses* 1.607: "potui poenas tibi, Phoebe, dedisse . . . "

report is accurate, it bears the condemnation of limited truth, and in making everything hinge upon that to the exclusion of the rest of the original story, the Manciple also becomes, as *"li corbiaux"* in the *Ovide Moralisé*, both *"l'accuseor"* and *"le decevable."* His tale lacks a sense of closure: he would leave us with mere condemnation; at best he leaves us with more questions than answers.

Traditional iconography for the crow (or raven) strongly associates the bird with advice or report in two senses: he can be either the raven of Noah that fails to report at all (the opposite of the white dove that returns with word of God's mercy and grace),[23] or, more favorably, the bird who brings the bread, or the Law of the Lord, to Elijah in the desert.[24] Both of these tend to give the crow an association with the Synagogue, or the Old Law, and indeed, in a parallel elaboration on the Phebus-Coronis story in the *Ovide Moralisé*, this association is adduced. The trusted companion of Palladis (an equivalent figure to Phebus in the main story), and here also the reporter of miscreance, is now, exactly as in Chaucer, the crow. His signification:

> C'est Signagogue, qui jadispoe
> Ot la grace et la bien vueillance
> De la devine sapiance,
> Et trop estoit plesans et bele,
> Si fu la principal ancele,
> Sor toutes autres esleüe,
> Plus amee et chiere tenue:
> Ore est desposee et demise
> De s'amour et de son servise,
> Et forsclose de Paradis. (*Ovide Moralisé*, 2920–29)

> This is the Synagogue, separated
> From the grace and good will
> Of divine Wisdom.
> So much more pleasant and lovely might it have been
> If the original handmaiden

23. Gen. 8:7; also *Glossa Ordinaria*, in *Patrologia Latina* 113:109; cf. col. 1074; see also L. Réau, *Iconographie de l'art Chrétien* (Paris: Presses Universitaire de France, 1955), 1:127, who sums up one bestiary and exegetical tradition: "Juifs que refusent d'entrer dans la Barque de saint Pierre et s'accrochent au cadavre de l'Ancienne Loi."

24. 1 Kings 17:4–6; cf. *De Bestis Aliis et Rebus*, in *Patrologia Latina* 177:31–33, where the *corvus* is identified with the "praedicator qui magna voce climat, dum peccatorum suorum memoriam, quasi quamdam coloris nigredinem portat." The *corvus* is further said to prepare men to hear the words of God, to receive sound doctrine, and to make true confession (177:32). Cf. the discussion of the contrast between the Manciple's Tale and the Parson at the end of this chapter.

Had eschewed all others
—more loved and cherished then:
Now she is disenfranchised, dismissed
From his love and service
—shut out of Paradise. (my translation)

I think that there is considerable reason to believe that the *Moralisé*'s expansion, parallel to the Phebus-Coronis story (not in the original Ovid) from which this "sentence" derives, provides the answer to Chaucer's apparent interchange of raven and crow in his reshaping of the original story—actually, he seems to have borrowed from both moralized tales.

Justice or Mercy?

In any case, however true its words may be, we see that the report of the Manciple's crow produces in Phebus only condemnation, and does not extend to remedy. The report of the bird comes, indeed, as the natural effect of the Old Law, which—though from the beginning loved by God and the king as beautiful and just—in discovering adulterous and "feyned loves" ("*terriennes delices et a faire les morteulz vices*," as the *Moralisé* describes Coronis's lover) proves insufficient for the preservation of "*nostre humanité.*" The report reminds us, with St. Paul (e.g., Rom. 3:20; 8:3) and the Parson (Parson's Tale, 366ff.), that, discovered as we are under the Law, so by the Law we are condemned—that, as St. Augustine has it, the law is "prejudicial": it "discovers, but it does not heal"; it provides "not the cure, but only the knowledge of sin."[25] What Chaucer has made clear to us, from the judgment of Theseus to the counsel of Prudence to the remedy of the Parson, is our need for a grace that goes beyond the truth of guilt and the Law's just condemnation. At the conclusion of *The Canterbury Tales*, our eternal hope is that such grace becomes available to us, by penitence, in Christ's mercy; our hope for society, that such a model for princely judgment is available by this example to the adjudications of temporal power.

If the Manciple's reiterated assertion that he is "nought textueel" sufficiently alerts us to the possibility that he may be distorting both the narrative

---

25. "The law . . . is absolutely prejudicial, unless grace assists it, and the utility of the law may be shown by this, that it obliges all whom it proves guilty of transgression to betake themselves to grace for deliverance and help to overcome their evil lusts. It rather commands than assists; it discovers disease, but does not heal it; nay, the malady that is not healed is rather aggravated by it, so that the cure of grace is more earnestly and anxiously sought for. 'The letter killeth, but the spirit giveth life' (2 Cor. 3:67)." Augustine, *On the Grace of Christ* 1.9, in *The Works of Aurelius Augustine*, ed. and trans. M. Dods (Edinburgh, 1874), 12:10. Cf. *Epistle* 145.3.4.

and the "sentence" of his story, thus making us watchful readers, then when that same caveat is uttered by the Parson immediately afterward in his prologue, it must lead us to consider the two men in juxtaposition. When we do, we discover that the Parson's relationship to his text is not, of course, the same:

> "But nathelees, this meditacioun
> I putte it ay under correccioun
> Of clerkes, for I am nat textueel;
> I take but the sentence, trusteth weel." (Parson's Prologue, 55–58)

Willing to have his "meditacioun" submitted to higher authority, the Parson would have us recognize that his concern is for "sentence," and this bias helps to justify his first response to Harry Bailly's request:

> "Thou getest fable noon ytoold for me,
> For Paul, that writeth unto Thymothee,
> Repreveth hem that weyven soothfastnesse
> And tellen fables and swich wrecchednesse.
> Why sholde I sowen draf out of my fest,
> Whan I may sowen whete, if that me lest?" (Parson's Tale, 31–36)

Since the immediate context of the Parson's remarks, in the mind of Chaucer's audience, is the preceding tale of the Manciple with its half-told Ovidian fable, the Parson's words deserve careful notice. St. Paul's warning to Timothy about those who "weyven soothfastnesse" with "fables" turns out to be extremely relevant to our Manciple:

> Neither give heed to fables and endless genealogies, which minister questions, rather than godly edifying which is in faith: so do. Now the end of the commandment is charity out of a pure heart, and of a good conscience, and of faith unfeigned: From which some having swerved have turned aside unto vain jangling: Desiring to be teachers of law; understanding neither what they say, nor wherof they affirm. (1 Tim. 1:4–7)[26]

We are brought back to the context of the Manciple's "moral" through stark contrast with his more worthy successor. The Parson was given to us in the General Prologue as the very embodiment of the "end of the commandment," the "ensample" and perfect practitioner of the "godly edifying which is in faith."[27] He that "Cristes gospel trewely wolde preche" (General Prologue, 481)

---

26. See also 1 Tim. 4:7; 2 Tim. 4:2–5.
27. Robinson, *Works of Geoffrey Chaucer*, 477ff.

> was to synful men nat despitous,
> Ne of his speche daungerous ne digne,
> But in his techyng discreet and benygne. (General Prologue, 516–18)

The sort of man who gave freely of his own sustenance to others, "out of the gospel he tho wordes caughte" (General Prologue, 498), and without apology for "knavyssh speche," kindly but unflinchingly fulfilled his office:

> But it were any persone obstinat,
> What so he were, of heigh or lough estat,
> Hym wolde he snybben sharply for the nonys.
> . . . .
> He waited after no pompe and reverence,
> Ne maked him a spiced conscience. (General Prologue, 521–23,
>   525–26)

The Manciple, from the Inns of Court, who could of his thirty-odd masters of law "sette hir aller cappe" ("set all their caps"—i.e., outwit them all), is hardly such a counselor (General Prologue, 586). He knows by hearsay something of the Law, but nothing of mercy. He gives us, by contrast with the Parson, a half-told fable that avoids an element critical to the whole truth, swerving aside from "sentence" into vain jangling so thoroughly that the imprudence of jangling is all the point he can any longer see. In view of his relationship in the Manciple's Prologue with the Cook, his attenuated perception seems naturally enough the consequence of failing to understand how the end of the Law is "charity out of a pure heart, and of a good conscience, and of faith unfeigned" (1 Tim. 1:5). Each of these qualities receives its precise negation, in order, in his malicious treatment of the Cook.

Perhaps, as elsewhere, Chaucer is getting at someone through his functionary, and the Manciple may represent those who desire to become counselors, teachers of the law, advisers to the king. Chaucer himself may have once been a student at the Inner Temple, and personal memory might have contributed a perspective on the denizens of that place to add incentive to his criticism.[28] Whatever the case for his own connections with the immediate world of his chosen narrator, Chaucer has the Manciple refer to the source of his sententious moralizing not as his thirty masters but rather as his "olde dame." It may not be entirely coincidental that the most important commentary on

28. A list of studies on the subject can be found in Martin M. Crow and Clair C. Olson, *Chaucer Life-Records* (Oxford: Clarendon, 1966), 12n, 21n. They also include the record that Chaucer was once sued by a manciple (340).

the Parson's Timothy reference makes a distinction between helpful fables and those that are *sine fructu* (fruitless), comparing the author of vain fables to the foolish woman of Proverbs (9:12, 18).[29] The Proverbs of Solomon, of course, is the biblical book from which the Manciple so ineptly quotes, in his moralizing counsel, as the advice of his "olde dame."

As for Phebus's "rakel ire," the Parson has a full section on the subject, in which "janglyng" and bad counsel are both given as subspecies of ire (Parson's Tale, 638–50). He notes "two maneres" of wrathful behavior, one good and one wicked. The latter is "hastif Ire" (Parson's Tale, 540), which it is appropriate for good princes to eschew; the "goode Ire is by jalousie of goodnesse, thurgh which a man is wrooth with wikkednesse . . . nat wrooth agayns the man, but wrooth with the mysdede of the man" (Parson's Tale, 537–40).[30] We appreciate in the Parson's concluding context that the justice tempered with mercy of Theseus is surely to be preferred to the swift wrath of the Manciple's Phebus. It seems to me that, at one level, the Manciple's Tale is intended to provoke us, like the character from a fourteenth-century dramatized sermon on advice and good judgment, to ask:

> Telle me now quate is pi rede [counsel]
> Thorgh moises law I am but dede.[31]

On another level, we are moved to hold in admiration the quality of noble judgment modeled in Theseus, in the reformed Melibee, and in the Parson, to whom the Manciple stands in such stark relief.

Whether or not we know the full story in the *Ovide Moralisé*, and even if we fear that what happens to the wife, however unhappy, is not unjust, we may still feel as though there must be something missing from the tale. Would the Phebus "fulfild of Gentilesse, / Of honour, and of parfit worthynesse," who slays the primeval Phiton, so carefully fosters the crow, and so reverently loves his bride "moore than his lyf," wish that bride to perish? The answer to this, even in the Manciple's foreshortening, is, of course, an emphatic no: Phebus

29. *Glossa Major*, in *Patrologia Latina* 192:379; cf. 192:348; see also John of Wales, *Compendiloquium*, part 8, in *Communiloquium Summa Collationum ad omne genus* (1511; repr., London: S. R. Publishers, 1964). The Manciple's first citation of his dame ("Thus taughte me my dame: / 'My sone, thenk on the crowe, a Goddes name'" [Manciple's Tale, 317–18]) is not, of course, from Proverbs, but evokes the warning of Christ against too much concern for self-preservation: "Consider the ravens: for they neither sow nor reap; which neither have storehouse nor barn; and God feedeth them: how much more are ye better than the fowls?" (Luke 12:24).

30. It should be noted that jealousy, the most apparent taint in the character of Phebus (Manciple's Tale, 144), is at least a characteristic he shares with the God of Moses and Hosea.

31. MS Bod. Lat. ThD 1. fol. 124r, a collection of fraternal sermons.

is filled with remorse. The part of the tale the Manciple has left sadly untold is, in reality, fulfilled in the Parson's sermon, where the "no" is qualified by the remedy of God made available to those who will seek it:

> Oure sweete Lord God of hevene, that no man wole perisse but wole that we comen alle to the knoweleche of hym and to the blisful lif that is perdurable, / amonesteth us by the prophete Jeremie, that seith in thys wyse: / "Stondeth upon the weyes, and seeth and axeth of olde pathes (that is to seyn, of olde sentences) which is the goode wey, / and walketh in that wey, and ye shal fynde refresshynge for youre soules, etc." (Parson's Tale, 75–78)

Conclusion

In the weighty political chess game of the medieval court, many moves avail to a king, and there are many ways to make him counsel. In this instance, the "olde sentence" that Chaucer gives his Parson is the completion of an episodic metacounsel to seek higher wisdom, the tale of a new law of justice tempered by mercy for those who are penitent. In considering the effect of Chaucer's poem, we ought not to forget the performance context of *The Canterbury Tales*. Both for courtly morality and for spiritual guidance, the Parson's counsel here proves more "fructuous" than the Manciple's and becomes, indeed, as does the Parson himself, the measure of the Manciple's shortcoming. In the last analysis, the most pointed irony in his tale for the Manciple is perhaps the most subtle—namely, that his weakness for "janglyng" is both proof and consequence of a failure to understand "the end of the law" with which he has supposedly spent his life surrounded. The larger frame of *The Canterbury Tales*, now about to conclude, unfolds to fulfill that irony with an accumulation of discoveries which amply hint that, in failing to go on from the limitations of Ovidian story to the biblical remedies of the Parson, the present company could well make a similar mistake.

five

IRONY AND MISREADING

Courtly Love and Marriage according to Henry VIII

This chapter was first ventured as a conference paper at a Catholic university (Notre Dame) during Lent (I have left it largely in that oral format here). As an Anglican, I was uneasy with the combination of venue and topic. I concluded that this probably had something to do with my rather too fragile Protestant evangelical identity. I owe at least part of this fragility, I suspect, to having been the only such person on my high school basketball team, dominated as it was by Catholics. One story from those days may help my reader get a sense of my purpose in what follows.

We were comfortably ahead at halftime in a basketball game. A couple of the guys, as was sometimes their wont, decided to tease me a little for my eccentric religion. In the accents of our tribe, if you will forgive their colloquial indelicacy, the ditty they chose on that occasion goes like this:

> Beware the Protestant minister:
> his false reason, false creed, and false faith;
> the foundation stones of *his* temple
> are the balls of Henry the Eighth.

This, just as we were called back out onto the court. The poem struck me as so funny that I couldn't stop laughing until the forward I was supposed to be guarding scored on me three times straight. We nearly lost the game. On the bus afterward our coach demanded to know "what in the [expletive, expletive] had happened" to me. One fellow confessed to the hijinks, upon which the coach roared, "Alright you guys—from now on there'll be no [blankety-blank] theological discussion in my locker room!" Years later I learned that the poem was a Gaelic witticism made popular by the Irish writer Brendan Behan—something of which my teammates were equally unaware.

History, like poetry, offers up such wisdom as it has to teach unpredictably, and often in a fashion flagrantly obverse to any possible intention in the mind of the original players or authors. This can easily lead to unwarranted fantasizing. Scholars, including modern medievalists, are not exempt from this temptation. What I will try to show in this chapter is that, recent modern fantasies notwithstanding, the much-romanticized notion of "courtly love" in the Middle Ages was pretty much always just a literary convention of sorts, a vehicle for social satire. Moreover, in that the very rules of this elite-society party game depended on an undergirding high cultural value for the normative *regulae* of Christian marriage as found in Scripture and the teaching of the church, courtly love was a potent device for teaching the value of those very principles by means of the ironic fancifulness of ludicrous contraries. Even the jokes of this genre (and there are many), I want to say, depend on unquestioned security in the assumption that fruitful Christian marriage was the glue upon which social stability and cohesion depended, perhaps most especially at the level of regal authority and the state.

Courtly Love as a Social Construct

One might not necessarily know this from the fantasies of Victorian medievalists or the remnants of their tribe in the academy today. The soft-pornographic realism of the Pre-Raphaelite painters—for example, Dante Gabriel Rossetti's *Beata Beatrix* (1863), Sir Edward Burne-Jones's *The Love Song* (1877), or, in the second generation, Sir Frank Dicksee's *End of the Quest* and *Chivalry*, along with John Collier's *Tannhauser in the Venusburg* (1894)—provides examples of a modernist taste for the aesthetic reconstruction of an ethical legacy of medieval culture for which no facts can be demonstrated. Attractive as they may be, such depictions bear no more correspondence to their ostensible medieval prototypes than does their plausibility of costume or, in many cases, lack of costume.[1]

---

1. A good general work on the Pre-Raphaelites and Victorian medievalism is *Beyond Arthurian Romances: The Reach of Victorian Medievalism*, ed. Jennifer Palmgren and Lorretta M. Holloway (London: Palgrave Macmillan, 2005); see also Marcus Waithe, *William Morris's Utopia of Strangers* (Cambridge: D. S. Brewer, 2006).

I do not mean to suggest that blithe falsifications of history and contra-dictions of plain sense are entirely without value. A complete incapacity for irony, coupled with an appalling ignorance of the actual anthropology out of which a text is written, will sometimes lead to an interpretation much more entertaining than the text itself. One academic whose place in the history of medieval literary study has been assured more by this dubious sort of fantasia than by his better work is the nineteenth-century French medievalist Gaston Paris. In an inventive essay on Chrétien de Troye's *Le Conte de la Charrette* (1883), he introduced the term *amour courtois* to describe the illicit, secret, demeaning, and ultimately disastrous love of Lancelot and Queen Guenevere.[2] In this relationship, which Paris tellingly described as "a kind of idolatry," Lancelot's first article of faith is in the goddess-like superiority of his mistress; the great knight grovels before her most trivial requests for feats by which he may hope to prove his undying ardor. Now the frank objective of this most famous "courtly lover" is nothing less than an adulterous liaison with the queen of his own liege lord, Arthur. Yet for Paris, Lancelot's amorous ambi-tion signaled a new and inspirationally modern moment in the history of medieval literature and provided the model by which, accordingly, all other medieval narratives about love should henceforth be understood.

Since then, as they say in the Bronx, a lot of folks have bought the bridge. It would be extraneous to our purposes here to provide a list,[3] but two other figures probably merit notice. The first I have in mind is Denis de Rouge-mont, whose *Love in the Western World* (1939; rev. 1972) begins with a close analysis of *Tristan und Isolde* and, following Gaston Paris, talks about the great nobility of a courtly lover who subjects himself repeatedly to intense sexual torment while remaining stoically resigned to unconsummated desire. De Rougemont finds the origin of this "higher" form of love in the heretical practices of the Cathars, among whom tormented eros was allegedly intrinsic to a kind of gnostic mysticism. Now, despite the fact that de Rougemont was a well-respected writer on a number of topics, and that the *National Review* lists *Love in the Western World* as one of the "100 Best Non-Fiction Books of the Century," this particular idea is utter rubbish. (While Mozarab verse with non-Christian ideas about sex clearly influenced the Provençal poets,

2. *Amour courtois*, the French nineteenth-century academic term, is a neologism coined to name the fantasy. It is not a medieval term. It should be distinguished from the medieval term *fin amour*, first found in the thirteenth-century Provençal poet Marcabrú, which describes courtliness or, sometimes, genteel practices of courtship—a refinement of manners character-ized by a preference for honor and by virtues such as self-effacement, fidelity, and a willingness to delay gratification.

3. One might consult here the sources cited in C. S. Lewis's *Allegory of Love* (Oxford: Oxford University Press, 1936).

few (if any) of them were Cathari heretics, and such Arabic influence as can be demonstrated was in any case more formal and metrical than topical.)

It may be helpful to recall that Provençal poems whose manner and subject matter were what Marcabrû was first to call "*fin amor*" were almost invariably performed aloud by the poet himself in court before an assembled regal company. Cultured medieval people were, on all the available evidence, more sensitive to political allegory than we are; a poet would certainly need to be thoughtful about the risk of offense to his courtly superiors if he were seen to commend a kind of pseudo-nobility that they viewed not only as inherently foolish but even as treasonable to figures in authority such as themselves.

That there were artificial conventions for a genteel sort of amorous poetry, as there were in Ovidian Rome, is certain. But, as Robert Briffault in his book *The Troubadours* has put it, the "stylized passion" of such poetry should not in any literalistic fashion prompt us to attach to it a greater suspicion of realism than we would to the "stage-love tunefully bestowed by an Italian tenor upon a prima donna graced with a lengthy career and Junonic presence."[4] As a point of comparison, Briffault instances Bernard de Ventadorn, who "celebrates in lascivious terms the personal charms" of Eleanor of Aquitaine "at a time when she was well into her late fifties." This, in an age without silicone and Botox. To put it in Briffault's words again, "the pedantic rules of courtly love were poetical fictions, and were in large measure consciously and admittedly such."[5]

No less a scholar of Christian literary history than C. S. Lewis, at least when he wrote his first major monograph, had not yet understood these conventions. Inspired to study medieval literature by Victorian poets such as William Morris, and finding the fantasy world of such poetry as "The Well at the World's End" too beauteous, as he touchingly put it, not to be true, he came to think of courtly love as a kind of proto-Protestant revolt, in the name of love, against the distressingly pragmatic view of the medieval Catholic Church regarding conjugal acts.[6] Accordingly, his *The Allegory of Love* (1936), initially attractive to many readers with like romantic tastes, has come to be regarded by most contemporary critical readers as not only fanciful but a bit embarrassing. Even his friend and colleague Gervaise Matthews, in his magisterial book *The Court of Richard II* (1968), with its pertinent chapters on literature, chivalry, and marriage, does not once mention *The Allegory of Love*.

    4. Robert Briffault, *The Troubadors* (Bloomington: Indiana University Press, 1965), 91.
    5. Briffault, *Troubadors*, 92.
    6. Lewis, *Allegory of Love*, chap. 1; cf. David Lyle Jeffrey, "Medieval Literature," in *Reading the Classics with C. S. Lewis*, ed. Thomas Martin (Grand Rapids: Baker Academic, 2000), 77–80.

Scholarly Corrective and Lessons Learned

The first literary critic to more or less definitively scotch the romantic idealism surrounding *amour courtois* was D. W. Robertson Jr. He was self-consciously correcting Lewis as well as de Rougemont and Gaston Paris, though he politely mentions only Paris, by then safely dead. By his own confession, Robertson was at most an agnostic where Christianity was concerned, yet his command of Christian biblical exegesis from the church fathers through the fourteenth century was virtually unequaled in his time.[7] Robertson's point was that, whether in the Ovidian satire called *The Art of Courtly Love* presented to the court of Marie de Champagne by her Mass-priest, Andreas, or in burlesque allegories such as *Le Roman de la Rose* and, from his point of view, the elegant *faiblesse* of Chrétien's *Lancelot*, "what is being satirized . . . is not 'courtly love' at all, but idolatrous passion."[8] Robertson's observation was that such a pseudo-religious elevation of carnal misdirection was not a peculiarly medieval phenomenon, but appears, only to be denigrated, also in the Old Testament and Roman classical literature. In other medieval literature, the ribald indelicacies of *Le Lai du Lecheur*, for example, are offered in the same high courtly style: the ironic contrast between high medium and low message affords a good part of the humor.[9] Robertson does not try to cast his medievals as Puritans; he allows, in fact, that "no one expected medieval noblemen to observe strict chastity." "But it is one thing," he says, "to engage in occasional dalliance and quite another to abandon oneself completely to idolatrous passion."[10] The so-called doctrine of courtly love, Robertson suggests, would be utterly inappropriate to a genuinely noble lover.

The historian John F. Benton names Paris, Lewis, and de Rougemont in his own renunciation of the myth. Benton's critique has the added advantage, for our purposes, that his analysis contextualizes the discussion in terms of both the laws and the practices associated with actual medieval marriage. These provisions were indeed, as Lewis observed, highly practical rather than romantic. The first of these, notwithstanding the canonical principle *consensus facit nuptias* (agreement to marry), was that "a legal marriage began with a

7. Robertson, in several articles and in his *Preface to Chaucer* (Princeton: Princeton University Press, 1962), was among the first American scholars to commend Henri de Lubac's *Exégèse Médiévale*, 4 vols. (Paris: Aubier, 1954).

8. D. W. Robertson Jr., "The Concept of Courtly Love as an Impediment to the Understanding of Medieval Texts," in *The Meaning of Courtly Love*, ed. Francis Xavier Newman (Albany: SUNY Press, 1968), 1–18.

9. Robertson, *Preface to Chaucer*, 204.

10. Robertson, "Concept of Courtly Love," 14.

financial contract between two families."[11] As Benton summarizes it, "The influence of family alliances, property rights, desire for legitimate offspring, social status, and the prospect of companionship all worked to make marriage attractive to the participants."[12] He adds, "We cannot know how much our medieval ancestors looked forward to what we would call a satisfying personal relationship—surely much less than do modern Americans." Love was something to be developed under the mutual obligations of obedience (cf. Eph. 5:23ff.); our own concern for "chemistry" and "fatal attraction" had no comparable primacy. The "participants" in a marriage included the extended families and communities, and numerous medieval texts, from *Urbain le Courtois* to St. Thomas Aquinas's *Summa contra Gentiles*, suggest that in marriage physical beauty is less to be sought than the highest order of friendship; in fact, Aquinas uses the term *amicitia* along with *amor* to avoid any possible confusion with "the love of concupiscence"[13] or, as we might more accurately call it, "falling in lust."

Adultery, especially that form of adultery in which a knight or vassal seduced the wife of his lord, was regarded in medieval law as a form of treason on a level with regicide.[14] The punishments accorded in the few known cases were severe.[15] In light of these harsh historical realities, a "Lancelot" story such as *Le Chevalier de la Charette* will seem quite a different tale than Gaston Paris imagined. As Benton puts it, "Chrétien has in fact gone out of his way to describe behavior he could be sure his courtly audience would condemn. . . . The knight who rides in a shameful cart is no casual lover but one who betrays his lord. . . . If we find Lancelot a sympathetic figure because he was guided by love rather than reason," he concludes, "it is because modern attitudes differ from medieval ones in ways Chrétien could not foresee."[16] For both Benton and Robertson, then, what Paris and others missed entirely was contextual irony.

One form of irony Chrétien uses in *Lancelot* is antiphrasis, an example of which, in the words of a medieval manual on the subject, is "to praise a lecher

---

11. John F. Benton, "Clio and Venus: An Historical View of Medieval Love," in Newman, *Meaning of Courtly Love*, 19–42.

12. Benton, "Clio and Venus," 21.

13. Cf. F. J. E. Raby, "Amore and Amicitia," *Speculum* 40 (1965): 599–610.

14. Benton, "Clio and Venus," 27.

15. Benton, "Clio and Venus," 40n26.

16. Benton, "Clio and Venus," 28. Similarly, noting that, in his version of the Philomela tale, Chrétien begins the rape scene with a courtly lover's supplication to his lady, Edith Joyce Benkov suggests that the juxtaposition "indicates a definite scorn on Chrétien's part for the ideal of courtly love"; see "Philomela: Chrétien de Troyes' Reinterpretation of the Classical Myth," *Classical and Modern Literature* 3, no. 1 (1983): 209.

for his chastity." Tonally, Chrétien's mode is *astysmos*, or mild sarcasm—a mode familiar to medieval readers of Ovid. To be scrupulous, not only modern English readers, according to W. T. H. Jackson, but medieval German authors often fail to "perceive the ironical overtones in French literature,"[17] so perhaps the subtleties of the conventions themselves have more than a little to do with our modern propensity to find charming what more probably the French authors were mocking. Dante's fifth canto of the *Inferno*, in which Paolo and Francesca are found among the damned for reading the Lancelot story as a prompt to adulterous *amor*, indicates clearly enough not only that literalistic romanticizing was even then a possibility, but also that a sophisticated medieval reader accepted that such a failure of interpretation might well make you eternally culpable. By comparison, it now seems pretty clear that most modern interpretations since the late nineteenth century have been telling us far more about modern sensibilities than medieval ones. What we thus learn about our own culture is not only that we tend to have a tin ear for irony. We learn also that, in our departure from earlier views of marriage that saw it as a sacred bond not merely spiritually but socially, we have come to view as entertaining, even admirable and ennobling, behavior that medieval men and women were most likely to have found ignoble and socially destructive—and also, on occasion, risible. In their setting, humorous and satirical literary "send-up" became a means of cautionary wisdom, a bas-relief framework for reflecting on the values actually thought commendable. In the hands of Victorian sentimentalists or Hollywood movie producers, the genre can become indistinguishable from soap opera, and almost as mindless.

Chrétien de Troyes

Our subject can be more reliably explored, I think, by reflecting on courtly custom and literary expression in the courts of three monarchs, one each from the twelfth, fourteenth, and sixteenth centuries. The *locus classicus* is France in the twelfth century. In the eminent case of Chrétien, whose work included translations of Ovid and a contribution to a Christian biblical allegorization of the *Metamorphoses*, the *Ovide Moralisé*, the first romance in his famous collection, *Erec and Enide*, explores qualities a worthy marriage was thought to engender. This poem clearly celebrates marriage as a unifying social force. Notably lacking in the devices of "love-service" or "*fin-amors*," our poem begins with a contract for marriage between Erec and Enide's father. Enide

17. W. T. H. Jackson, "Faith Unfaithful: The German Reaction to Courtly Love," in Newman, *Meaning of Courtly Love*, 55.

is attractive to Erec, but there are no verbal protestations of love or amorous passion. By contrast, their immoderately extended honeymoon is character-ized by concupiscent self-indulgence on Erec's part: he treats his wife more like a paramour or mistress—"*De li fist s'amie et sa drue*" (line 2435)—the word *drue* here having commonly ignoble connotations. Her embarrassment at the negative social consequences of his initially self-indulgent, idolatrous preoc-cupation with sex precipitates a quest that severely tests the marital bond, proving it to be one in which both parties must necessarily mature as the plot unfolds: Enide is repeatedly demonstrative of her absolute fidelity, and Erec is finally won over to reciprocate her fealty, not to mention her prudence, with his love and trust. This, as Jackson has observed, is in startling contrast to the weak marriage of Arthur and Guenevere and the false chivalry of Lancelot. He notes in particular that "the concluding *Joie de la Cort* episode makes very clear the difference between the servile bondage of a knight to a lady's whim and the free association of lovers in a purposeful life."[18]

Erec and Enide is thus not, in fact, a celebration of *amour courtois* but, as its concluding eschatological overtones suggest, a poem through which we are to increase our appreciation for the way in which the medieval Christian ideal of marriage reveals its sacramental value by forming a model for rightly ordered desire at several levels, ultimately expressive of and participating in God's redemptive love for the world. "My lord is in every way the son of a king," Enide tells her confused alter ego, "yet he took me when I was poor and naked" (lines 6254–55). This is a very different Erec than the one we find at the beginning of the poem. The concluding coronation banquet is on Christmas Day, and after Mass a thousand knights serve the bread, a thousand wine, all dressed in white, and we have a distinct sense that the ending of the poem is itself an epithalamion. This work sets the standard, I suggest, by which Chrétien's other "romances" may be judged.

The point about epithalamium as a genre was not, of course, incidental to the medieval view of marriage or to the particular performance of this poem in the court of Marie de Champagne. Marie was also the recipient and dedicatee of a rather elegant poetic commentary on Psalm 44 (Vulgate [45 KJV]) called, from the first word of the original Latin text, *Eructavit*. Medieval readers would recall that the psalm is a marriage poem, and commentaries from that of Augustine forward identified it allegorically with the "sacred marriage feast of the Bridegroom and the Bride, the King and his people." For Augustine it connects also with conversion, metamorphosis, transformation, as he puts it, "from the old to the new man . . . from an adulterer to a man of

18. Jackson, "Faith Unfaithful," 57.

chastity."[19] For Augustine preeminently "the Church is the Bride, Christ the Bridegroom." "There are commonly spoken by balladists," he adds, "certain verses to Bridegrooms and Brides, called *epithalamia*" (*supra* Ps. 45:3 [44 Vulgate]), and he notes that this psalm rejoices in such a poet's task, one whose "tongue is become the pen of a ready writer" (Ps. 45:1).

It is typical of late medieval Catholic doctrine that symbolic images applied to the church *generaliter* may apply to Mary *specialiter*, as *figura* for the church, the bride of Christ. In early Gallican liturgies Mary's feast included a celebration of her role as Queen of Heaven's King and thus featured Psalm 44.[20] Echoes of these images are likewise present in the Countess of Champagne's Commentary, in which the traditional lectionary placement of Psalm 44 in the Christmas-morning Mass ("*Le jour de Noel au matins*") is reiterated, but with the interesting touch that the epithalamion is sung by King David, who appears in the opening lines as a penitent outcast, dressed in sackcloth and ashes outside the nuptial chamber of the Bridegroom. This aspect of the poetic framework is not, of course, in the biblical text of Psalm 44, but calls to mind David's repentance following his adultery with Bathsheba (2 Sam. 11) and possibly another repentance recorded in 1 Chronicles 21. In the *Eructavit*, David is cast as the poet's own double, a medieval *jongleur* or balladeer, singing and pleading to be admitted to the cosmic marriage feast so that he can sing his epithalamion directly to the eternal Bride and Groom and their assembled noble guests. The Court of Heaven is portrayed in the *Eructavit* as an elegant feudal court, and it is said that the "*joie de la cort*" is a celebration that attends the King's crowning of his son and reception of his bride into the royal family. In such a context the "Joy of the Court" could not but be associated in the minds of Marie's court with the "joy of the court" at the conclusion of *Erec and Enide*.

The beautifully composed *Eructavit* is largely celebratory anagogy, but on occasion also includes explicit practical Christian teaching at the moral level. For example, it includes a stern injunction against any devaluation of marriage on the part of either party, suggesting among other things that even the "custom of the world" has it that, if a woman deserts the love of her husband for another, either through willed sin or a careless mistake, and though she should come to a full repentance, the husband has "no obligation to take her back and she would in fact be better off in the grave."[21] Nor should we imagine

19. See Augustine, *On the Psalms* 44 (in the Latin versions from which Augustine worked, the Old Latin, like the Vulgate, numbered this Ps. 44; in the KJV it is Ps. 45).

20. See George Scheper, "Bride and Bridegroom," in *A Dictionary of Biblical Tradition in English Literature*, ed. David Lyle Jeffrey (Grand Rapids: Eerdmans, 1992).

21. Newman, *Meaning of Courtly Love*, 26n24.

that such doctrinal reminders might be taken amiss by the thoughtfully pious Marie de Champagne. Among her chaplains, her personal confessor was Adam de Perseigne, a learned Cistercian and librarian. As it happens, Adam, at one time confessor also to England's King Richard I (Coeur de Leon), was the author of the *Eructavit*. This very same Adam was the priest called by Marie to her deathbed. Partly on account of the exemplary Christian fidelity associated with her court, Adam's commentary on Psalm 44 circulated widely as a text of spiritual instruction, in Anglo-Norman England as well as on the Continent. Later, *La Chronique de Gislebert de Mons* noted—of the next generation of this royal family—that Baldwin of Hainault, husband to the daughter of King Henry and Marie de Champagne, was a praiseworthy exemplar of male fidelity, saying, "It is rarely found in any man that he should cleave so much to one woman and be content with her alone."[22] None of this makes Marie de Champagne's court sound like much of a paradise for the modernist fantasies of would-be "courtly lovers." Further, it certainly casts the gravest of doubts upon the proposition that Chrétien de Troyes was an ardent proponent of "courtly love" so called.

The "Marriage Group" of *The Canterbury Tales*

About the same time that academics and artists took so much pleasure in the apparent discovery of "courtly love," it became fashionable in literary criticism to refer to some of Chaucer's *Canterbury Tales* as a "marriage group." In fact, however, almost every tale deals in some way with marriage, from the Knight's Tale to the Parson's, and several in such a way as explicitly to ironize—much less subtly than Chrétien—the literary conventions (or affectations) associated with "courtly" (i.e., illicit) love. The Knight's Tale sets off its Boethius-quoting protagonist, Theseus, against a pair of comically jejune and ineffectual knights. They, in turn, act out in wonderfully humorous hyperbole all of the pains attributed to frustrated "courtly love" (for a woman they have yet even to meet), offering a paradigmatic exposé of the social calamities occasioned by the pursuit of disordered affections—especially among persons whose responsibilities include governance.

This tale is followed by two tales that parody such disorder at another level by stripping off the fine clothes and upper-class manners—in low and vulgar humor nevertheless satirizing essentially the same sort of amorous intemperance. That most profoundly "learned" burlesque of marriage, the

---

22. Newman, *Meaning of Courtly Love*, 39n17.

Prologue and Tale of the Wife of Bath, specifically permits the garrulous Alison to misquote and misrepresent central church teachings on the "full gret sacrament," as she calls it, making a hilarious but utter hash of Christian canonical texts from Scripture through Jerome and Augustine. This sets up her own tale, a Breton *lai* in which a Guenevere-led court is blithely willing to pass over a maiden's rape in exchange for a "politically correct" answer in a courtly parlor game: what women universally most desire, the rapist must acknowledge, is total mastery over men. The Wife of Bath's tale is much more entertaining than a bare-bones synopsis can reflect, but readers may remember that it concludes with an ugly hag's entrapment of the rapist knight by blinding him with magical charms, then deluding him into believing that by accepting her shape-shifting capacity to be any woman he wants her to be, he can live out the fantasies he has really been pursuing all along.

Other disordered marriages—the tyranny of an irresponsible husband that fails to break the *feodas* (covenant promise) of his forbearing wife (Clerk's Tale), a beast-fable satire on the foolishness of excessive concupiscence (the Nun's Priest's Tale), and the impotent carnality and mockery of sacramental marriage by the old knight Januarie (the Merchant's Tale)—all deconstruct the conventions of "courtly love," literary or otherwise. The Franklin's Tale shows how, in fact, women most of all would be made victims by a culture of such notions of secret *amour* and "honorable" dalliance, even as the men in their lives became shabby parodies of true chivalry.[23] Conversely, the Tale of Melibee, with its exemplary reification of the virtues of the *mulier fortis* of Proverbs 31 and the *amicitia maxima* that Augustine and Aquinas, especially, found among the goods of accountable marriage, suggests worthy marriage as a means to living wisely. Finally, it must be said, the Second Nun's Tale shows us spiritual marriage as a good complete in itself, even though the sexuality of such a marriage be sublimated; and the Parson in his sermon gathers up the embedded scriptural commentary in most of these tales to recapitulate with a direct reference to biblical texts the essentials of Christian teaching on marriage.

Marriage is thus a central theme of *The Canterbury Tales* as a whole, though it is developed in such a way that the reader can appreciate its evident social and spiritual goods all the better for having observed the poor facsimiles that try to pass as something more attractive. Chaucer writes about the social and communal goods of well-ordered marriage elsewhere, in his political allegory *The Parliament of Foules*, in *Troilus and Criseyde*, and in

23. See, e.g., Alan T. Gaylord, "The Promises in the Franklin's Tale," *English Literary History* 31 (1964): 331–65.

his lyrics, notably when he is admonishing the carnally self-indulgent Richard II, among whose early preoccupations were behaviors not dissimilar to the early indulgences of Chrétien's Erec. Here, in a plea for Richard to be constant in his covenant to rule his people in justice, Chaucer bids him to "cherish" his people, to

> Dred God, do law, love trouthe and worthinesse
> And wed thy folk again to stedfastnesse. ("Steadfastnesse")

The idea that the obligations of a king in *feodas* with his people constituted a kind of marriage, with those duties being of a sort consistent with those enjoined by St. Paul in Ephesians 5, is as deeply embedded in the political philosophy of medieval Christendom as the *mysterion* or *sacramentum* of marriage is in Scripture figural, as the *Eructavit* declares, in reference to the coming parousia, for the eschatological union of Bridegroom and Bride in the kingdom of God. This is why Chrétien's contemporary, Hugh of St. Victor, likewise elaborates on Augustine's *De bono coniugali* to say that the intended liturgical office "proposed marriage in a compact [*feodas*] of love, that in it might be the sacrament of that society which exists in the spirit between God and the soul."[24] *Feodas*, like *sacramentum*, has here the full connotation of a covenant, or *pactum*; without this character, it could not be a sacrament. This is how one is to understand the canon—namely, as a "compact of mutual agreement" (2.11.4); it is the mutual verbal consent or compact that makes the marriage (2.11.5), not sexual union.[25] In this way, what medievals called

24. Hugh of St. Victor, *On the Sacraments* 2.11.3, trans. Roy Deferrari (Cambridge, MA: Medieval Academy of America, 1951), 325. Cf. St. Augustine, *De bono coniugali*, trans. P. G. Walsh (Oxford: Clarendon, 2001), 32–33. Hugh was writing in retrospect on an evolution in the Western European practice of marriage that, because of Christian doctrine, was under way but still not in his time complete. See here Glenn W. Olsen, ed., *Christian Marriage: A Historical Study* (New York: Crossroad, 2001), especially his essay "Marriage in Barbarian Kingdom and Christian Court: Fifth through Eleventh Centuries," 146–212.

25. Hugh of St. Victor, *On the Sacraments* 2.11.4–5. It is noteworthy that Chrétien and Adam de Perseigne were writing during the papacy of Alexander III (1159–81), during which time, prompted by the writings of Peter Lombard and other masters at Paris, canonical reform and a greater precision were being introduced in regard to marriage. To this point, the definitive indication that marriage had taken place was evidence of sexual union (*commixto sexuum*). All that preceded it was at most an espousal (*desponsatio*), and the relationship might be dissolved if either party perfected marriage carnally (*commixtione perficitur*) with a third person. Under the new reforms, betrothal (*sponsalia per verba de futuro*) was to become public as much as possible, and, in a fashion similar to modern practices of formal "engagement," it indicated to the community a period of chaste commitment following the verbal commitment and prior to the even more public marriage vows (*sponsalia per verba de praesenti*). The desire to remove abusive forms of "secret marriage" was one motivation for these elaborations, and discussion of the potential of secret vows to create social disorder features largely in the documents. See

the "faith of the betrothal" is, properly speaking, the beginning of marriage. The breach of that betrothal pledge—as, for example, by Angelo's perfidy in Shakespeare's *Measure for Measure*—is in itself adultery. Conversely, to fulfill one's betrothal vow even in unpropitious or inadvertent circumstances is to act in troth, or fidelity. Hugh of St. Victor's words, summarily then, speak for medieval Christianity: "Marriage, according as it is *worthy*, is a sacrament of that society which exists in spirit between God and the soul" (2.11.3). Accordingly, its ceremony is as communal a celebration as that of most other sacraments; like each of them, it bears witness of a pledge to a higher Troth. Erec and Enide's eventual coronation, in this light, is at once a declaration of the realized sacramental worthiness of their marriage and a consecration in *feodas* of their regency, in all that that signifies for the community at large. The eschatological overtones in Chrétien's final verses are not an incidental allegorical flourish but a reminder of the eternal archetype or exemplar by which Psalm 44 and Ephesians 5 ground the meaning of marriage in the mystery of human redemption itself.

Henry VIII and the Making of Modern Fantasy

I turn now to a very different court, that of Henry VIII, not to recount the unsavory details of his six wives, his five violated betrothals, or his many other dalliances, nor yet to show what his insistence on sexual freedom was to cost in the lives of his own worthy courtiers, among them a most noble bishop and a truly extraordinary chancellor. All this is well known, not least, alas, because modern cinema has made a lovable playboy out of this monster of the concupiscent appetites. I return to him because none of his legendary yet quite authentically documented exploits would be much remembered if he had not at the same time been a kind of Renaissance paragon: a genuine scholar, bibliophile, accomplished musician, theologically literate layman, and, not least, the founder of English Protestantism—largely on the grounds (as I am sure Eamon Duffy no less than Brendan Behan and my locker-room teammates would each in their fashion agree) of justifying personal sexual indulgence, slanderous intrigue, and judicial murder in a fashion that definitively out-burlesques the "courtly love" of medieval ironists. It has been shown

here Michael Sheehan, *Marriage, Family, and Law in Medieval Europe* (Toronto: University of Toronto Press, 1996); James A. Brundage, *Law, Sex, and Christian Society in Medieval Europe* (Chicago: University of Chicago Press, 1987); and Dorothea Kullman, "Hommes amoureux et femmes raisonnables: *Érec et Énide* et la doctrine ecclésiastique du marriage," in *Geschlecter-rollen im mittelalterlichen Artusroman*, ed. Friedrich Wolfzettel (Atlanta: Rodopi, 1995).

that the pursuit of the literary and social conventions associated with "courtly love," including reading romances aloud in the company of ladies, persisted through the time of the court of Richard II down to the Tudor court, and with a good deal of elaboration in the artifice of polite social game.[26] At the same time, there is abundant evidence that these courtly social fictions were becoming more vulnerable to factual enactment. Henry's courtly theatrics, as literalizing as his reconstructions of British history, effectively strip the earlier French literary conventions of their irony, play out polite and public flirtations as private fantasy, then legislatively normalize the consequences. Thus Henry, if not "the onlie begetter" of modernity in these matters, certainly deserves a lot of credit.

Henry's royal library was rich in theological writings. But it listed also sixteen medieval romances, including three versions each of *Lancelot* and *Lancelot du Lac*—more copies, it would appear, than for any other work. He had also Boccaccio's *Decamerone* and *De claris mulieribus* both in the original and in French translation, Guillaume de Lorris's *Roman de la Rose*, and a lot of Ovid. This suggests a certain preoccupation. Yet in his own work he fancied himself a theologian. For his book refuting Luther, ironically ghostwritten in part by Thomas More and titled *Assertio Septem Sacramentorum* (1521)—marriage therefore included—Henry won from Pope Leo X the now even more ironic title of "Defender of the Faith." Having perhaps acquired in his own mind personal grounds for entertaining doubts about the doctrine of papal infallibility, he then went on effectively to abolish the papacy as far as England was concerned, declaring himself the head of the church as well as of the state. There are other things about Henry VIII that discomfit, such as his lifelong "zeal in the outward practices of religion,"[27] and in particular his edition of what he called his *Sacra Biblia* (1535), essentially a Vulgate New Testament with selected parts of the Old Testament, omitting (notably, for his purposes) more than half of the latter. In this he is a prototype for much modernist biblical interpretation. The omissions include all of the Chronicles of Israel's kings, the books of the Prophets, Job, and the Song of Songs: that other epithalamion inseparable in Christian imagination from the *sacramentum* of marriage and calling us especially to the spiritual marriage of divine Bridegroom and sanctified Bride, Christ and the church. Henry's

---

26. See John Stevens, *Music and Poetry in the Early Tudor Court* (London: Methuen, 1961), 154–202. Henry's instinct for reducing the fictional elements of history to "facts" is evident in his charge to Polydore Virgil, the Italian brought in to produce a myth-free history of Britain, the *Historia Anglia* (London, 1555).

27. F. L. Cross, *The Oxford Dictionary of the Christian Church* (Oxford: Oxford University Press, 1953; 1990), 634.

preface to this work (which survives in only four copies) is, for all its show of piety, not less licentious than any other aspect of his life. Hear what he says to his readers—presumably a favored few:

> You know well how our Lord God, whose words or scriptures we are discussing, ordered that when a king sat on the throne of his kingdom, he should write for himself the law of God, and, having it with him, should read it every day of his life, so that he should thus learn to fear the Lord his God, and guard his words.[28]

We may note that Henry's accurate though hypocritical evocation of Deuteronomy 17:18–19 is as learned a gesture as his deletion of the accounts of Nathan's condemnation of David's adultery and of Elijah's denunciation of Ahab from "The Bible according to Henry VIII." He had heard enough about these passages already from the likes of Bishop John Fisher and Lord Chancellor Thomas More, both of whom he had executed (June 22 and July 5, respectively) within a month of his "personal" Bible's private publication, perhaps even as he was writing down these deceitful words for the preface. A month later he was himself (finally) excommunicated.

One's mind moves to analogues, of course, not many of which make a Christian who takes the authority of Scripture seriously very comfortable: Thomas Jefferson's Bible, for example, bowdlerized to suit Enlightenment and deistic sympathies;[29] or the pseudo-academic revisionist antics of the Jesus Seminar, not to mention the pitiable, Scripture-abusing marriage self-help books one now finds in Christian bookstores. When it comes to marriage in a putatively Christian society in general, however, the effects of our selective denials of Scripture and the canonical teaching of the church, however fashionable and entertainingly presented, have cost us dearly. On the court and off the court, we have too often laughed at all the wrong places. In court and

28. See Arthur Freeman, "The Gospel according to Henry VIII: The Selectivity, Conservatism, and Startlingly Personal Nature of a Bible Designed by Henry VIII," *Times Literary Supplement*, December 12, 2007; James P. Carley, *The Books of Henry VIII and His Wives* (London: British Library Publishing, 2005); and Carley's more complete *The Libraries of Henry VIII* (London: British Library Board, 2000). Henry owned copies both of Bruno Astensis's *De Sacramentis Ecclesiae* and Hugh of St. Victor's *De Sacramentis Chrisianae Fidei*. Carley notes that Catherine of Aragon, whom Erasmus thought more learned even than Henry, in 1525 asked the Dutch humanist to write a book on Christian marriage for Princess Mary. This was published in 1526 as *Christiani Matrimonies Institutio* (Carley, *Books of Henry VIII and His Wives*, lv). She then asked Thomas More to translate this book into English, a task he delegated to his children's tutor, Richard Hyrde; it was published in 1529 as *A Very Fruitful and Pleasant Boke Called the Instruction of a Christen Woman* (lvi). By this point Anne Boleyn had been openly installed in the court for a year, her adulterous liaison with Henry having begun well before the divorce of Catherine, in 1523.

29. *The Jefferson Bible* (New York: Beacon Press, 2001).

out of it, we have shrugged off all the most destructive of social consequences to families, to church, and to state.

As a result, here we stand, in the English-speaking culture of the declining West, on the verge of social bankruptcy where marriage as an institution is concerned. Our tabloid-dulled imaginations have unconsciously accepted the glamorization of marriage's opposite; burlesque, in a variety of contexts, has refashioned our cultural memory to the point where the notion of marriage as a sacrament has become, for many, of merely academic interest. Living like Henry VIII (or Hugh Hefner) has become a kind of archetypal modernist fantasy that has eclipsed in our social discourse most of the spiritual capital by which marriage was understood by our Christian forebears to be integral to our pursuit of the common good. In this lapsus we have lost contact with the scriptural imagination of poets such as Chrétien de Troyes and Geoffrey Chaucer—much to our cost.

Conclusion

In this chapter I have argued two things. The first is that what some modern medievalists have called "courtly love" is effectively a social construction of modernity, an outgrowth of romantic idealism as a substitute for Christian biblical ideals, and that it depends upon the neglect or subversion of biblical teaching regarding marriage. The second argument is tacit but ultimately more fundamental—namely, that in the process of "romanticizing" medieval Christian texts, we have distorted and helped to undermine in their Christian values what was perhaps their signature advance over the crudities of northern barbarism: a cultivation of gentility and self-sacrificing love as the hallmark character of Christian community. This, of course, includes centrally the noble ideals that marriage, if it is to be truly Christian, must always seek to realize. Understood in the medieval writers' own biblical terms and not our substitutes for them, marriage is among the higher goods to which medieval literature would direct our attention.

PART 2

SCRIPTURE *and the* ENGLISH POETIC IMAGINATION *after the* REFORMATION

It has been sometimes assumed, out of ignorance, that the great Reformers were opponents of the arts, ascetic rather than aesthetic in their temperament. The opposite pertains in the case of poetry. The Reformers came along at a time when vernacular poetry was in decline, and they provided inspiration by examples of sufficient vigor and accomplishment that would-be serious poets looked to them just as, in painting, had Lucas Cranach and Albrecht Dürer. The resulting new energies considerably complicate and enrich our sense of English literary history in particular.

The previous century had not been a glorious one for vernacular poetry. By 1500 the memory of Geoffrey Chaucer and such medieval poets as Langland and the *Pearl* poet had grown dim; the Scottish imitators of Chaucer—Henryson, Dunbar, and Lyndsay—found only a regional audience. By the beginning of the sixteenth century, spheres of intellectual activity other than the court were gaining in importance; currents of controversy swirled about the halls of northern European universities. While some of these were eddies from the turbulence of scholastic attempts to integrate Aristotle fully into medieval theology, and to navigate withal the challenges of nominalism, there was another, equally powerful set of conflicting energies. These were a result of newly intensified study of classical literary texts, Greek as well as Latin. Much excitement attached to the preparation of sound editions of authors from Homer and Aeschylus to Cicero and Seneca. Commentaries were written on these and other classical authors, reflecting closely on philological matters as well as on historical and cultural context. The ancient world was opening up its treasures in a new and vital way, not just as a means of learning grammar, rhetoric, and logic, but as a great library filled with literature of astonishing power and eloquence.[1] Students flocked to the study of classical literature. When we use the term "Renaissance," this is the rebirth to which we refer.[2]

Textual Reformation

Desiderius Erasmus of Rotterdam is an emblem for the brilliant scholarship that ensued. As a young professor of Greek at Cambridge, he attended John Colet's lectures on Romans. Having already become resistant to what he regarded as the depredations of the scholastic method, he was astonished by the richness and eloquence of the unadorned biblical text. He had begun arguing for a return, *ad fontes*, to biblical texts that would parallel the new engagement with classical literature, but when he heard Colet open up the text of Romans with careful philological and literary analysis, his commitment to the biblical sources intensified dramatically. He now regarded Scripture as the chief source for Christian humanism, with classical texts subtending them in a vital *philosophia Christi*.[3] But he saw also that the rigorous textual and philosophical methods of the new classical humanism were an indispensable ally for creating a literary education that could produce in the Christian learner sound judgment and right action.[4] This would require that primary attention be given to the text itself.

As with many a humanist scholar in his era, the frustrations Erasmus felt with ossified scholastic methodology were not greater than his impatience with corruption in the social fabric, in both church and state. His *Praise of Folly*, written while he was in England, is a devastating satire reminiscent of

1. A. G. Dickens and Whitney R. D. Jones, *Erasmus the Reformer* (London: Methuen, 1994), 19–40; also Peter Mack, *A History of Renaissance Rhetoric, 1380–1620* (New York: Oxford University Press, 2011), chap. 1.

2. In my comments on the affection of leading Reformers, I have by permission drawn here briefly on my essay "Classical Foundations, Vernacular Edifice: Literature in the Reformation," in *Reformation 500: How the Greatest Revival since Pentecost Continues to Shape the World Today*, ed. Ray Van Neste and J. Michael Garrett (Nashville: B&H Academic, 2017), 105–20.

3. Dickens and Jones, *Erasmus the Reformer*, 41–62.

4. Lisa Jardine, *Erasmus, Man of Letters: The Construction of Charisma in Print* (Princeton: Princeton University Press, 1993), 4–5.

Sebastian Brant's *The Ship of Fools*. Both *The Ship of Fools* and *Praise of Folly* were works of "protest"—"protestant" before the name.

Erasmus was not otherwise a writer of popular fiction; he was a biblical scholar and theologian. His hero was the great polyglot and translator of the Bible, St. Jerome, and he made it a long labor of love to edit Jerome's known works.[5] But because in his own right he was a sound scholar of biblical Greek, he worked also to produce a reliable Greek New Testament (1516), and his edition provided a text superior to any that had previously been available.[6] Suspicious of the paraphrases and faulty Latin translations of the Bible still widely in use, Erasmus made it his business to direct his peers to go back to the Greek text in as accurate a version as possible, and to read the commentaries of early fathers of the church as guides more useful than more recent commentaries and theological digests. This was characteristically expressive of his humanist bias, a tendency to trust careful, linguistically competent study of the biblical text itself rather than secondary scholarship. In other words, he believed that theology, to be sound, must be grounded in *philology*. Primary texts took precedence.

The Poetics of *Sola Scriptura*

From the perspective of intellectual history, it is the humanist bias toward philology—both classical and biblical—and weariness with the schemata and logical arguments of philosophers whose methods were ultimately Aristotelian that most clearly set the stage for what was to appear in the Reformation. What the classical humanist strove for in his students was a fresh encounter with an ancient text, classical or biblical. But we should not fail to recognize that the revolutionary literary encounters with texts of the Bible that mark the Reformers' break with the paradigms of their time owe greatly to their rigorous philological training and close reading of classical texts, chiefly poetry. Luther tells us that when he first entered the monastery, he left behind all his books except his copies of Plautus and Virgil, authors he would quote all his life.[7] His chief colleague Philip Melanchthon was a renowned Greek scholar

5. Jardine, *Erasmus*, 9. See James F. Brady and John C. Olin, eds., *Patristic Scholarship: The Edition of St. Jerome*, vol. 61 of *Collected Works of Erasmus* (Toronto: University of Toronto Press, 1992).

6. Printed at Basel in 1516 by Johan Froben, it is the first Greek New Testament to be published and bore the title *Novum instrumentum omne*. The third edition (1522) was used by Tyndale for his translation (1526). See David Daniel, *The Bible in English* (New Haven: Yale University Press, 2003), 113–59.

7. Heiko A. Oberman, *Luther: Man between God and the Devil* (New York: Doubleday/Image, 1982), 122n.

who at Heidelberg lectured on Virgil and Livy; his own first publications were an edition of Terence (1516) and a celebrated Greek grammar (1518).[8] John Calvin was educated as a classical philologist as well as trained as a lawyer; his first published work was an edition of Seneca the Younger's *De Clementia* (1532), and his theological works contain many evidences of his knowledge of classical literature. Theodore Beza, Calvin's chief disciple and successor, began his career as a widely admired Latin poet,[9] and he became professor of Greek at Lausanne. Later he would publish a satire in Latin verse, *Passavantius*, and a work on Cato, *Cato Censorious* (1591).[10] His *Abraham Sacrifiant* (1550, 1553), a play written in French, was influential for later French writers such as Racine, and it had a following also in England.[11] As the most luminous work of literature by a prominent Reformer, it merits more attention than it has received.

Summarily, for the leading Continental Reformers, great texts from the ancient pagan as well as the Jewish and the Christian past were thought worthy of attention in themselves as well as to provide a necessary apprenticeship for biblical study. Unlike most of their predecessors, the Reformers were prepared thus to read the texts of the Bible just as they would any other great works in Greek, as deserving of close study and better editions. Employing their knowledge of languages and humanistic literary methods, they discovered and declared that the Holy Scriptures were, in effect, a noble literature, the greatest of the "great texts." This discovery was to produce an intellectual excitement and fertility of imagination that would ensue in literary as well as theological writing. It also made the texts of the Bible itself the basis for humanistic learning—what Barbara Lewalski has been pleased to denominate "the Bible as *Ars Rhetoricae*"[12]—and eventually the preeminent source for Christian instruction in the arts of the trivium (grammar, rhetoric, and logic) in Puritan and dissenting schools down through the works of Isaac Watts and beyond.[13] The advent of vernacular Bible translation would soon spur on a

---

8. Thorsten Fuchs, *Philipp Melanchthon als neulateinischer Dichter in der Zeit der Reformation* (Tübingen: Narr, 2008).

9. Philip Schaff, *A History of the Christian Church*, 8 vols. (Peabody, MA: Hendrickson, 2006), 8:167.

10. Beza, *Epistola responsiva ad commissionem sibi datum a Petro Lyseto* (1504).

11. The translation by Arthur Golding, *A Tragedie of Abraham's Sacrifice*, has been edited by Malcolm William Wallace (Toronto: University of Toronto Library, 1906) and is available on demand in the BiblioLife Reproduction Series. The original French text is printed as an appendix (91–127).

12. Barbara Lewalski, *Protestant Poetics and the Seventeenth-Century Religious Lyric* (Princeton: Princeton University Press, 1979), 72–86.

13. David Lyle Jeffrey, "Modernism and the English University in 1789," in *The Idea of the University: 1789–1989*, ed. Kathleen Jaeger (Halifax: Institute for Advanced Studies Press, 1990), 3–17.

broadening of the audience for this literature,[14] and private reading encouraged a more dramatic appreciation of biblical narratives. In the Abraham play by Beza, the patriarch has become already an existentially challenged poetic hero, much as he will later appear in the reading of Søren Kierkegaard. Printed at Geneva in 1550, it had ten more editions in the sixteenth century and thirteen editions in the seventeenth; it was translated into Latin, Italian, and English. Few works of the period had more success.[15] Focus on the biblical text itself rather than on theological formulae let the Bible come to life on its own terms as literature—indeed, as poetry; and, as a corollary of private access to the text alone, personal reading opened the way to creative, often individualistic responses. These were to include John Milton's *Samson Agonistes* and *Paradise Regained* (both in 1671), but also Giles Fletcher the Younger's long poem in eight-line stanzas, *Christ's Victory and Triumph in Heaven and Earth, over and after Death* (1610).[16] Fletcher's poem is clearly indebted to Calvinist theological thought and to the Geneva Bible (kept in print in England until 1644). This partisanship perhaps accounts for his nervousness about retelling the story of the atonement in a poetic paraphrase; in a preface to the reader, he draws heavily on Sidney's *Defence of Poesie* to justify his medium. That first great English work of literary criticism, printed also in 1595 under the title *An Apology for Poetry*,[17] begins with Sidney's defense of the superiority of individual imagination to traditional views and convention. This was effectively a secularization, for poetics, of the *sola scriptura* theological stance of the Reformers. In postmodern times, what has survived of it is even more radically individualistic.

Scripture and Poetry in Late Modernity

Poetry in the medieval centuries, though circulated only in manuscript and even then encountered most often as a work read aloud in communal settings, was not a private matter, as even the case of Caedmon representatively shows. Poets were expected to address matters of public interest. They did not, therefore, write about themselves—their own feelings or personalities; as a result, one may read all of Chaucer's poetry without getting much sense

14. Ian Watt, *The Rise of the Novel: Studies in Defoe, Richardson, and Fielding* (Berkeley: University of California Press, 1957; reissued by Kessinger, 2010).

15. Wallace, *Tragedie of Abraham's Sacrifice*, xxxviii.

16. Giles Fletcher the Younger, *Christ's Victory and Triumph in Heaven and Earth, over and after Death*, ed. William T. Brooke (London: Griffith, Farran, Okeden, and Welsh, 1888).

17. *A Defence of Poetry by Philip Sidney*, ed. J. A. Van Dorsten (Oxford: Oxford University Press, 1971), has useful annotations.

of what he may have been like on the personal level. The obligation of such poets to their readers was to give a bright articulation to the hopes and dreams of their community, to proclaim a common vision.

Poets in late modernity, by contrast, are widely published, read in print, and infrequently heard reading aloud, yet their poems are most commonly personal and subjective utterances by persons who often stand over and against their communities, choosing themes as well as accents that proclaim their alienated identity. Philip Larkin's *The Less Deceived* (1955) and *Whitsun Weddings* (1964) are representative of a stance of English poets in the twentieth century for whom T. S. Eliot's *The Wasteland* (1922) marked both the final demise of the poet as a voice of public vision and the legitimation of the late-modern poet as a pessimistic, even cynical, critic of all such hopefulness. This general ethos for modern poetry accordingly participates in a very different general response to the Bible, one in which its literary power lingers even though its religious authority has largely faded away.

Part of the challenge of late modernity, even for a Christian convert such as T. S. Eliot, has been the fading from common vocabulary not merely of a rural, pastoral ethos but of biblical language and, in a growing urban alienation, of a public vision of Christian values and virtues. Thus, for Eliot in "Ash Wednesday," the question is "Where shall the word be found, where will the word / Resound?"—that is, not just for himself as a poet with now something different to say, but as a man reborn out of season, seeking to speak to "those who walk in darkness," upon whom the light has not yet shined (cf. Isa. 9:2). Eliot's has not been an easy question for late-modern poets writing from a Jewish or Christian perspective to answer, or for others of less certain faith even to negotiate, when, merely out of admiration for the resonant poetic idiom of the King James Version of the Bible especially, they seek to draw upon the music of biblical language. Each of the poets discussed in this second half of the book is among those who have wrestled with this question; each has come to conclude that the value of biblical language to the possibility of poetry is great—indeed, of such potency that they have crafted ways to reinsert biblical idiom into literary discourse. These ways differ dramatically as we move from the churched to the unchurched, from a still vestigially Christian to a post-Christian world.

The essays in the second half of this volume trace the path from the Reformation humanists forward to a modernity in which the emergence of the self as authority and arbiter of moral obligation would increasingly make of the Bible an aesthetic rather than a spiritual touchstone. The process was gradual, the realization of the Reformation's unintended consequences almost imperceptible until the Enlightenment took the high ground from Christian humanism in the eighteenth century. Without doubt, the pace of the shift even then was slowed by the enormous appeal of the KJV Bible, the most influential translation of Scripture into any European vernacular.

It is necessary to acknowledge that the road to Reformation was both rocky and irregular in England, and that there was fallout from the politics of it in the universities, where most of the great poets of the period were educated. What the corruptions of power and usurpation of status were to the confusions of Henry VIII, the conflicts and contestations of Reformation and Counter-Reformation theology were to the formal study (in Latin translation) of biblical texts in the universities. Though his academic intention is more complex, it becomes clear that one of the chief vices of Christopher Marlowe's protagonist, the beginning of his decline into satanic ritual and covenant with Lucifer, is a willful misreading of the Scriptures. In Marlowe's brilliant play *The Tragicall Historie of Doctor Faustus*, the self-promoting misreader is, notably, a Wittenberg professor. Though Marlowe was not himself an orthodox Christian, his poetic imagination, fired by the very texts his protagonist abuses and betrays, permits him to write one of the most theologically penetrating works in all of English literature. In Shakespeare's *Hamlet* of the same period, the morally confused protagonist is a Wittenberg undergraduate on leave to deal with a family crisis for which he proves tragically unprepared. These are not compliments to the Reformation.

Then came the monumental work of the forty-seven (or fifty-four) scholars who, at the command of King James I of England (formerly King James VI of Scotland), produced the Authorized Version of the Bible published in 1611. Though it was intended to replace the English version of the Geneva Bible of 1560, Shakespeare used the Geneva Bible primarily, and it was consulted along with the Vulgate Latin text even by most Anglican divines until midcentury. We shall examine the growing power of the KJV in the work of two of the most remarkable poets in the English language, John Donne, a near contemporary of Marlowe, and George Herbert, his younger friend. Both were priests in the Anglican Church, and both were deeply shaped by patristic and medieval biblical commentary, as well as by the Bible itself. Each uses Scripture beautifully, both by way of illumination of the human condition and in the pastoral cure of that condition in their vocations. For both, poetry shaped by Scripture becomes a means of prayer; like Augustine before them, they write in specific response to the poetry of God. Each permits the divine voice, antiphonally, to respond to their poetic prayer. They are a high-water mark in the redemption of the tradition begun by Caedmon more than nine centuries before them.

From the seventeenth century on, the KJV Bible would become the wellspring of moral and religious interchange, the source of proverbial wisdom and parental counsel, as well as the foundational literary text of English-speaking

Christendom, by the nineteenth century eclipsing the influence of Latin and Greek poetry because it was so much more widely accessible. The eighth chapter here explores the way in which its cadences became habitual not only among poets but in the work of novelists, playwrights, and politicians. No other translation would ever come up to the beauty of its language; hence, even though a large majority of Bible-reading Christians have abandoned it for other translations, it continues to be "the poets' Bible."

This is notably the case even with Jewish poets; our examination of Anthony Hecht, among others such as Howard Nemerov, amply warrants the contention of modern Hebraists that the KJV best captures the Hebrew poetry of the Psalms, Job, and Isaiah. Modern Jewish poets have not, for the most part, been observant, halachic Jews. Yet as they have grown older, most have shown signs of beginning to remember their early formation, and, as might for any of us be the case, remembrance has led to reflection and sometimes repentance, even a classic biblical "calling out to the Lord." This too overflows into some remarkable poems.

Margaret Avison is a poet less well known than she should be. As with T. S. Eliot, the decisive moment in her poetic career was a conversion to Christianity, but in her case it was as an evangelical Presbyterian, working throughout her life in a Toronto street mission, that she would move from her early formation in the Black Mountain school of poetry to embrace the Bible. Her work is marked by an intensity, an acuity of perception, irony, and frankness, all of which are shaped by Scripture.

Richard Wilbur, in some ways a successor to Robert Frost in being a poet laureate of the United States, is one in whose work the unpretentiousness of modern plain speech has fused almost seamlessly with the rhythm and diction of the KJV Bible. One of our contemporaries whose use of the Bible has been part of his disciplined use of traditional poetic forms, Wilbur is, I suggest, a poet whose work is less likely than that of many to become dated. His is a gracious and graceful art, a poetry to be reread and cherished.

We then consider two other contemporary American poets, the late Anthony Hecht and the still-flourishing Harvard poet-in-residence Gjertrud Schnackenberg. Here are two excellent practitioners, one Jewish, one Christian, each of whose work has been attuned to beauty by the poignancy and eloquence of biblical language. In their poems examined here, the characteristically modern tension between broken conversations and a desire for transcendence has been magnificently graced by a biblically informed imagination of the potential for a well-wrought poem—even in a prosy time—to provide a structure for projecting a future with satisfying possibilities of closure, and thus to lift broken hearts to a hope beyond themselves.

In the final essay I return to Christopher Marlowe's *The Tragicall Historie of Doctor Faustus* (1616), but here to consider the strategic difficulties in presenting it to an audience that lacks the familiarity with Scripture that fired Marlowe's imagination, despite his atheism, to write the most brilliant of Reformation-era theological expositions of the contest between willful disobedience and prevenient grace. The question I wish to engage, however, is not primarily theological but literary and cultural: Have we arrived at a point at which poets, religious or otherwise, will no longer know and be able to make use of the Bible as a resource for the poetic imagination?

six

POETRY in PREACHING, PRAYER, and PASTORAL CARE

John Donne and George Herbert

J ohn Donne and George Herbert are generally regarded, and with justice, as the finest English lyric poets of the seventeenth century. Donne had been a friend of Magdalen Herbert, George's widowed mother, since the lad was about seven years old, and through friendship with the family is reported to have had a role in persuading the younger man to become, like himself, a priest in the Church of England. They had much in common by way of intellectual gifts as well as ultimate vocation, yet very different personalities and contrasting approaches to their callings, both as pastors and as poets. We must concern ourselves with their differences as well as similarities if we are to appreciate the complementary yet distinctive quality of their poetry, their prayer, and in Donne's case, also preaching.

When now we think of the uses of poetry, prayer is not usually the quickest thing to come to mind, if indeed it comes to mind at all. In the biblical tradition, however, from the songs of Moses, Miriam, and Deborah on through the Psalms of David, the association is direct. The Psalms in particular have been fundamental to worship not only in Jewish but also in early Christian tradition. New poetry reflective of the Psalms and written for communal as well as personal prayer is common among the early Latin Christian poets such as Prudentius, Fortunatus, and Theodulf of Orleans, and it is still a prominent expression of meditative spirituality among scholastics of the thirteenth century such as St. Bonaventure (e.g., *Laudismus de Sancta Cruce*):

> Jesus crucified, support me,
> That so long as life is in me
> I with joy may mourn your death.[1]

The essential paradox in Bonaventure's lines captures a feature of Christian poetry that persisted well into the seventeenth century, as instanced by both Donne and Herbert. Devotional poems of the medieval period, focused on the cross, often became liturgical hymns; the *"Adoro de devote"* of Thomas Aquinas, composed about the same time, is still regularly sung as a eucharistic hymn. Medieval poets writing in the vernacular likewise formalized prayer poetically in virtually every European language; and, as we shall see, prayed poems, set to music as hymns, remained a strong part of English poetic tradition—in particular through the eighteenth century—by virtue of the efforts of poets such as Isaac Watts, Charles Wesley, William Cowper, John Newton, and Christopher Smart.[2] Yet, Watts and Wesley perhaps excepted, no finer examples of the prayer-poem in English have been written than the best of those by John Donne and George Herbert.

John Donne: A Passion for Learning

Donne now appears, on many counts, to be the more complicated of these two great figures, a man of restless curiosity, intense intellectual interests, and volatile temperament, strong in his passions both sexual and spiritual, a dashing courtier with far more friends than enemies. Mercurial temperament and bouts of depression notwithstanding, he could seem a charming extrovert. Everyone who knew him was impressed by his intellectual gifts as well as by his social presence and energy. Though he refused to sign the oath of allegiance to the Church of England that was then required to receive a degree, he took the full three-year course of study at Oxford and then another at Cambridge, during which, unusually, he focused more on Hebrew than Greek, possibly

---

1. Clemens Blume and Guido M. Dreves, eds., *Analecta Hymnica Medii Aevi* (Leipzig, 1906), 49–50; translation by Jose de Vinck, *The Works of Bonaventure* (Patterson, NJ: St. Anthony Guild Press, 1966), 3:1–10.

2. See David Lyle Jeffrey, *The Early English Lyric and Franciscan Spirituality* (Lincoln: University of Nebraska Press, 1975); Jeffrey, *The Law of Love: English Spirituality in the Age of Wyclif* (Grand Rapids: Eerdmans, 1980); Jeffrey, *English Spirituality in the Age of Wesley* (Grand Rapids: Eerdmans, 1986).

with the assistance of Tremellius, the Jewish scholar who had converted to Calvinism.[3] This effort clearly involved much more than merely dutiful study. Though his expertise falls short of that of Lancelot Andrews, the translator responsible for most of the King James Bible's Pentateuch, Donne would later frequently make good use of Hebrew philology in expounding a biblical text in his sermons.[4] Languages were a forte: Walton records in his biography of Donne that, after the young poet's sojourn of a few years in Italy and Spain, he was completely fluent in both Italian and Spanish; indeed, his library was apparently richer in Spanish volumes than in those of any other language.[5] That one of his passions was learning itself, and that he was a lifelong scholar, is everywhere apparent in his sermons.

But it is apparent also in his poetry, and that from early on (e.g., "A Valediction: of the Booke").[6] Though much of his earliest verse was famously of the cavalier erotic sort, not credibly innocent of the amorous adventures they solicit or celebrate,[7] it is also clear that Donne took seriously the idea that poetry offers a means of understanding, including self-understanding, that in important respects was superior to deductive reasons and argument for spiritual insight.[8] This forms a link between even his erotic poetry, most of which was written before his late twenties, and his preaching, in which he remains superbly poetical, weaving images and poetic phrases from Scripture for his congregation in such a way that, as George R. Potter so admirably puts it, "he stirred their imagination and appealed to their subconscious."[9] He learned to do this, I would suggest, while studying the Hebrew Scriptures intensively

3. George R. Potter and Evelyn M. Simpson, eds., *The Sermons of John Donne*, 10 vols. (Berkeley: University of California Press, 1962–68), 10:306–12. Henceforth referred to as *Sermons*. More recently it has been speculated that Donne may have studied Hebrew with Dr. John Layfield; see the study by Chanita Goodblatt, *The Christian Hebraism of John Donne: Written with the Fingers of Man's Hand* (Pittsburgh: Duquesne University Press, 2010).

4. E.g., Sermon no. 11, on Hosea 2:19, preached at a marriage (May 30, 1621); Potter and Simpson, *Sermons*, 3:11.241–43. He also prepared commentaries on both Genesis and Exodus for his *Essayes in Divinity*, ed. Anthony Raspa (Montreal: McGill-Queen's University Press, 2001).

5. H. J. C. Grierson, ed., *The Poems of John Donne* (London: Oxford University Press, 1933), xvi–xvii. Hereafter referred to as *Poems*.

6. Grierson, *Poems*, 27–29.

7. Grierson (*Poems*, xxii–xxiv) refers to the amorous language as "conventional," but also thinks that Donne "sowed his wild oats," especially between 1593 and 1595 (*Poems*, xvi).

8. A good in-depth study is Frances Cruickshank, *Verse and Poetics in George Herbert and John Donne* (London: Routledge, 2016). See also her "Broken Altars: The Work of Form in George Herbert's *Temple*," *Christianity and Literature* 66 (2016): 24–38.

9. Potter and Simpson, *Sermons*, 10:300 (appendix on Donne's sources). See also Peter McCullough, ed., *The Oxford Edition of the Sermons of John Donne*, vol. 1 (Oxford: Oxford University Press, 2015), for newly published sermons from 1615 to 1619.

just as he was beginning to write poems of his own. Raymond-Jean Frontain has observed that "Donne's poetic development can be mapped in terms of his shift from secular to sacred models"—from Ovid, Horace, Juvenal, and other poets of the Latin tradition (central to an Oxford education) to what Donne describes as the "figurative . . . metaphorical God."[10] By this Donne means simply that the God who reveals himself in Scripture, the one to whom a believer prays, is imagined biblically, incarnationally, in figurative terms:

> He is our Father, for he made us: Of what? Of clay; So God is *Figulus*, so in the Prophet; so in the Apostle, God is our Potter. God stamped his Image upon us, and so God is *Statuarius*, our Minter, our Statuary. God clothed us, and so is *vestiarius*; he hath opened his wardrobe unto us. God gave us all the fruits of the earth to eate, and so is *oeconomus*, our Steward. God poures his oyle, and his wine into our wounds, and so is *Medicus*, and *Vicinus*, that Physitian, that Neighbour, that Samaritan intended in the Parable. God plants us, and waters, and weeds us, and gives the increase; and so God is *Hortulanus*, our Gardener. God builds us up into a Church, and so God is *Architectus*, our Architect, our Builder; God watches the City when it is built; and so God is *Speculator*, our Sentinell. God fishes for men, (for all his *Iohns*, and his *Andrews*, and his *Peters*, are but the nets that he fishes withal), God is the fisher of men; And here, in this Chapter, God in Christ is our Shepherd. The book of *Iob* is a representation of God, in a Tragique-Comedy, lamentable beginnings comfortably ended. The book of Canticles is a representation of God in Christ as a Bridegroom in a Marriage-song, in an Epithalamion: God in Christ is represented to us, in divers forms, in divers places, and this Chapter is his Pastorall. The Lord is our Shepheard, and so called, in more places, then by any other name.[11]

Donne's theory of poetry becomes available to us retrospectively to his poems, and most explicitly in his later prose writings, including his sermons. It is in these genres that he is most at liberty to explain and encourage a means of relationship with God which he himself discovered earlier, but which he fears can be lost to Christian learning if the poetry of Scripture itself is not

10. Raymond-Jean Frontain describes Donne's poetic career as a movement from Ovid through Petrarch to God. See Raymond-Jean Frontain and Frances M. Malpezzi, eds., *John Donne's Religious Imagination: Essays in Honor of John T. Shawcross* (Conway: University of Central Arkansas Press, 1995), 13. As Katherine Calloway puts it, "Donne's creator is a poet, and the natural world is a divine poem in which his wit and wisdom can be discerned by the willing and wondering reader." See "A 'Metaphorical God' and the Book of Nature: John Donne on Natural Theology," *Studies in Philology*, forthcoming.

11. Potter and Simpson, *Sermons*, 9:5.131–32, in a mature sermon for Christmas Day, 1629. This observation would be turned into a poem by George Herbert; "The Call" begins "Come my Way, my Truth, my Life." See *The Works of George Herbert*, ed. F. E. Hutchinson (Oxford: Clarendon, 1941; 1972), 156.

engaged with both spiritual and aesthetic appreciation. This appreciation has much to do, Donne suggests, with how we think about God and how we comport ourselves in approaching him.

How are we to speak to God if we cannot imagine him in something like personal, human terms? For Donne, *simpliciter*, we need a language similar to that so much used for prayer and praise in Scripture itself. This is a point of prospect that he assumes in his divine poems and *Devotions*, but that also recurs frequently in his sermons as a reminder to his congregation:

> All the words of *God* are always sweete in themselves, says *David*; but sweeter in the mouth, and in the pen of some of the *Prophets*, and some of the *Apostles*, then of others, as they differed in their naturall gifts, or in their education: but sweetest of all, where the *Holy Ghost* hath beene pleased to set the word of *God* to Musique, and to convay it into a Song.[12]

Poetry has a special register of authority, he will argue; thus Paul "cites sometimes the words of *secular Poets*, and approves them; and then the words of those Poets become the word of God."[13] It seems clear that Donne increasingly felt that his hearers needed to aspire more to biblical poetry than to academic philosophy where matters of faith and even theological insight were concerned. In a later sermon he quotes Calvin to say that

> there is no secular Author . . . which doth more abound with persuasive *figures* of Rhetorique, nor with musical *cadences* and *allusions*, and assimilations, and conformity, and correspondency of words to one another, than some of the *Secretaries of the Holy Ghost*, some of the authors of some books of the Bible doe.[14]

We find him equally attuned to the figural eloquence of Scripture in a very early sermon on Ezekiel 33:32, preached during Lent in 1618 at Whitehall.[15] Here he argues that the preacher's words should imitate the *musicum carmen* of Scripture itself, conveying not merely the matter but the manner of it (166–67). "There are not so eloquent books in the world as the Scriptures," and it is only fitting that, since "a great poem [is] . . . in a musical, in a metrical, in a measured composition, in verse" (171), the preacher in his sermon should compose a "love song (as the text speaks) in proposing the love of God to man, wherein he loved him so, that he gave his onely begotten Son for him" (170).

12. Potter and Simpson, *Sermons*, 4:7.179.
13. Potter and Simpson, *Sermons*, 4:6.163.
14. Potter and Simpson, *Sermons*, 10:4.103.
15. Potter and Simpson, *Sermons*, 2:7.164–78.

Donne's *Devotions* likewise give us a rich sense of his conviction in the matter, and, once again, almost as much in the KJV cadences and allusions in his diction as in the point he endeavors to argue:

> My God, my God, thou art a direct God, may I not say a literal God, a God that wouldst be understood literally and according to the plain sense of all that thou sayest? But thou art also (Lord, I intend it to thy glory, and let no profane misinterpreter abuse it to thy diminution), thou art a figurative, a metaphorical God too; a God in whose words there is such a height of figures, such voyages, such perigrinations to fetch remote and precious metaphors, such extensions, such spreadings, such curtains of allegories, such third heavens of hyperboles, so harmonious elocutions, so retired and so reserved expressions, so commanding persuasions, so persuading commandments, such sinews even in thy milk, and such things in thy words, as all profane authors seem of the seed of the serpent that creeps, thou art the Dove that flies. O, what words but thine can express the inexpressible texture and composition of thy word, in which to one man that argument that binds his faith to believe that to be the word of God, is the reverent simplicity of the word, and to another the majesty of the word; and in which two men equally pious may meet, and one wonder that all should not understand it, and the other as much that any man should.[16]

This is a very important prayer for our understanding of Donne's theology; it bears fuller quotation:

> Neither art thou thus a figurative, a metaphorical God in thy word only, but in thy works too. The style of thy works, the phrase of thine actions, is metaphorical. The institution of thy whole worship in the old law was a continual allegory; types and figures overspread all, and figures flowed into figures, and poured themselves out into farther figures; circumcision carried a figure of baptism, and baptism carries a figure of that purity which we shall have in perfection in the new Jerusalem. Neither didst thou speak and work in this language only in the time of thy prophets; but since thou spokest in thy Son it is so too. How often, how much more often, doth thy Son call himself a way, and a light, and a gate, and a vine, and bread, than the Son of God, or of man? How much oftener doth he exhibit a metaphorical Christ, than a real, a literal?[17]

---

16. *John Donne's Devotions upon Emergent Occasions, together with Death's Duel* (Ann Arbor: University of Michigan Press, 1965), 124–35. Donne subscribed to a version of the "double literal sense" in which obviously figurative language is to be taken as the face value of meaning in the text. Yet he is careful to warn against allegorical excess and mistaking genres— e.g., "In the first book of the Scriptures, that of Genesis, there is danger in departing from the letter; in this last book, this of the Revelation, there is much danger in adhering too close to the letter" (Potter and Simpson, *Sermons*, 6:2.62).

17. Donne, *Devotions*, 125.

Any imagination that poetic speech about God or biblically grounded poetic speech directed *to* God are somehow less appropriate or reliable than discursive or analytic language is here firmly rejected. It is equally apparent that the claim of H. J. C. Grierson that Donne is "the only poet of the first rank who is also a great orator"[18] is amply warranted in his sermons and devotional writings, many passages of which are in fact superb poetry—and biblical poetry. In a passionate plea for the centrality of Holy Scripture in the reading of any who would be learned, Donne makes his case in language as poetic as that of the authors he commends:

> Dost thou love learning, as it is expounded, dilated, by *Orators*? The Father of Orators testifies, *Nihil tam perspicuum*, there is nothing so evident, as that there is a soveraigne power, that made, and governes all. Dost thou love learning, as it is contracted, brought to a quintessence, wrought to a spirit, by *Philosophers*? The eldest of all them in that whole book, *Quod Deus latens, simul & patens est*, testifies all that, and nothing but that, that as there is nothing so dark, so there is nothing so cleare, nothing so remote, nothing so neare us, as God. Dost thou love learning, as it is sweetened and set to musique by *Poets*? The King of the poets testifies the same, *Mens agitat molem, & magno se corpore miscet*: that is, a great, an universall spirit, that moves, a general soule, that inanimates, and agitates every peece of this world. But *Saint Paul* is a more powerfull Orator than *Cicero*, and he says, *The invisible things of God are seen by things which are made;* and thereby man is made *inexcusable*: *Moses* is an ancienter *Philosopher* then *Trismegistus*; and his picture of God is the Creation of the world. *David* is a better *Poet* then *Virgil*; and with *David, Caeli enarrant, the heavens declare the glory of God*. The power of *oratory*, in the force of perswasion, the strength of conclusions, in the pressing of *Philosophy*, the harmony of *Poetry*, in the sweet-nesse of composition, never met in any man so fully as in the Prophet *Esay*, nor in the Prophet *Esay* more then where he says, *Levate Oculos, Lift up your eyes, on high, and behold who hath created these things;* behold them, *therefore*, to know that they are created, and to know who is their creator.[19]

This, in a sermon that began with the claim that even secular poetry, in a God-ordained context, has in Holy Scripture become grafted into the word of God.

Desire for God: The Holy Sonnets

Donne seems to have written a number of his divine poems not long after his erotic verse, and some of the best known were surely composed almost

18. Grierson, *Poems*, xlii.
19. Potter and Simpson, *Sermons*, 4:6.166–67.

simultaneously with many of his cavalier Petrarchan praises, nothing if not erotically extravagant. "Twicknam Garden," "The Primrose," and "The Relique"—all of which were likely sent to Mrs. Magdalen Herbert, as were most certainly his *La Corona* sonnets (sometime between 1608 and 1609)—on such evidence as we have would seem to have been from the same period.[20] These ostensibly quite different sorts of poems—praise of and implicit pleadings to ladies, and praise and pleadings directed to God—have in Donne more in common than not. Donne's voice in both is impassioned, impatient, immodest; the temperament of the persona in both categories is importunate and audacious:

> License my roving hands, and let them go
> Before, behind, between, above, below.
> O my America! My new-found-land,
> My kingdom, safeliest when with one man manned,
> My mine of precious stones, my empery,
> How blest am I in this discovering thee!
> To enter these bonds is to be free;
> Then where my hand is set, my seal shall be.[21]

Compare that verse to this:

> Batter my heart, three-person'd God, for you
> As yet but knock, breathe, shine, and seek to mend;
> That I may rise and stand, o'erthrow me, and bend
> Your force to break, blow, burn, and make me new.
> I, like an usurp'd town to another due,
> Labor to admit you, but oh, to no end;
> Reason, your viceroy in me, me should defend,
> But is captiv'd, and proves weak or untrue.
> Yet dearly I love you, and would be lov'd fain,
> But am betroth'd unto your enemy;
> Divorce me, untie or break that knot again,
> Take me to you, imprison me, for I,
> Except you enthrall me, never shall be free,
> Nor ever chaste, except you ravish me.[22]

20. Among his more frankly Ovidian poems, one would include Elegie XIV, "A Tale of a Citizen and His Wife"; Elegie XVII, "Variety"; Elegie XVIII, "Love's Progress"; and of course Elegie XIX, "Going to Bed." The divine poems in his *La Corona* series (1608–9) were dedicated to Lady Herbert (Grierson, *Poems*, xx–xxi and xli). George Herbert would have been then about sixteen years old; by some accounts Lady Herbert may not have received them until as late as 1610, in which case he would have been seventeen.

21. Elegie XIX, lines 25–32 (Grierson, *Poems*, 107).

22. Holy Sonnet XIV (*Poems*, 299). Cf. "To the Countess of Bedford" (*Poems*, 167; lines 1–4).

Indeed, in the amorous poems there is much deliberately religious language, while in the divine poems appears erotically amorous language; so, in one of his Petrarchan admirations of Lady Bedford, he calls her a "divinity":

> Reason is our Soules left hand, Faith her right,
> By these wee reach divinity, that's you;
> Their loves, who have the blessings of your light,
> Grew from their reason, mind from faire faith grew.[23]

In Holy Sonnet XVIII, by way of comparison,

> Betray kind husband thy spouse to our sights,
> And let myne amorous soule court thy mild Dove,
> Who is most trew, and pleasing to thee, then
> When she'is embrac'd and open to most men.[24]

It is fair to say that, just as Donne's sermons are, if anything, more poetic than his poems, so his prayer-poems can, even in a sonnet sequence, become a form of preaching, as in their totality both the *La Corona* poems and the Holy Sonnets illustrate. Often these preacherly poems are a species of self-examination; the one he admonishes is himself (e.g., "The Annunciation and Passion," "The Cross," Holy Sonnets XV, XIII, and III through VI). Some, especially his penitential poems (penitential psalms are a biblical prototype for him), move from a hortatory invitation to others to a personal plea to God for forgiveness.[25] This is the strategy in his "Goodfriday, 1613. Riding Westward," which begins:

> Let mans Soule be a Spheare, and then, in this,
> The intelligence that moves, devotion is,
> And as the other Spheares, by being growne
> Subject to forraigne motion, lose their owne,
> And being by others hurried every day,
> Scarce in a yeare their naturall forme obey:
> Pleasure or businesse, so, our Soules admit
> For their first mover, and are whirld by it. (lines 1–8)[26]

23. "To the Countess of Bedford" (*Poems*, 167; lines 1–4); cf. Holy Sonnet XVIII (*Poems*, 301; lines 11–14).

24. Holy Sonnet XVIII (*Poems*, 301; lines 11–14). Cf. *Poems*, 306–7; lines 1–8.

25. One view is that this is involuntary; see Ryan Netzley, "Loving Fear: Affirmative Anxiety in John Donne's Divine Poems," in *Reading, Desire, and the Eucharist in Early Modern Religious Poetry* (Toronto: University of Toronto Press, 2011), 106–48.

26. Cf. Holy Sonnet XVIII, *Poems*, 301; lines 11–14.

"Hence," he says, the cares of life call him to journey westward, even though his "Soules forme bends toward the East," as on such a day it ought (lines 9–10). That sets up a tension between the cross and its burden of self-denial (Luke 9:23), and the desire to bypass Calvary in haste to get on with life. To look upon the cross endangers such evasion: "Who sees Gods face, that is selfe life, must dye; / What a death were it then to see God dye?" (lines 17–18). Evasion can be a powerful motive for Donne, but the Spirit keeps tugging away at his heart:

> If on these things I durst not looke, durst I
> Upon his miserable mother cast mine eye,
> Who was Gods partner here, and furnish'd thus
> Halfe of that Sacrifice, which ransom'd us? (lines 29–32)

Here compassion has a human exemplar, and his mind is flooded with memories of Calvary. With an imagination now stirred to engage the Passion narrative of the Gospels, he remembers more—namely, that though he may have an aversion to contemplating the cross because of his complicity in the sin that brought it about, Jesus on the cross has been looking directly at him all along:

> Though these things, as I ride, be from mine eye,
> They'are present yet unto my memory,
> For that looks towards them; and thou look'st towards mee,
> O Saviour, as thou hang'st upon the tree;
> I turne my backe to thee, but to receive
> Corrections, till thy mercies bid thee leave.
> O thinke mee worth thine anger, punish mee,
> Burne off my rusts, and my deformity,
> Restore thine Image, so much, by thy grace,
> That thou may'st know mee, and I'll turne my face. (lines 33–42)

The poem is thus an exercise in self-examination, expressing contrition and offering a confession; it ends in a plea for identification with Christ, accepting the burden of the cross. What Margret Fetzer has said about the Holy Sonnets applies equally here—namely, that these poems illustrate the persona's need "to establish a relationship to God" and that "a relationship is begun in verse, before it can move on to the lesser formality of prose."[27]

27. See Margret Fetzer, *John Donne's Performances: Sermons, Poems, Letters, and "Devotions"* (Manchester, UK: Manchester University Press, 2010), 266–68. Cf. Helen B. Brooks, who in discussing the Augustinian character of the poem suggests that "the meditative state at the

In a poem such as this, the gospel has been set before us, and we are on the threshold of Donne's sermons.

Donne also wrote poems of spiritual counsel and pastoral care, hymns, poetic prayers set to music (one of which was performed for him in divine service at St. Paul's), and "The LITANIE," a liturgical prayer sequence.[28] All of these are worthy examples of his poetic genius turned toward prayer both personal and communal. Regarding liturgy, Donne had a strong commitment to common prayer as the central focus of Christian life, as Jeffrey Johnson has admirably demonstrated.[29] The highest achievement in the art of poetic prayer in the seventeenth century, however, was to come from the pen of his younger contemporary, Lady Magdalen Herbert's son.

George Herbert: Poet at Prayer

As modern readers, we find it natural to look at the poems of George Herbert as if they were, in effect, a kind of prayer journal, a record of his private, most personal conversations with God. They are that, but much more than that.[30] In his "Prayer (I)" the first line bids us to consider prayer as a communal rather than merely personal spiritual exercise:

> Prayer the Churches banquet, Angels age,
>> Gods breath in man returning to his birth,
>> The soul in paraphrase, heart in pilgrimage,
> The Christian plummet sounding heav'n and earth;
> Engine against th'Almightie, sinners towre,
>> Reversed thunder, Christ-side-piercing spear,
>> The six-daies world transposing in an houre,

---

end of 'Goodfriday' may be read . . . not as a falling short of union with God, but as a sign of the sinful soul's gift of grace and progress toward that day when the soul will stand face to face with God" ("Donne's 'Goodfriday, 1613. Riding Westward' and Augustine's Psychology of Time," in Frontain and Malpezzi, *John Donne's Religious Imagination*, 298). Cf. Patrick Grant, *The Transformation of Sin: Studies in Donne, Herbert, Vaughan, and Traherne* (Amherst: University of Massachusetts Press, 1974), 40–72.

28. E.g., "To the Countess of Bedford" (Grierson, *Poems*, 192–94); "To the Countess of Huntingdon" (*Poems*, 177–79); for his hymns and "The LITANIE," see *Poems*, 308–39.

29. Jeffrey Johnson, "Wrestling with God: John Donne at Prayer," in Frontain and Malpezzi, *John Donne's Religious Imagination*, 306–23. Johnson here argues that Donne "pursued a devotional rather than dogmatic understanding of prayer" (321), a point as fully applicable to George Herbert.

30. C. S. Lewis cited Herbert's *The Temple* as one of the ten books that had most influenced him (no. 4). See the chapter by Don King in *C. S. Lewis's List: The Ten Books That Influenced Him Most*, ed. David Werther and Susan Werther (New York: Bloomsbury Academic, 2015).

A kinde of tune, which all things heare and fear;
Softnesse, and peace, and joy, and love, and blisse,
    Exalted Manna, gladnesse of the best,
    Heaven in ordinarie, man well drest,
The milkie way, the bird of Paradise,
    Church-bels beyond the starres heard, the souls bloud,
    The land of spices; something understood.[31]

This poem, a veritable concordance of biblical images drawn from both Testaments, suggests that the transforming power of prayer owes to its participation in a world not its own, vocalization by means of invoking God's Word rather than the invention of any individual supplicant.[32] The subject here is common prayer, prayer based on Scripture, as in the Book of Common Prayer, and this poem is consistent with Herbert's conviction, as we find it earlier in "The Church-Porch" (stanza 67), that public, corporate prayer catches us up and moves us along toward God more effectively than private prayer.[33] John Drury notes that Herbert "even had the people joining with him in the collects, or seasonal prayers, which were assigned by the book to the minister."[34] For Herbert, common prayer was an expression of the priesthood of all believers, an office in which all members were united, one in heart before their Lord. That he intended the ostensibly private prayer-record of his major collection *The Temple* to be of adjunct to common prayer, even preparation of the heart for Communion, is evidenced in the fact that he offered it to his friend Nicholas Ferrar to judge if there might be help to others if his poems were made public posthumously, to "turn to the advantage of a dejected poor soul . . . and enrich the World with pleasure and piety."[35] Herbert's motives parallel, in this sense, Augustine's in publish-

31. Hutchinson, *Works of George Herbert*, 51. A readable popular study of this poem as a means of discussing its subject is Dennis Lennon's *Turning the Diamond: Exploring George Herbert's Images of Prayer* (London: SPCK, 2002).

32. Chana Bloch, *Spelling the Word: George Herbert and the Bible* (Berkeley: University of California Press, 1985), 87–91. Terry G. Sherwood, *Herbert's Prayerful Art* (Toronto: University of Toronto Press, 1989), offers a valuable in-depth study of the poems as primarily personal prayer.

33. See Ramie Targoff's *Common Prayer: The Language of Public Devotion in Early Modern England* (Chicago: University of Chicago Press, 2001) for her excellent study of Herbert and Donne in this regard.

34. John Drury, *Music at Midnight: The Life and Poetry of George Herbert* (London: Allen Lane, 2013), 243.

35. Izaak Walton, *The Life of Mr. George Herbert* [1670], in *The Lives of John Donne, Sir Henry Wotton, Richard Hooker, George Herbert, and Robert Sanderson*, intro. George Saintsbury (London: Humphrey Milford, 1927), 74–75; cf. Helen Wilcox, ed., *The English Poems of George Herbert* (Cambridge: Cambridge University Press, 2007), xxx.

ing his *Confessions,* a work Herbert knew well, and mark his intentions to leave a legacy of pastoral care.

Common Prayer and Biblical Poetry

The Temple is Ferrar's title. Herbert seems not to have had one for the overall collection other than "The Church-Porch" and "The Church." We can understand Ferrar's choice by remembering that the image of the Jewish temple was most often invoked, in the seventeenth century, in the New Testament sense, referring to Christ's body (John 2:19–21), to the church (Eph. 2:19–22), and even to the bodies of individual believers (1 Cor. 6:19). To be in Christ is to be joined together as stones in an edifice in which the faithful "are the temple of the living God" (2 Cor. 6:16), "built upon the foundation of the apostles and prophets, Jesus Christ himself being the chief corner stone" (Eph. 2:20).[36] To construe prayer primarily in an individualistic sense is not the manner of New Testament Christianity, nor is it the manner of Herbert's notion of prayer.[37] In fact, it might be most useful to think of Herbert's poems as a species of prelude, preparing the heart for worship. Such seems to be the purpose of "H. Baptism (I)" and "H. Baptisme (II)," for example, which, if read as preparatory prayers, attune believers to the reaffirmation of vows made on their own behalf as they witness the baptism of a child, a new member of Christ's body and therefore his temple, his church.

An objection to this view of the poems might be that they are not sufficiently accessible because of their learnedness, their immersion in Scripture, not just at the level of allusion but in structure, assumed typology, and metonymic or paroemic invocation of substantial narratives. Yet Herbert could count upon his audience being immersed in Scripture to a degree available now to no poet writing in English. If, as John Drury observes, "deep and thorough knowledge of the Bible, with the ability to handle and interpret it, was a major part of Herbert's education, read daily at school and often at home,"[38] it was to some degree the bedrock of learning for anyone who regularly attended church in this period. That said, it is clearly the case that not only Herbert's mind but also his heart was unusually saturated with the language of Scripture; he could hardly think of anything without some biblical analogue or enrichment of it infusing his thought. In her superlative study of Herbert's

36. Bloch, *Spelling the Word,* 113–21, offers a rich exposition.
37. Ramie Targoff, "The Poetics of Common Prayer: George Herbert and the Seventeenth-Century Devotional Lyric," *English Literary Renaissance* 29, no. 3 (1999): 468–90.
38. Drury, *Music at Midnight,* 70; cf. 222–23.

use of the Bible, Chana Bloch speaks of his close attunement to "inner cor-respondences," "collation," "marriage of texts," and "juxtaposition"[39] as habits of his mind that were a direct reflection of Scripture itself. Like many within the English Protestant world, he applied Scripture to himself as a di-agnostic and a medicine, but not in any sterile academic or clinical fashion. Biblical knowledge for him was not a matter merely of acquired learning, but the object of his heart's deepest affections. Ferrar commends him for it in his preface to *The Temple*:

> Next God, he loved that which God himself hath magnified above all things, that is, his Word: so as he hath been heard to make solemne protestation, that he would not part with one leaf thereof for the whole world, if it were offered him in exchange.[40]

Ferrar was honoring his friend not merely as one who subscribed to Article VI of the official Anglican Book of Common Prayer Articles of Religion ("Of the Sufficiency of the Holy Scriptures for Salvation"); many could answer to that affirmation. Rather, he was commending Herbert as one who had been unusually scrupulous not to add to or edit out anything in the entirety of Scripture (see Rev. 22:18–19), who did not merely know the Bible well and use it sagely but whose heart's deepest affection kept centering him, again and again, in God's words rather than his own. Love of Scripture fired his imagination. That kept him ever seeking to deepen his understanding of its meanings and thus always reading each text in the light of the whole canon in which it is found.[41] Love of learning, yes, but above all a desire for God made of the Scriptures one light after another to his poetic imagination.

> Oh that I knew how all thy lights combine,
>   And the configurations of their glorie!
>   Seeing not onely how each verse doth shine,
> But all the constellations of the storie.
> This verse marks that, and both do make a motion
>   Unto a third, that ten leaves off doth lie:
>   Then as dispersed herbs do watch a potion,
> These three make up some Christians destinie:

39. Bloch, *Spelling the Word*, 47, 54, 63, 65, etc.

40. Nicholas Ferrar, "The Printers to the Reader," in Hutchinson, *Works of George Herbert*, 4.

41. Cf. Chauncey Wood, "Herbert's Biblically-Titled Poems," *George Herbert Journal* 26 (2002/3): 35–45.

> Such are thy secrets, which my life makes good,
>   And comments on thee: for in ev'ry thing
>   Thy words do finde me out, & parallels bring,
> And in another make me understood.
>   Starres are poore books, & oftentimes do misse:
>   This book of starres lights to eternall blisse.[42]

Herbert's poems are thus commentaries on Scripture, not so much on this biblical text or that, but on the *totum integrum* of the Word of God, ingested, digested, and now overflowing with the exuberant health of a grateful heart. In such a heart there is left no room for pride or for the telltale reflexes of elitism; like a child, Herbert offers what gifts he may to the Lord and to all who will receive them:

> The shepherds sing; and shall I silent be?
>   My God, no hymne for thee?
> My soul's a shepherd too; a flock it feeds
>   Of thoughts, and words, and deeds.
> The pasture is thy word: the streams, thy grace
>   Enriching all the place.
> Shepherd and flock shall sing, and all my powers
>   Out-sing the day-light houres.
> Then we will chide the sunne for letting night
>   Take up his place and right:
> We sing one common Lord; wherefore he should
>   Himself the candle hold.
> I will go searching, till I finde a sunne
>   Shall stay, till we have done;
> A willing shiner, that shall shine as gladly
>   As frost-nipt sunnes look sadly.
> Then we will sing, and shine all our own day,
>   And one another pay:
> His beams shall cheer my breast, and both so twine,
> Till ev'n his beams sing, and my musick shine.[43]

In our day, someone who believes as Herbert believed and speaks as he spoke may conceivably be denigrated as a "fundamentalist," even by fellow Christians, but a life of listening to and gratitude for the wisdom of the Bible

42. "Holy Scriptures II," in Hutchinson, *Works of George Herbert*, 58; cf. Wilcox, *English Poems of George Herbert*, 210.
43. "Christmas," in Hutchinson, *Works of George Herbert*, 80; cf. Wilcox, *English Poems of George Herbert*, 290.

would be recognized by Christians of the apostolic era itself as the evidence of his authentic calling.

Conversion and New Vocation

The artful simplicity that marks so many of Herbert's poems is the result of much discipline and self-restraint in the writer. He had to come a long way to achieve it; a masterful writer of Latin poems most highly praised in the academic circles of his day, a teaching fellow of Trinity College (1614–18), a holder of the prestigious post of Public Orator at Cambridge (1620–24), and a member of Parliament (1624), Herbert was both by birth and education an eminent member of the privileged class.[44] He was regarded in his Cambridge years as brilliant and yet too much proud of it, extravagant in his dress and aloof in a way that seems to have owed to more than his introversion. He did not, like Donne, circulate his poems in manuscript, but, as something of a perfectionist, kept them to himself to the very end. He was a skilled musician (lute, viola), but that discipline was not in his early years sufficient to temper his outbursts of intemperance, especially ire; the opening lines of "The Collar" suggest it could recur (the obvious pun "collar"/"caller" may have a third resonance, "choler"), and the rebelliousness he goes on to depict ("But as I rav'd and grew more fierce and wilde") may well allude to his state of mind in resistance to the pastoral calling to which, in September 1630, he finally submitted.[45] But submit he did, to a village church and rector's collar. Ferrar observes in his "The Printers to the Reader" (Walton repeats it) that Herbert soon began, "when he made mention of the blessed name of our Lord and Saviour Jesus Christ, to adde, *My Master*."[46] This was not a pose; "The Collar" is a confession:

> I struck the board, and cry'd, No more.
>   I will abroad.
>   What? shall I ever sigh and pine?
> My lines and life are free; free as the rode,
>   Loose as the winde, as large as store.
>   Shall I be still in suit?
>   Have I no harvest but a thorn
>   To let me bloud, and not restore
>   What I have lost with cordiall fruit?
>   Sure there was wine

44. Drury, *Music at Midnight*, 57, 110–29, 141.
45. Drury, *Music at Midnight*, 203.
46. Ferrar, "Printers to the Reader," in Hutchinson, *Works of George Herbert*, 4; see Drury, *Music at Midnight*, 212–13.

Before my sighs did drie it: there was corn
　　Before my tears did drown it.
　Is the yeare onely lost to me?
　　Have I no bayes to crown it?
No flowers, no garlands gay? all blasted?
　　　All wasted?
　　Not so, my heart: but there is fruit,
　　　And thou hast hands.
　Recover all thy sigh-blown age
On double pleasures: leave thy cold dispute
Of what is fit, and not. Forsake thy cage,
　　　Thy rope of sands,
Which pettie thoughts have made, and made to thee
　　Good cable, to enforce and draw,
　　　And be thy law,
　While thou didst wink and wouldst not see.
　　　Away; take heed:
　　　I will abroad.
Call in thy deaths head there: tie up thy fears.
　　　He that forbears
　　To suit and serve his need,
　　　Deserves his load.
But as I rav'd and grew more fierce and wilde
　　　At every word,
Me thoughts I heard one calling, *Child*!
　　And I reply'd, *My Lord*.[47]

Herbert's newfound ability to identify with the ordinary farm laborers who composed his parish clearly contributed to the character of holy life attributed to him by them and kept in memory. When his marriage was almost as fresh as his ordination, he and Jane (Danvers) adopted the three orphaned daughters of his sister Margaret,[48] and they too seem to have entered fully into his life at Bemerton, attending daily morning and evening prayer along with a good number of the local parish. The comment of his brother, Lord Herbert of Cherbury, that "his life was most holy and exemplary; insomuch, that about Salisbury, where he lived . . . he was little less than sainted,"[49] is well supported by other testimony.

Yet Herbert's deep sense of obligation to care for his local parish was not exclusive of his desire to provide pastoral care to pastors. His *A Priest to the*

47. Hutchinson, *Works of George Herbert*, 153–54; cf. Wilcox, *English Poems of George Herbert*, 524.

48. Drury, *Music at Midnight*, 164; cf. 229.

49. Hutchinson, *Works of George Herbert*, xxxvi.

Temple, or, The Country Parson: His Character and Rule of Holy Life, which was not printed till 1652,[50] is so great and timeless a classic that it commends itself even yet to any person who has such a calling. Here he contends that, while a country parson should be at pains to acquire a knowledge "of tillage, and pastorage" and make use of them in his teaching, yet

> the chief and top of his knowledge consists in the book of books, the storehouse and magazine of life and comfort, the holy Scriptures. There he sucks, and lives. In the Scriptures hee findes four things; Precepts for life, Doctrines for knowledge, Examples for illustration, and Promises for comfort. . . . But for the understanding of these; the means he useth are first, a holy Life, remembering what his Master saith, that *if any do Gods will, he shall know of the Doctrine, John 7*. and assuring himself, that wicked men, however learned, do not know the Scriptures, because they feel them not, and because they are not understood but with the same Spirit that writ them.[51]

A great deal of the character, though not the style, of Herbert the poet is here declared. Beyond that, we enter here into an appreciation of Herbert the dedicated pastor. For such a one, he says, literary means can assist: "Sometimes he tells them stories, and sayings of others, according as his text invites him; for them also men heed, and remember better than exhortations." But above all, "the character of his sermon is Holiness; he is not witty, or learned, or eloquent, but Holy."[52] Herbert the country priest had an entirely different audience than did Donne; he accepted that. But no less did he pray "for his people, that the Lord would be pleased to sanctifie them all, that they may come with holy hearts, and awfull [i.e., reverential] minds into the Congregation."[53]

In sum, he wished to bring his flock safely to the place he himself had come. The courtly manners that thinly disguised his early, self-directed life are brought to their undoing, in the end, by the Master he has learned also to call Love:

> Love bade me welcome: yet my soul drew back,
>   Guiltie of dust and sinne.
> But quick-ey'd Love, observing me grow slack
>   From my first entrance in,
> Drew nearer to me, sweetly questioning,
>   If I lack'd any thing.

50. Hutchinson, *Works of George Herbert*, 223–90.
51. Hutchinson, *Works of George Herbert*, 228.
52. Hutchinson, *Works of George Herbert*, 233; cf. 278, where Herbert says succinctly, "The Country Parson's Library is a Holy Life."
53. Hutchinson, *Works of George Herbert*, 235.

> A guest, I answer'd, worthy to be here:
> > Love said, You shall be he.
> I the unkinde, ungratefull? Ah my deare,
> > I cannot look on thee.
> Love took my hand, and smiling did reply,
> > Who made the eyes but I?
>
> Truth Lord, but I have marr'd them: let my shame
> > Go where it doth deserve.
> And know you not, sayes Love, who bore the blame?
> > My deare, then I will serve.
> You must sit down, sayes Love, and taste my meat:
> > So I did sit and eat.[54]

Chana Bloch has brilliantly expounded this final poem in Herbert's *The Temple*; I refer my reader to her work gladly, rather than make a poor effort at innovating upon her excellently informed exposition.[55] Nevertheless, I would stress that the banquet to which Herbert's "speaker" or persona here accedes is not exclusively either the eucharistic meal in which the believer participates or the eschatological feast in heaven, but both together, the one inseparable from the other. This poem is, poetically, Herbert's last will and testament; it is also, in all appropriate evangelical senses, his confession of faith.

A Complementarity of Voices

It might seem that, in many ways, Donne and Herbert are a study in contrasts, so different from each other that one can scarcely imagine them as family friends, products of the same institutions, sharing at various times similar public aspirations, priests in the same church. There is much evidence to sharpen the case for contrast. When we think of Donne the young poet, his cavalier erotic verse (conventional or not) comes immediately to mind. Herbert seems to have had the same thought. When he began to write poems (ca. 1610), being perhaps a bit too aware of the amorous verse of his family friend, he wrote to his mother Magdalen, their frequent recipient, to announce that he was not going to produce anything like it, declaring his resolve "that [his] poor abilities in poetry shall be all and ever consecrated to God's glory."[56] Perhaps unsurprisingly, Donne seems to have lived his whole life in remorse for sins

---

54. "Love III," in Hutchinson, *Works of George Herbert*, 188–89; cf. Wilcox, *English Poems of George Herbert*, 658.

55. Bloch, *Spelling the Word*, 99–122.

56. Letter quoted in full in Drury, *Music at Midnight*, 85.

committed, most likely involving his youthful excesses; the theme of repentance emerges repeatedly in his sermons, especially notable in his recurrence to the penitential psalms. Herbert seems to have worried more about sins of omission; many of his poems effect a kind of examination of conscience and repentance for his initial reluctance to serve. If Donne remained flamboyant in style, image-conscious and extroverted even in his preaching, Herbert's youthful aloofness was softened into a genuine humility by his final yielding to Christ, and he made no effort to preserve his sermons. So with progeny. After his controversial marriage in 1609, Donne was as prolific in the begetting of children as heretofore he had been in the pursuit of mistresses; Herbert, by contrast, married at the age of thirty-five and adopted children, fathering none of his own. One might go on.

If one goes to matters of theology, spirituality, and pastoral care, however, one sees immediately that here were the two main impulses of English Christian churchmanship. It is sometimes said of Donne that he represents the Catholic roots of English faith,[57] and of Herbert that he represents the Puritan strain and voice.[58] Actually, Donne drew upon John Calvin and Theodore Beza as much as he did upon Francisco Suarez and Cornelius à Lapide, and Herbert's biblical commentaries included not only those of Calvin but also of the Catholic Lucas Brugensis, which he valued enough to leave in his will to John Hayes, his successor in the parish.[59] I would suggest that what we have in Donne and Herbert are certainly distinct emphases of the Catholic and the Reformed style and temperament; yet, in that both men were deeply Augustinian,[60] catholic rather than Catholic or Protestant, they offer complementary expressions of Christian spiritual life that are of universal value. Both are necessary; for every Magdalen, there needs to be a Mary of Bethany to teach us what we are when we pray.

---

57. E.g., Louis Martz, *The Poetry of Meditation* (New Haven: Yale University Press, 1962).

58. E.g., Barbara Lewalski, *Protestant Poetics and the Seventeenth-Century Lyric* (Princeton: Princeton University Press, 1979).

59. Drury, *Music at Midnight*, 10. Rosamund Tuve's Herbert is deeply Catholic in *A Reading of George Herbert* (Chicago: University of Chicago Press, 1952); Joseph H. Summers's *George Herbert: His Religion and Art* (London: Chatto and Windus, 1954; rev. 1981) and "George Herbert and Anglican Traditions," *George Herbert Journal* 16 (1992–93): 21–39, offer a better balance. See also Philip Donnelly, "The Triune Heart of *The Temple*," *George Herbert Journal* 23 (1999–2000): 35–54.

60. Patrick Grant's *The Transformation of Sin* locates both poets squarely within Augustinian modes of prayer and theological formation (40–99); Katrin Ettenhuber's *Donne and Augustine: Renaissance Cultures of Interpretation* (Oxford: Oxford University Press, 2011) is an excellent in-depth study of Donne's reading in general.

seven

HABITUAL MUSIC

The Influence on English Poets of the King James Bible

I n his influential book *A History of English Prose Rhythms*, George Saintsbury, professor of rhetoric and English literature at Edinburgh University,
makes a startling claim with respect to the literary influence of the King
James Version of the Bible (KJV):

> So long as a single copy of the version of 1611 survives, so long will there be
> accessible the best words of the best times in English, in the best order, on the
> best subjects—so long will the fount be open from which a dozen generations
> of great English writers, in the most varying times and fashions, of the most
> diverse temperaments—libertines and virtuous persons, freethinkers and de-
> vout, poets and prosemen, laymen and divines—have drawn inspiration and
> pattern; by which three centuries of readers and hearers have had kept before
> them the prowess and the powers of the English tongue.[1]

As is typical of Saintsbury, that sentence is a mouthful. Actually, up until the
present century, more than a modest case may be made for his rather sweep-
ing judgment. While from our twenty-first-century perspective Saintsbury's
claim might seem as extravagant as his diction, in part this is because we can
no longer, as he did, reckon *aurally* with the poets and novelists we read when
they echo a standard, authorized translation of the Bible in English. But to

---

1. George Saintsbury, *A History of English Prose Rhythms* (London: Macmillan, 1912),
157–58.

anyone still familiar with the public reading of Scripture in weekly services of worship, Saintsbury's claim will seem less hyperbolic.

Though the last century spawned a cornucopia of biblical translations in English, few of these modern efforts have had much of an impact upon the novelists, poets, and dramatists of either the old British Commonwealth or America. Instead, however counterintuitively, these writers have tended overwhelmingly to make recourse to a translation that they themselves would regard, at least in respect of vernacular idiom, as thoroughly outdated. Yet even a casual survey will confirm that the KJV—now of nearly four hundred years' standing—still bears the poet's laurel crown. Why? Some reasons for the sustained preeminence of the KJV are worth thinking about.

A Persistent Voice

Anyone familiar with both late twentieth-century poetry and the KJV will have observed that not merely allusions and citations but also the cadences, rhythms, and syntax of the most beloved of English Bibles still shape a considerable amount of poetic language. In Richard Wilbur's "A Christmas Hymn," with its epigraph from Luke 19 in the KJV, influence might be expected:

> This child through David's city
> Shall ride in triumph by;
> The palm shall strew its branches,
> And every stone shall cry.
> And every stone shall cry,
> Though heavy, dull, and dumb,
> And lie within the roadway
> To pave his kingdom come.[2]

Yet in this poem, as the excerpt reveals, not merely direct citation and borrowed phrasing but also biblical parallelism and repetition work together to achieve a hymnody evocative of the Psalms as the KJV presents them.

What may be surprising is that not only in Christian poets (Wilbur is an Episcopalian) but also in Jewish poets this more comprehensive order of KJV influence can easily be discerned. For example, in Anthony Hecht the language of the KJV is not only used for epigraphs (as in the citation from Job 38:28 in "Adam": "Hath the rain a father? Or who hath begotten the drops of dew?")

---

2. Richard Wilbur, *New and Collected Poems* (San Diego: Harvest/HBJ, 1988), 225; now set to music, it is found as a hymn in the Episcopal hymnbook.

but also works its way into the narrative form and, by way of his sonorous phrasing, into whole poems—even poems in which the subject mater might seem to make the old biblical language most alien. In "Ostia Antica," for example, as if in words spoken by Augustine to his mother, Monica, in their last conversation in AD 387, the cadenced phrasing and Hebrew parallelism of Isaiah, the Psalms, and Wisdom books "becomes" the Latin speaker's "Englished" voice. The poem's "Augustine" thus speaks in accents unmistakably evocative of the Hebraized English of the KJV:

> "If there were hushed
> To us the images of earth, its poles
> Hushed, and the waters of it,
> And hushed the tumult of the flesh, even
> The voice intrinsic of our souls,
> Each tongue and token hushed and the long habit
> Of thought, if that first light, the given
> To us were hushed,
>
> So that the washed
> Object, fixed in the sun, were dumb,
> And to the mind its brilliance
> Were from beyond itself, and the mind were clear
> As the unclouded dome
> Wherein all things diminish, in that silence
> Might we not confidently hear
> God as he wished?"[3]

The KJV provides Hecht with titles and sometimes, by means of a captured, evocative phrase, both theme and allusion. This is true even in his poems "Behold the Lilies of the Field," "The Man Who Married Magdalene," and "Seven Deadly Sins"—where in fact skeptical irony regarding Christian verities is the mode of poetic engagement. In "Imitation" Hecht evokes the biblical psalmist in irreverent fashion: "Let men take note of her, touching her shyness." Here the KJV-attuned reader readily hears purloined echoes of Psalm 45, on which Hecht's poem is a kind of profane yet worshipfully eloquent meditation.

Examples might be multiplied almost indefinitely, and it is a witness to the cultural weight of the KJV's authority that it does not seem to require much piety in the poet, whether a Christian or of other religious heritage, for the influence to be substantial. The examples I have chosen here are winners of

---

3. Anthony Hecht, *The Hard Hours* (New York: Atheneum, 1967), 15.

the Pulitzer Prize for poetry in 1968 (Hecht), 1957 (Wilbur), and 1989 (Wilbur). A third Pulitzer winner, Howard Nemerov (1978), also Jewish, writes poetry rich in biblical language generally and King James language specifically. Nemerov quotes with precision from both Testaments of the KJV verbatim, even in something so oblique as a poem about the fall of Lucifer ("Dialectical Songs"). Likewise he ironically inverts familiar KJV phrases and incorporates phrases and fragments as paroemia in other unexpected places, such as in his wry poem "Einstein and Freud and Jack," which concludes:

> Of making many books there is no end,
> And like it saith in the book before that one,
> What God wants, don't you forget it, Jack,
> Is your contrite spirit, Jack, your broken heart.[4]

This wry juxtaposition of Ecclesiastes 12:12 and Psalm 51:17 is a reflex of deeply synthesized biblical memory, evidently fostered by years of familiarity with the KJV. That it comes in a wry seventy-fifth birthday poem for Allen ("Jack") Tate, the great Southern writer and New Critic, himself formidably familiar with the King James Bible, makes Nemerov's witticism about writerly life and the religious purpose of Scripture reading all the more trenchant. There is expectation, moreover, that other literate readers will similarly relish the intertextually poignant biblical wordplay, repentantly or not. What such examples show us, then, is that even while the KJV was rapidly falling out of currency in the churches, the poets were far from ready to let it go.

Writerly Education and the King James Bible

It may fairly be said of great writers that they are first of all great readers. Fluency arises from a well-stocked, rich reservoir in which not only story but also memorable items of choice phrasing, cadenced epithet, and wisdom sayings have been gathered and stored. The novelist D. H. Lawrence (1885–1930) reflects the process in his autobiographical final book, *Apocalypse*, itself effectively a species of commentary on the last book of the Bible:

> From earliest years right into manhood, like any other nonconformist child I had the Bible poured every day into my helpless consciousness, till there came almost a saturation point. Long before one could think or even vaguely understand, this Bible language, these "portions" of the Bible were *douched* over the

4. Howard Nemerov, *The Collected Poems* (Chicago: University of Chicago Press, 1977), 458–59.

mind and consciousness, till they became soaked in, they became an influence which affected all the processes of emotion and thought.[5]

Though he was a rebel against the evangelical Christianity in which he was raised, Lawrence's immersion in the KJV affected everything from his parallelistic prose style to his subject matter. His stage play *David* replicates much of the "original" KJV language, as to a lesser degree does his rewriting of the life of Jesus, *The Man Who Died* (1929), *Aaron's Rod* (1922), and his richly allusive but profane novel *The Rainbow* (1915). Thus, though he left behind the faith of his fathers, as a writer he lived off the literary and linguistic capital of the KJV and the biblical heritage in which his family had raised him.

Evangelical and other biblicist formations are now less frequently found among major writers in Britain than once was the case. Where biblical influence is currently prominent is among the writers of postcolonial Africa such as Chinua Achebe (*No Longer at Ease* [1960]) or Wole Soyinka (*The Swamp Dwellers* [1963]), or in American novelists such as Wendell Berry (*A Place on Earth* [1967; 1983]; *Jayber Crow* [2000]), Marilynne Robinson (*Gilead* [2004]; *The Death of Adam* [1998]), or Leif Enger (*Peace Like a River* [2001]).[6] But in such cases the process of ingestion of the Bible has been more or less the same, and the version almost invariably the KJV. What George Bernard Shaw (1856–1950) says of himself—namely, "That I can write as I do without having to think about my style is due to my having been steeped as a child in the Bible, *The Pilgrim's Progress*, and *Cassell's Illustrated Shakespeare*"[7]—may still be said in some fashion of many recent authors writing in English.

Shaw's triumvirate of personal formation reveals much about the close linkage in English literary history between the KJV as a foundational text and the foundational role played by Bunyan and Shakespeare, each often associated with the King James Bible, but neither in fact much influenced by it. Shakespeare's language, undeniably, can seem more proximate to the KJV in general than that of almost any other well-known early modern author

---

5. D. H. Lawrence, *Apocalypse and the Writings on Revelation*, ed. Mara Kalnins (Cambridge: Cambridge University Press, 1980), 59–60.

6. The religious tradition of a writer need not dictate the version of the Bible employed. Berry would presumably have, as a Baptist, been more often exposed in church to the American Standard Version, and Robinson, as a Presbyterian, to the Revised Version and Revised Standard Version. But James Joyce, who was of course raised Catholic, preferred the KJV to the Douai-Rheims for citation, as later did Catholic Flannery O'Connor in her short stories and in her novel *The Violent Bear It Away* (1960). In Berry's essay "The Burden of the Gospels," he admits to being "more affected than I knew by the King James Version, which is the translation I still prefer." See *The Way of Ignorance and Other Essays* (Berkeley: Counterpoint, 2006), 127.

7. George Bernard Shaw, *Everybody's Political What's What* (London: Constable, 1944), 181.

except, perhaps, Bunyan. But this effect arises mostly from the cadences of formal, oratorical sixteenth-century language, such as in Hermione's "unveiling" speech by Paulina in *A Winter's Tale* or Isabella's imploring of Angelo in *Measure for Measure*. Shakespeare seems to have known the Bible in several versions, and probably most often made use of the English Geneva Bible (1560).[8] The legend that he may have assisted in the King James Bible translation is just that—legendary.[9] What helps perpetuate the legend, as T. R. Eaton put it in *Shakespeare and the Bible* (1858), is simply that

> Shakespeare perpetually *reminds* us of the Bible, not by direct quotation, indirect allusion, borrowed idioms, or palpable imitation of phrase and style, but by an elevation of thought and simplicity of diction which are not to be found elsewhere.[10]

John Bunyan (1628–88), on the other hand, has been thought, rightly enough, to be steeped in the KJV Bible. But here also the verbal evidence of his own work points less obviously to the KJV *verbatim* than to biblical narrative and the theology of the Puritans. There is, nonetheless, much biblical parallelism and borrowed KJV phrasing in *The Pilgrim's Progress* (1678), and Bunyan adopts there many sayings from the Psalms and Proverbs. The KJV was clearly his Bible, and in *Grace Abounding to the Chief of Sinners* (1666) in particular, its language is abundantly evident as he celebrates Scripture as the "wisdom of God."

John Milton (1608–74) was enough of a learned scholar to consult many Bible versions, not only in English but also in Latin—as well as the Hebrew and Greek originals. He owned a KJV from his childhood, and evidently read it regularly from a very early age.[11] Thus, although Milton's intellectual and theological concerns drove him to consult the original-language texts

8. See Naseeb Shaheen, *Biblical References in Shakespeare's Plays* (Newark: University of Delaware Press, 1999); also David Daniel, *The Bible in English* (New Haven: Yale University Press, 2003), 295, 350–54.

9. In one of the more notorious attempts to "prove" this hypothesis, it has been noted that Shakespeare was forty-six in 1610, when, as David Norton nicely puts it, "the King James Bible was receiving its final rubbing and polishing. The forty-sixth word of the forty-sixth Psalm is 'shake,' and the forty-sixth from the end of the Psalm is 'spear.'" Norton's magisterial two-volume *A History of the Bible as Literature* (Cambridge: Cambridge University Press, 1993) is a treasure trove of such material and a highly recommended resource for anyone interested in a deep background study of its subject. I am gratefully indebted to it at several points in what follows.

10. T. R. Eaton, *Shakespeare and the Bible* (London: James Blackwood, 1858), 4–5 (italics added).

11. Norton, *History of the Bible as Literature*, 1:299.

as needed, and to regard them—rather than any translation—as definitively authoritative, William Riley Parker is surely close to the mark when he says, of the influence of the KJV upon Milton, that "its diction, its imagery, its rhythms early became a part of him."[12] Anyone who reads long in Milton's prose or poetry will recognize the hold the KJV has upon the great Puritan, not only as a theological but also as a literary model.

Cultural Authority

Genuine cultural authority is complex to the point of being a kind of mystery; in many ways, what the recent proliferation of Bible translations has split asunder—namely, the relationship between the theological or even cultural authority of Scripture, on the one hand, and the literary authority of the KJV as its standard translation, on the other—had not yet in the seventeenth century even come together. That fusion began to occur only after several decades of the King James Bible's regular use in churches.

One can sense the sometimes grudging but growing acceptance of the KJV as authoritative for faith, for worship, and for literary culture—more or less in that order—by reading the incidental remarks of prominent eighteenth-century divines and poets. John Locke (1637–74), the Enlightenment philosopher, was raised in a Dissenting household with the KJV; while he had doubts about the intelligibility of its chapter-and-verse divisions, he wrote his own paraphrase of and commentaries on the KJV text and quoted from it in his work.[13] Alexander Pope (1688–1744), a homeschooled Catholic, also sometimes used the KJV, especially for allusions to the Old Testament. Jonathan Swift (1667–1745), the satirist and Anglican dean of St. Patrick's, Dublin, regarded the KJV as not only the best English translation but also as a perdurable source of beauty and strength in the English language, as well as a primary means of anchoring the better qualities of the language for posterity. In his typically conservative fashion, arguing for a fixed standard for "correct" English, Swift says, "I am persuaded that the translators of the Bible were masters of an English style much fitter for that work than any we see in our present writings."[14] Like many another commentator, Swift sets off to advantage the Hebraisms of the KJV against what he regarded as the

12. Norton, *History of the Bible as Literature*, 1:299.

13. Especially valuable, from a number of points of view both theological and historical, is John Locke's preface to *A Paraphrase and Notes on the Epistles of St. Paul* (London, 1707).

14. Jonathan Swift, "A Proposal for Correcting, Improving and Ascertaining the English Tongue" (1712), in *The Prose Works of Jonathan Swift*, ed. Herbert Davis, 14 vols. (Oxford: Blackwell, 1957), 4:14.

labored latinity of "present writings," a judgment all the more notable in light of his championing, in other literary contexts, of the "ancients" (Greek and, especially, Roman authors) against the "moderns" (his contemporaries).

Later in the century, his fellow clergyman and literary critic Vicesimus Knox (1752–1821) allows that the KJV, the *Iliad* (in Pope's translation, one suspects), and Shakespeare are the triumvirate of sublime achievement. Knox also indicates a significant reason for the preeminence of the King James Bible when he says,

> We have received the Bible in the very words in which it now stands from our fathers; we have learned many passages of it by heart in our infancy; we find it quoted in sermons from the earliest to the latest times, so that its phrase is become familiar to our ear.[15]

It is in this way that authors as diverse as the Scottish philologist James Burnet (Lord Monboddo) and the English lexicographer, poet, and critic Samuel Johnson began to regard the KJV, with Swift, as instrumental to a dignified, pure standard of written English.[16]

This order of authority is much in evidence well throughout the nineteenth century. It is interesting that Sir James G. Frazer, the famous mythologist of *The Golden Bough* (1890; 1900), compiled his *Passages of the Bible Chosen for Their Literary Beauty and Interest* (1895) from KJV quotations, and that no less a religious skeptic than T. H. Huxley (1825–95), an apologist for Darwin, wrote of the KJV that "it is written in the noblest and purest English, and abounds in exquisite beauties of a merely literary form."[17]

In America, much the same pattern of appreciation is evident. Timothy Dwight (1752–1817), the New England poet, Calvinist, and eventual president of Yale University, wrote his master's thesis there on "The History, Eloquence, and Poetry of the Bible" (1772), and KJV language thoroughly permeates his major long poem, *The Conquest of Canaan* (1785).[18] The KJV was the book of books for Dwight, the English version of biblical eloquence that he championed throughout his life. Walt Whitman (1819–92), whose poetry could hardly have been to Dwight's theological taste, wrote of the KJV Bible as if it were entirely

15. Vicesimus Knox, *Essays Moral and Literary* (1778), from *The Works of Vicesimus Knox*, 7 vols. (London, 1824), 1:267.

16. Norton provides a good selection from the late eighteenth-century debate among a host of commentators (*History of the Bible as Literature*, 2:94–134).

17. T. H. Huxley, quoted in George P. Eckman's *The Literary Primacy of the Bible* (New York: Methodist Book Concern, 1915), 39, 162.

18. See the article on Dwight by Vincent Freimarck, "Timothy Dwight's *Dissertation* on the Bible," *American Literature* 24 (1952): 73–77.

poetry, and phrases from the KJV are amply and notoriously present in his work,[19] even as they are in Herman Melville's fiction, despite what critic Lawrence Thompson has reasonably called Melville's lifelong "quarrel with God."[20]

On this point, then, the evidence is clear: as its influence grew steadily through the eighteenth century and came to the point of irrefragable command in the nineteenth, on both sides of the Atlantic, the KJV achieved among poets, novelists, dramatists, and intellectual statesmen a generally supreme authority as the standard of stylistic and literary excellence. The KJV had become thoroughly established as a cultural authority, a source and resource for writers and readers of English literature. Very few since then have resisted the KJV on these grounds, though two of weighty acumen must be acknowledged: neither C. S. Lewis nor T. S. Eliot in the early twentieth century could any longer approve of the KJV, not because it lacked literary power, but precisely because what Lewis regarded as an unthinking idolatry of the KJV's style tended to prevent modern people from hearing the text as to its substance. In Eliot's complementary view, "the Bible has had a *literary* influence upon English literature *not* because it has been considered as literature, but because it has been considered as the report of the Word of God."[21] One might indeed confirm Eliot's convictions in this regard, though there remain, as we have seen, complexities for which to account.

Readerly Education

It was inevitable that cultural and literary authority, coupled with religious and spiritual authority, should have made the KJV a staple in early childhood education. In fact, in a gesture almost impossible to imagine today, T. H. Huxley advocated the use of the Bible in the British schools, and the translation he proposed—for cultural and literary rather than religious reasons—was the KJV.[22] His precedent in this regard was Matthew Arnold (1822–88), who, for all his hatred of evangelistic biblical preaching by those such as D. L. Moody (*God and the Bible* [1875], xiv–xv), wanted to preserve the Authorized English Bible as a literary and cultural resource. Arnold was thus willing—especially,

19. Walt Whitman, *The Critic* 3 (February 3, 1883): 39–40.
20. Lawrence R. Thompson, *Melville's Quarrel with God* (Princeton: Princeton University Press, 1952).
21. Lewis states his disapproving position in a lecture of 1950, then essay, "The Literary Impact of the Authorized Version," in *They Asked for a Paper* (London: Geoffrey Bless, 1962), 46–49. T. S. Eliot's essay "Religion and Literature" (1935) is found in *Selected Prose*, ed. John Hayward (Harmondsworth, UK: Penguin, 1953), 32–33.
22. Eckman, *Literary Primacy of the Bible*, 397.

perhaps, in view of the perspective he acquired when he was Inspector of Schools—to engage in an appeal to vaguely religious sentiments, with which he had little sympathy, to achieve his cultural objective.[23] For evidently cultural and stylistic reasons, Arnold believed Isaiah to be a "literary work of the highest order . . . a monument of the Hebrew genius at its best" (*Works*, 7:58). This led him to try his hand at preparing a text: *A Bible Reading for Schools: The Great Prophecy of Israel's Restoration (Isaiah, Chapters 40–66), Arranged and Edited for Young Learners* appeared in 1872.

But if we are to consider the basis of the KJV's influence, we need not only to reflect on the impact of King James Bible reading in British schools upon the formation of nineteenth- and early twentieth-century writers but also, in America, to reckon with the enormous influence of *McGuffey's Eclectic Readers* (recently repopularized as a classic of American educational history). These may have been the most popular textbooks of all time (David Norton reports that 122 million copies were published by the 1920s), and their most frequent textual authority for grammatical standards is the KJV. The same can be said of *Brown's Grammar* (1856; 1863), a less massively popular influence than McGuffey, but nevertheless pervasive in both Canadian and American schools for decades. Most poets and novelists have been pupils in elementary school classrooms; and many of the most recurrent KJV citations are phrases and passages that have entered into mainstream literary discourse on this side of the Atlantic through such school texts. What texts such as McGuffey and Brown established in America was fully parallel to what Arnold's and Huxley's efforts finally established in Britain: the King James Bible entered the canon as a work of English literature.

But, as the biologists say, there were still other vectors, not least among them the musical enshrining of specific biblical passages from the King James translation. To appreciate this, we need to visit only a single example.

Handel and the King James Version

An important element in biblical transmission, from the time of the early Christian church, is the setting of texts to music. We might have considered in this study hymns, especially ones composed by the likes of Isaac Watts, Philip Doddridge, William Cowper, John Newton, and Charles Wesley, for hymns have been one of the most important means of transmission of biblical idiom, especially in the eighteenth and nineteenth centuries, but these would oblige a

23. See the excellent account of Arnold's reflection over a period of years in Norton, *History of the Bible as Literature*, 2:272–76.

full-length study in themselves.[24] There is more to musical settings of the KJV than hymns, however, as G. F. Handel's *Messiah* (1742) well illustrates. This popular eighteenth-century oratorio remains an annual concert fixture in the English-speaking world. The libretto by Soame Jenyns was adapted directly from the King James Bible, and countless millions, in one medium or another, still hear its celebrated passages from Isaiah and Revelation year after year. In a spectacular rerun of its first performance in 1784, Handel's musical presentation of the biblical text was popular enough that John Newton, author of the hymn "Amazing Grace" and rector of St. Mary Woolnoth in London, elected to preach a full year's cycle of sermons (fifty in all) on the biblical excerpts in the oratorio. In those sermons, as for most who have ever heard Handel's great oratorio sung, one of the most memorable passages is from Isaiah 40, beginning with the words "Comfort ye, my people." Handel's rich musical setting does not drown out the crisp choral diction; many listeners still have the first verses of Isaiah 40 by heart because of it.

In yet other ways the KJV language of the "poetical books," and the book of Isaiah as an exemplary specimen of it, was experiencing in the lifetime of Newton and Handel an increased order of attention. Where English literature is concerned, an important instigator was the Reverend Robert Lowth (1710–87). In 1753, Lowth, the Oxford Professor of Poetry, published a book of Latin lectures under the title *De Sacra Poesi Hebraeorum Praelectiones*. While the content of these lectures was not completely available in English translation until 1787, partial translations began to appear in monthly installments of *The Christian's Magazine* in 1767, and the gist of Lowth's argument was expressed in his widely respected translation of and commentary on Isaiah, *Isaiah: A New Translation* (1778). The essence of Lowth's contention regarding the Hebrew of biblical poetry (of which many of his examples come from Isaiah) is that it is superior to the poetry of classical Greek and Latin authors, an opinion, as we have seen, held also by John Donne in his sermons. Chief among its particular beauties is its metrical form, especially that feature captured rather successfully by the KJV translators—namely, Hebrew parallelism. That Hebrew parallelism translates so well into English Lowth reckons to be a property primarily of the Hebrew, but he regards as a providential grace its English rendering. While parallelism is not equally apparent in all parts—for example, of Isaiah—it is nonetheless, as we have seen, the basis of the *poesis* expressed in the Old Testament. Finally, Lowth argues that the Bible, to be considered properly, must be regarded as a great literary achievement, not

---

24. An excellent resource is J. R. Watson's *The English Hymn: A Critical Study* (Oxford: Oxford University Press, 1999).

merely as a religious source text. Nothing is "more elevated, more beautiful or more elegant" than Hebrew poetry; in it "the almost ineffable sublimity of the subject is fully equaled by the energy of the language and the dignity of the style."[25] In his own translation of Isaiah 40, Lowth retains more of the KJV idiom than any of his successors among English translators do.

While Handel was making such magnificent use of the KJV in the *Messiah*, John Newton, though himself a minor poet, was more concerned with the theological content of the texts than their poetry. His collaborator on the *Olney Hymns*, the better-known poet William Cowper (1731–1800), wrote verse saturated with the KJV, much as did his older contemporary Christopher Smart (1722–71). But whereas it is biblical content—as much or more than KJV phrasing—that is evident in Cowper, repetition, metricality, and parallelism come to the fore in Smart's late poetry. To compare: in Cowper's long poem *The Task* (1785), he writes,

> I was a stricken deer, that left the herd
> Long since; with many an arrow deep infixt
> My panting side was charg'd, when I withdrew
> To see a tranquil death in distant shades.[26]

Here the specter of KJV Psalm 42:1 is apparent ("As the hart panteth after the water brooks, so panteth my soul after thee, O God"), but direct verbal parallelism with the KJV is subsumed to a parallelism of personal application in the mode of Calvinistic spiritual autobiography. Cowper calls upon the KJV more directly in his long poems, but only rarely, as in "He is the freeman whom the truth makes free, and all are slaves beside" (*Task* 5:733–34), where both the content of John 8:32 and its proximate diction are employed.

If we set against this some lines from Smart's *Jubilate Agno* (written 1758–63), we sense at once the difference:

> For the SHADOW is of death, which is the Devil, who can
> make false and faint images of the works of Almighty God. . . .
> For SHADOW is a fair word from God. . . .
> For the shadow is his and the penumbra is his and his the
> perplexity of the phenomenon.[27]

25. Robert Lowth, *Lectures on the Sacred Poetry of the Hebrews*, trans. George Gregory, 2 vols. (London, 1787), 1:37.

26. *The Poetical Works of William Cowper*, ed. H. S. Milford, 4th ed. (London: Oxford University Press, 1934), 166, lines 108–11.

27. Christopher Smart's *Jubilate Agno*, written in the hospital, was published posthumously in 1939 by W. F. Stead under the title *Rejoice in the Lamb: A Song from Bedlam*, then reedited

In Smart's poem, the stylistic Hebraism, KJV idiom, is in fact its governing form.

When we come to William Blake (1757–1827), we have arrived at a place in which the poetic modes of KJV Hebraisms are not only naturalized but have become attached firmly to a notion of prophetic vision and essential to achieving the language of the "sublime" in poetic diction. Though Blake was a marginal figure in his own lifetime, he now looms large in the poetic canon, not least as a precursor of the Romantics. Blake is likewise a poet more of the Old than the New Testament: he too claims "Isaiah the Prophet" as a foundational influence in his middle years and writes that Isaiah, along with Ezekiel, spoke to him in a fancy or dream confirming his poet's role as a prophetic voice.[28] Blake's view of the King James Bible translation is that it was itself "inspired," and though his personal theology was heterodox and wildly eccentric, his King James Bible was apparently the most heavily used of all the books in his library.[29] In Isaiah, particularly, he found himself not so much "a hearer of the word" as an idolater of its poetic power. For Blake it was the voice of condemnation rather than of comfort in Isaiah that compelled; in *The Marriage of Heaven and Hell* he has Isaiah say, "As I was then persuaded & remain confirmed, that the voice of honest indignation is the voice of God, I cared not for consequences but wrote."[30] What Blake wanted and got from the KJV was a kind of poetic authority; yet what he used it for was often to subvert the authority of the Bible itself.

Samuel Taylor Coleridge (1772–1834), his opium use and early Unitarianism notwithstanding, was a much more learned critical reader of the Bible, and in the end his reading of it made him more orthodox. Though Coleridge made use of KJV idiom occasionally in his verse and thought it a positive influence both on the English language and on the writing and speech of those who read the KJV as children, his chief preoccupations were with formal biblical criticism and Christian apologetics. His notion of poetic inspiration was closely tied to his view of biblical inspiration, but as his writings in *The Statesman's Manual*, *Confessions of an Enquiring Spirit*, and even

---

by W. H. Bond in 1954. It was largely composed in the "Let/For" antiphonal model that Bishop Lowth had shown to be one characteristic form of Hebrew psalmody. I have quoted it here from David Lyle Jeffrey, *English Spirituality in the Age of Wesley* (Grand Rapids: Eerdmans, 1987, 2000; repr., Vancouver: Regent, 2004), 334.

28. See Leopold Damrosch, *Symbol and Truth in Blake's Myth* (Princeton: Princeton University Press, 1980), 16; Geoffrey Keynes, ed., *The Complete Writings of William Blake* (London: Oxford University Press, 1966), 799.

29. According to the *Blake Records*, ed. G. E. Bentley Jr. (London: Oxford University Press, 1969), 527.

30. *The Marriage of Heaven and Hell*, plate 12. See William Blake, *The Poetry and Prose*, ed. David V. Erdman (Garden City, NY: Doubleday, 1965), 38.

the *Biographia Literaria* all show, these are both connected to his conception of the faithful Christian imagination. Anthony Harding captures this point succinctly when he writes that "Coleridge's imagination was more imbued with Hebrew literature, imagery, and thought-forms than that of any other English poet of the time except Blake, and he found in Hebrew poetry the exemplary use of Imagination, the '*modifying*, and *co-adunating* Faculty.'"[31] Coleridge actually knew a little Hebrew, though his sense of it depended mostly on Johann Gottfried Herder's *The Spirit of Hebrew Poetry* (1783), Lowth's *Isaiah*, and, from his childhood, the King James Bible, two copies of which he kept by him to the end of his life. Coleridge's view that biblical Hebrew reached its pinnacle in Isaiah (*Table Talk*, February 24, 1827) was by then beginning to be a consensus.

In Percy Bysshe Shelley (1799–1822) we meet another resistant but compulsive reader; Shelley, along with Mary Wollstonecraft Shelley, with whom he read the KJV aloud for entertainment in the evening, was an atheist. Lord Byron (1788–1824) was a lapsed Christian but was influenced literarily by the KJV, nowhere more apparently than in the diction of some passages of *Childe Harolde's Pilgrimage* and in his *Hebrew Melodies*, in both of which the recurrent voice and the allusions are primarily from Isaiah.

By now the historical trajectory of the King James Bible's formidable influence upon writers in English should be sufficiently clear. That influence is more immediately apparent in the poets than in novelists and other prose writers; among their works we can appreciate the aural and oral qualities of the KJV that have, evidently, been most formative. But it would be a mistake to think that primary canonical writers of prose, including prose fiction, stand apart from this general pattern. Charlotte Brontë (1816–55), for example, a deeply Christian novelist, in her major novel *Jane Eyre* (1847) alludes to and quotes the KJV repeatedly; indeed, her general style is thoroughly shaped by it.[32] She loved the Psalms, and the parallelism of both the Psalms and Isaiah appears everywhere. If we look into novels such as George Eliot's *Scenes from a Clerical Life* and *Adam Bede*, for example, or the work of Sir Walter Scott and Charles Dickens, we find variants of the same plenitude.

John Ruskin (1819–1900) is yet another prose writer who confessed gladly to having read aloud with his family two or three chapters of the Bible daily

---

31. See Anthony John Harding, *Coleridge and the Inspired Word* (Kingston, ON: McGill-Queen's University Press, 1985), 7; also the excellent discussion by Norton in *History of the Bible as Literature*, 2:153–63.

32. Catherine Brown Tkacz, "The Bible in Jane Eyre," *Christianity and Literature* 44, no. 1 (1994): 3–28; and Linda Morra, "Charlotte Bronte's Books of Revelation: Apocalyptic and Prophetic Allusion in the Novel" (MA thesis, University of Ottawa, 1994).

after breakfast, being required to "learn a few verses by heart," as well as "the fine old Scottish [metrical] paraphrases" of the Psalms; and to these, he says, together with the KJV itself, he owes the "first cultivation of [his] ear in sound." He was made to memorize the whole of Psalm 119 (C. H. Spurgeon would have been delighted by this), though he hated it at the time. Significantly, this psalm is, of course, the great alphabetic poem in praise of the Scriptures as *Torah 'emeth*, the Law of God *aleph* to *tov*, and Ruskin confesses

> that of all the pieces of the Bible that my mother thus taught me, that which cut me most to learn, and which was, to my child's mind, chiefly repulsive—the 119th Psalm—has now become of all the most precious to me, in its overflowing and glorious passion of love for the law of God.

Later he adds, "I have with deeper gratitude to chronicle what I owe my mother for the resolutely consistent lessons which so exercised me in the Scriptures as to make every word of them familiar to my ear in habitual music—yet in that familiarity reverenced, as transcending all thought, and ordaining all conduct."[33] Here is yet another representative case in which the memorized and ingested word, the word "taken to heart" in an aural and oral transmission, has become the abiding word in the heart and on the lips of prominent shapers of English language and literature.

Inclination of the Heart

The power of the KJV to influence oratory and poetry alike, as I have already implied, is a result of the fact that this translation, more than any since, was made to be read aloud.[34] Since not long after the invention of printing, literate people have been able to read privately, but often at the cost of a rich appreciation of the aural and oral "Hebraic" qualities of biblical language. Modern translations of the Bible, by comparison, often read aloud colorlessly, even badly, because too little attention has been given to public voice.[35] In a context where oratorical register is highly valued, such as in the African American churches, the KJV tends still to be much preferred for use in worship, despite

33. John Ruskin, *Praeterita* (London, 1885–89), 31; see also Mary Gibbs and Ellen Gibbs, *The Bible References in the Works of John Ruskin* (New York: Oxford University Press, 1898).

34. "Appointed to be read aloud in churches," the KJV was heavily punctuated so as to guide public readers. See F. F. Bruce, *The English Bible: A History of Translations from the Earliest English Versions to the New English Bible* (New York: Oxford University Press, 1961), 108–10.

35. See David Lyle Jeffrey, "Biblical Translation and the Future of Spiritual Interpretation," *Modern Theology* 28, no. 4 (2012): 687–706.

its many archaisms. Consequently, the KJV marks distinctively the public oratory of figures such as Martin Luther King Jr. In the often-magnificent prose
of W. E. B. Du Bois, the KJV echoes on almost every page with a similar oral
authority and prophetic power:

> I sit with Shakespeare and he winces not. Across the color-line I move arm in
> arm with Balzac and Dumas, where smiling men and welcoming women glide in
> gilded halls. From out the caves of evening that swing between the strong-limbed
> earth and the tracery of the stars, I summon Aristotle and Aurelius and what
> soul I will, and they come all graciously with no scorn nor condescension. So,
> wed with Truth, I dwell above the Veil. Is this the life you grudge us, O knightly
> America? Is this the life you long to change into the dull red hideousness of
> Georgia? Are you so afraid lest peering from this high Pisgah, between Philistine
> and Amalekite, we sight the Promised Land?[36]

One "hears" the King James Bible in African American preaching, political
speeches, and public oratory because, in a way no subsequent translation has
been able to match, the KJV brings back to life the ancient biblical voice in
which the prophet and the poet are one and the same seeker. It is still a voice
with authority. This is a Bible to be *heard*, not merely looked into. "Hear! O
Israel" makes real sense in these accents: "Incline your ear, and come unto me;
hear, and your soul shall live" (Isa. 55:3)—this has a resonance that beckons.
So also do these verses: "Hear the word of the LORD, ye rulers of Sodom;
give ear unto the law of our God, ye people of Gomorrah" (Isa. 1:10); "Give
ear, all ye of far countries" (Isa. 8:9); "Let your ear receive the word" (Jer.
9:20); "Wherefore hear the word of the LORD, ye scornful men" (Isa. 28:14);
"Give ye ear, and hear my voice; hearken, and hear my speech" (Isa. 28:23).

This is the sort of power that both is poetry and makes for poetry. For
inner music, clarity of phrasing, rhetorical repetition, parallel, and emphasis,
there is nothing yet like unto the KJV for a translation that *sounds* like the
voice of God. To the Greek mind of the biblical scholar, such a notion is a
kind of foolishness; but to the ears of English writers, to whom the echoing
rill of Hebrew melodies has continued to seem sweet, the diction of the KJV
has been the authentic voice of biblical wisdom. Imagine, if you will, this
familiar passage from Isaiah as it might be read aloud by Dr. King or sung
beautifully to Handel's setting by one of the great choral ensembles of the
age, and you will know again the matchless art of the KJV and why it remains
beloved of writers:

36. W. E. B. Du Bois, *The Souls of Black Folk* (1903; repr., New York: Barnes and Noble,
2003), 81.

Comfort ye, comfort ye my people, saith your God.

Speak ye comfortably to Jerusalem, and cry unto her, that her warfare is accomplished, that her iniquity is pardoned: for she hath received of the LORD's hand double for all her sins.

The voice of him that crieth in the wilderness, Prepare ye the way of the LORD, make straight in the desert a highway for our God.

Every valley shall be exalted, and every mountain and hill shall be made low: and the crooked shall be made straight, and the rough places plain:

And the glory of the LORD shall be revealed, and all flesh shall see it together: for the mouth of the LORD hath spoken it.

The voice said, Cry. And he said, What shall I cry? All flesh is grass, and all the goodliness thereof is as the flower of the field:

The grass withereth, the flower fadeth: because the spirit of the LORD bloweth upon it: surely the people is grass.

The grass withereth, the flower fadeth: but the word of our God shall stand for ever.

O Zion, that bringest good tidings, get thee up into the high mountain; O Jerusalem, that bringest good tidings, lift up thy voice with strength; lift it up, be not afraid; say unto the cities of Judah, Behold your God! (Isa. 40:1–9)

This, though its flower fades, is still the translation that most moves a writerly heart to exaltation.

eight

CONCLUSION AND FORM FOR THE PERSONAL IN MODERN POETRY

One of the most obvious features of a correlative modern trend toward transferring obligation for coherence and structure from the writer to the reader is the literary phenomenon of multiple (or non-) conclusions. Whereas for a poet like Herbert his "closes," as he called them, were a signal of their communicable meaning as well as artful structure, many modern poets have resisted such architectonic completeness. The emergence of end-it-yourself art became, during the late 1960s, increasingly entertaining to students of language and culture. The problem of endings flourishes in novels like Richard Brautigan's *Trout Fishing in America*, with its mayonnaise chapter; in John Fowles's *The French Lieutenant's Woman*, where readers paste on whichever of two endings they like; and ultimately, perhaps, in Brautigan's *A Confederate General from Big Sur*, with its possible 186,000 endings per second but no real conclusion at all. Such texts experimented with a range of effects, from apparent conclusions that at the last dissolve, as in Mike Nichols's film production of *The Graduate*, to a play like Samuel Beckett's *Endgame* (*Fin de Partie*), which, with Zeno's paradox, is always ending, ever dying, yet never able to come to an end.

Although these examples come from novels, film, and theater, the *problématique* they share is one that has for some time preoccupied late-modern philosophers, historians, theologians, philologists, scientists, some educational theorists, and, not least of all, modern poets. Here, from the point of view of the poets primarily, we may reflect on the persistent yet frustrated search for poetic structures that can speak of some possible end point, an intentional or even inevitable telos, and accordingly develop its corollary, a form for meaning in poetry in which the reader can participate intelligibly. This too has obvious implications for how the Bible may or may not appeal to the poetic imagination in modernity, for the Bible is coherently teleological; from the beginning it looks forward to the end, "the fullness of time." Modernity resists—at all levels—the idea of such a form for conclusion, not least because that might imply a judgment.

Scripture and Structure

Aesthetically considered, closure in a work of art need not, as a notable book on the subject tells us, be identical with temporal conclusion; "that is, it is not always a matter of endings. . . . Whether spatially or temporally conceived, a structure appears 'closed' when it is experienced as integral: coherent, complete, and stable." In these terms, the experience of closure, of conclusion, becomes "a function, really, of the *perception* of *structure*."[1] In this sense, as the history of aesthetics suggests, literary criticism has typically assumed and almost always appreciated that a successful conclusion is the product of a structure understood, the form of a realized framework for interpretation that can evoke an affirmative response to a work's artistic integrity. We can see this reflected *en bref* in a modern poem that whimsically engages the resistance to this very expectation, Richard Wilbur's "Parable":

> I read how Quixote in his random ride
> Came to a crossing once, and lest he lose
> The purity of chance, would not decide
>
> Whither to fare, but wished his horse to choose.
> For glory lay wherever he might turn.
> His head was light with pride, his horse's shoes
>
> Were heavy, and he headed for the barn.[2]

A presumption of the poem's whimsical conclusion is the basic communality of *some* experience and its presumed communicability by the word or image. Quixote's horse, not so much a visionary as Balaam's ass, sees no further than its confused rider and chooses predictability and security. Measured

1. Barbara H. Smith, *Poetic Closure* (Chicago: University of Chicago Press, 1968), 2, 4.
2. Richard Wilbur, *The Poems of Richard Wilbur* (New York: Harcourt, Brace and World, 1963), 131.

against random chance, the barn will do. The poem is a modern one, a joke at the expense of resisters of responsibility but also a serious question about the meaning of endings. It invokes the same structure as the fictional narrative by Richard Fariña entitled *Been Down So Long It Looks Like Up to Me.* In this book, apropos of conclusions, one of the leading characters is made to say, "I've been on a voyage, old chap. I've seen fire and pestilence, famine and sword. A real pilgrimage. I'm exempt."[3]

Despite the allusion, the speaker is, of course, no Tiresias. Exemption can be no part of a credible conclusion, all the "immortalism" of our era notwithstanding. No amount of wishful thinking can hide the fact that none of us is finally exempt. As Qoheleth in Ecclesiastes says, "All go unto one place; all are of the dust, and all turn to dust again" (Eccles. 3:20), and in fact the wise man dies just like the fool (2:16).

Here, then, is an incoherence; in the quest for conclusion in modern literature and film, no subject other than sex has been more prominent than death, from the watery anticipations of T. S. Eliot to Ingmar Bergman's specters to the historical and poetic destiny of Sylvia Plath. The theme is so recurrent in poetry that it has been studied by many, including, notably, A. Alvarez in his book *The Savage God.*[4] But, though death may figure recurrently for characters and personas in literary texts as their release from the despair of a psychologically shapeless modern universe, it does not, unhappily, provide a formal experience of conclusion for the living. Thus Samuel Beckett's "Malacoda," with its carefully chosen title and grandiloquent fatigue, describes the measurement of a corpse for its coffin and preparations for funeral display as a ludicrously decorous ritual, vainly attempting to grant dignity and therefore meaning to the deceased for the sake of the living. "The undertaker's man, impassible behind his scutal bowler," works his art to disguise the corruption of death for the sake of little more than ritual illusion. What the mortician does "to coffin . . . to cover" and perfume with flowers is designed as one last frame for a photograph, a vestige of already fading memory:

> mind the imago it is he
> hear she must see she must
> all aboard all souls
> half-mast aye aye
>
> nay[5]

---

3. Richard Fariña, *Been Down So Long It Looks Like Up to Me* (New York: Random House, 1966).

4. A. Alvarez, *The Savage God* (London: Widenfeld and Nicholson, 1971).

5. Samuel Beckett, *Poems in English* (New York: Grove Press, 1963), 43.

Negation is emphatically the nihilist point of the poem. When the hope of perceiving any structure for meaning goes, it is natural enough, perhaps, that faith in communication itself should go, and in this poem vocabulary is already radically contorted to "mute the signal." Though from its title onward it finds the last syllables to despise its alienation made possible by an explicitly Christian and biblical vocabulary of affirmation (thus "Malacoda"), the poem also finds irrelevant or unintelligible the human measure of it. The real failure of structure experienced in this poem is not that of the cycle of life and death. That inevitability is beyond debate. The "nay" is an intense emotional denial that even death—the inexorable physical conclusion—can define, interpret, or give closure to the structure of human experience. The real failure of structure the poem decries is the loss of any intelligible form for the personal whatsoever, for a meaningful relation of the "she," the "coffined dead," the persona, the reader.

Private Mythologies

It seems that the most intractable maze for a modern poet—as for many another modern person—is the tangled web of self-preoccupation. The post-Romantic emphasis on the autonomous and independent character of human personality has increasingly come to define personal identity as a kind of psychological originality and spiritual individualism—even as a glorified and mutually exclusive quixotic vision in which each person lives entirely within his or her own private mythology (or, to recall Brautigan's marvelous chapter, his own "Kool-Aid reality"). But such private mythologies are often composed of flat contradictions between the felt reality of psychological experience and any intelligible description of it that might connect the interior self and that which lies outside but nevertheless impinges upon the self. In the relatively tranquil world of Robert Frost, for example, the contradictions can be seen in his poem "The Tuft of Flowers." For decades, schoolteachers of the sort Paul Simon used to sing about have been using the lines

> "Men work together," I told him from the heart,
> "Whether they work together or apart."

—as if Frost were here affirming the intrinsic community of all humankind, simply because the lines occur at the end of the poem and therefore seem final, seem a conclusion. But in modernity, as we have noticed, temporal endings are not necessarily conclusions. One need not dispute that the persona (the

"I") of the poem thinks there is some truth in this statement in order to appreciate that he believes his *first* statement as much or more:

> But he [the mower] had gone his way, the grass all mown,
> And I must be, as he had been—alone,
> "As all must be," I said within my heart,
> "Whether they work together or apart."[6]

Neither statement is more compelling than the other. What each depends upon is the mood of the persona—in this poem a mood tinged by a profoundly modern sense of alienation. The persona's depressive mood was lifted in the first place by a butterfly alighting on some flowers the mower had left by a brook; but a reader may well have the impression that if something different had happened—if, for instance, the flowers were snatched up by a cow and eaten—the poem could have as easily reverted to the original sentiment, which is private, ambiguous, and transient. Thus, instead of involving a convincing progression, the poem yields up a tension between two opposing conclusions. Instead of resolving the tension, potentially satisfying both poet and reader because it seems formally complete, the poem remains undecided. There is an uneasy truce, nowhere approaching rest; the persona appears to be pulled in two psychological directions, finding only a momentary harbor in either and a good deal of confusion in between. As one of my students once put it, it is Frost's *wavering*—his inability to formulate a consistent philosophy, to realize an integral structure to meet the problems of life—that speaks to us as persons living in a personally ambiguous time. As he fails to choose, his readers choose (or not) for him, and with heavy shoes.

Yet we ought not to make too much haste to blame Frost or anyone else out of context. Nor should we blame too much any modern writer if he or she seems inconclusive, privatistic, and apt to throw the choice of how to end it all back on us. For the modern poet has learned this maneuver, after all, from the educational tradition from which all Western culture has imbibed its worldview. Liberalism in its early stages, the very spirit of the humanities disciplines, has been an effort, however ambiguous, to subordinate the functional organization of society, the Many, to the "personal" life of its members, the Self. Possessed of an Aristotelian epistemology and a new natural theology, we have from the Renaissance forward proclaimed with Protagoras that "man is the measure of all things." But from the time of the French Revolution forward, as Camus in *The Rebel* so clearly saw, it became possible to pronounce

6. Robert Frost, *Collected Poems* (New York: Random House, 1930), 31.

the humanist credo in a more individualistic way. In the *Confessions* of Rousseau, in Fichte, and in Schiller, the word "personal" no longer means "having to do with persons, with the mutuality of beings, with human relationship," but comes to mean "individual," "self," "autonomous self." It is an easy subtlety to see in the old phrase not "Man is the measure" but "I, a man, am the measure" or "I am the measure of all things." With a few notable exceptions, the history of the Western poetic voice since Rousseau is a progression into the definition of the Self as subject, the individual subject to which all the outside world stands as objects to be understood with only the reflective "I" as measure. The implications of this shift are manifold: not only has it incurred disparate clamor from some quarters against self-contradictions in the liberal ideal, but it lies behind criticisms of the humanities offered by many of those who from within now suspect the enterprise of having become an educational failure. The contradiction? That while, on the one hand, liberalism claims to stand for personal human freedom, on the other, its licensing of egocentrism and its love for and cultivation of private mythology make it too easily in practice a defense of human exploitation. And certain kinds of poetry, words upon words, private mythologies half-lived by megalomaniac selves bent upon their right to public approval of private fantasies, may be judged (and not only by Marxist critics such as Terry Eagleton)[7] as emblematic of that exploitation. The contradiction is evident not only in modern literature but in all of modern thought.

The epistemological bias of our post-Reformation artistic culture is, like the perspective of modern philosophy, characteristically egocentric. As John Macmurray in his Gifford lectures pointed out, to say so involves no more than this: that "firstly modern philosophy takes the Self as its starting point, and not the world, or the community, or God; and that secondly the Self is an individual in isolation, an ego or 'I,' and never a 'thou.'" (This is shown by preoccupation "with questions like 'How does the Self know that other selves exist?'") "Further, the Self so premised is a thinker in search of 'knowledge'"[8]— namely, instrumentally useful information. The Self is conceived as the Subject, to which all that is not Self stands outside as object, as the "correlate in the experience of the object presented for cognition." Naïvely conceived, as in some Senate hearings or in Humpty Dumpty's declarations to Alice, this posture is the insistence upon the right to a private mythology; as with Humpty, the assertion is that "the words in this conversation shall mean exactly what I want them to mean." The meaning for you—is up to you. Create from these

7. Terry Eagleton, *After Theory* (New York: Basic Books, 2004).
8. John Macmurray, *The Self as Agent* (London: Faber and Faber, 1969), 31.

fragments your own mythology. Ultimately we get "The pigeons on the grass alas, alas, the pigeons on the grass alas . . ." (Gertrude Stein) or the rhythmic mockery of a Lenny Bruce. Too few understood their irony. With Alice, as with Gertrude Stein, the modern poet's audience often feels bewildered and left out; Humpty's fall is seen by children as just deserts for his arrogant Self-referentiality, but the connection is not always made by contemporary adults.

Humpty, in any of his modern guises, if he is to be listened to at all, must at some level of credibility acknowledge that he lives in our world too, participates in our experience. Humpty's inevitable fall and fragmentation in the nursery rhyme (where it is a cautionary tale) evokes what we might think of as a Babel-effect, or, if one is more classically minded, a Platonic myth of the fall complete with appropriate forewarnings against expecting too much of Aristotelian political solutions. Lewis Carroll's parable likewise has to do with the issue of mutual intelligibility; Humpty's egocentrism destroys the community of ideas along with the community of words. Hundreds of modernist treatises on political and educational theory to the contrary, not all problems are solvable by better organization, shrewder analysis, or the exchanging of roles and center points. As in the poem by Frost, for Humpty, whether we work together or apart, the end may well be, as in the beginning, that one is alone. As Lewis Carroll foresaw and Samuel Beckett lived out in dramatic form, the Self-Subject, the I-centered perspective, cannot by itself create or incarnate a coherent form for the personal. To do this, a private mythology must at some vital point transcend self and participate with others in a living public dream.

Living in a vulgarized present, disillusioned with a demythologized past, however intense his private vision, a modern poet often feels necessarily outside any viable public vision. Philip Larkin expressed this alienation memorably in his poem "Church Going" and in his *Whitsun Weddings*, yet found the language of pulpit and pew still rich enough to borrow, even as its meaning for him was hollowing out. Feeling the starker poverty of his own and his nation's religious vocabulary, Robert Frost turned for communicability to a bucolic version of the American dream. We are only mildly surprised to learn from his modern biographers that he really hated that farm. Yet, artificial as his myth was, it nevertheless proved, as he saw, vital to the creation of a shareable vision in his poetry, in that it had vestigial elements of commonality about it.

Point/Counterpoint

Perhaps a note from a poem published just a century ago may serve as a kind of epigraph for these reflections. Against the rising insistence on the preeminence of the reflective Self, of I-centered poetics, Gerard Manley Hopkins offered a particularly Christian corrective, one that hears modernity out but places its dominant worldview in conversation with more community-oriented antecedents, setting a possible course correction for future poets. His most concise statement of this dialectical invitation comes in an untitled sonnet that has increasingly come to be seen as one of his most profound:

As kingfishers catch fire, dragonflies draw flame;
As tumbled over rim in roundy wells
Stones ring; like each tucked string tells, each hung bell's
Bow swung finds tongue to fling out broad its name;
Each mortal thing does one thing and the same:
Deals out that being indoors each one dwells;
Selves—goes itself; *myself* it speaks and spells,
Crying *What I do is me: for that I came.*

I say more: the just man justices;
Keeps grace: that keeps all his goings graces;
Acts in God's eye what in God's eye he is—
Christ—for Christ plays in ten thousand places,
Lovely in limbs, and lovely in eyes not his
To the Father through the features of men's faces.[9]

Against the posy-like egocentrism in the first stanza or octave, subsuming all creation to Self-as-Subject, the second stanza or sestet is a psychological and aesthetic riposte. Speaking of the reconciliation of passive with active, alienation with community, "I" with "Thou," subject with object, it offers a better satisfaction for individual striving in terms the individual does not naturally perceive, pointing toward the incarnation of a more graceful inspiration, the Word in the words, God in the man, joining man and men together. Here Hopkins's resolution of the egocentric quest in a logocentric conclusion effects a conversion, offering out of poetry a hope beyond poetry, a grace beyond the reach of art.

Hopkins and others like him have often been dismissed, even by those who acknowledge their poetic mastery, as "merely" religious poets. But perhaps it is time for another look. We cannot go back to the Middle Ages, nor would we want to. But in the perspective afforded by our recent social fragmentation, we might wish to recapture some of its understanding. Of course, Hopkins, like the medieval prototypes he studied, understood words and knew how to

9. Gerard Manley Hopkins, *Poems of Gerard Manley Hopkins*, 4th ed. (London: Oxford University Press, 1967), 90.

use them. He could count on a love for language and history in his audience. Things have changed. One of the dilemmas for modern poets is that their audience knows fewer and fewer words. It has, moreover, cut itself off from conversation with the past. The genius of a good poem, expressing a form for the personal as relationship, is that it provokes not merely private experience but also shared memory—and thus gives us back some portion of common vision. Such poetry becomes a road home. On a biblical view, the ultimate creator of this vision is not the individual poet but the Word, the one behind the many, the Word in words. When such a vision informs poetic imagination, the power of the accessible Word is that each private insight may enter into a timeless communal story. Poetry, then, is a means of discovery, restoring words to form, making conclusions possible.

nine

THE CONVERSION POEMS
OF MARGARET AVISON

Margaret Avison (1918–2007) was an urban poet living in Toronto, but her primary sources of inspiration early in her career were the Black Mountain school of poets technically and the landscape and life of the Canadian Shield spiritually. In many ways she began as a nature poet, and throughout her career retained an attunement to nature:

> Otter-smooth boulder
> lies under rolling
> black river-water
> stilled among frozen
> hills and the still unbreathed
> blizzards aloft;
> silently, icily, is probed
> stone's secret. ("Stone's Secret," lines 1–8; *sunblue*, 21)[1]

Criticism of a finely balanced poetry such as Avison's—especially, perhaps, learned *explication de texte*—tends too easily to make of the critic a voluptuary. Remembering her caution, "That Eureka of Archimedes out of his bath / Is the kind of story that kills what it conveys" ("Voluptuaries and Others," lines 1–2; *Winter Sun*, 73), the critic of Margaret Avison ought probably to be

---

1. Editions used here are *sunblue* (Hantsport, NS: Lancelot Press, 1978; 1980); *Winter Sun / The Dumbfounding: Poems 1940–66* (Toronto: McClelland and Stewart, 1982).

drawn, in apprehension, through a slow measuring of her words to quietness and contemplation. Indeed, if it could remain articulate, this would be of all responses the most just, since it would faithfully mirror the transformation of her own perception, through language, toward the quiet understanding that became her strength. Yet she merits also our attempt at responsible acknowledgment, however exacting a self-critical prospect that may entail, for she is undeservedly neglected.

Poetry as Wisdom

Margaret Avison is a distinctive voice among late-modern poets for many reasons. Not least among these is her spiritual wisdom. Despite the centrality of her religious vision in her later poems, she seems less a mystic than a sage, and her poetry less lyric than gnomic. Her work as a whole rests securely as testimony to a philosophical and spiritual progress: it is a *chef d'oeuvre* on our slim shelf of modern "wisdom literature." One thing about the tone of her work seems safe to declare: that over its opened pages there descends almost immediately in the reading a perceptible and peculiar stillness, a composition of tranquility and tension in which one's head tilts forward and the ear strains to listen. And as we are drawn into her own sense of presence,

> Moving into sky
> or stilled under it
> we are in the becoming
> moved: let wisdom learn
> unnoticing in this. ("The Effortless Point," *sunblue*, 63)

To talk about conversion in Avison's poetry, and to do so without reduction or offense, seems hardly less difficult than probing the stone's secret before its time; who knows what is in a heartbeat? Yet the conversion of purpose, the transformation of perspective, and the metamorphosis of object and light to inner light are near to the heart of all of Avison's poetry, and in what she tells us of her life, there and elsewhere, the objective correlative for that movement in her poetry is the subjective experience of a spiritual awakening and reconstitution thereby of an intrinsically biblical imagination.[2] It seems

2. See the especially valuable discussion by George Bowering, "Avison's Imitation of Christ the Artist," *Canadian Literature* 54 (1972): 56–69; see also the recent studies by Elizabeth Davey, *A Persevering Witness: The Poetry of Margaret Avison* (Eugene, OR: Wipf and Stock, 2016); and David Kent, ed., *"Lighting Up the Terrain": The Poetry of Margaret Avison* (Toronto: ECW Press, 1987).

inescapable, then, that—with due respect to the inevitable shortcoming of whatever distance and self-consciousness we have as readers—we nonetheless should take her at her word and consider what it means for her that

> The evasive "maker"-metaphor,
> thank God, under the power
> of our real common lot
> leads stumbling back to what it promised to evade. ("Creative Hour,"
> *sunblue*, 99)

To consider Avison's work responsibly, we should begin by asking about her earliest expressions of her poetic vision, the poetic it implies, and the nature of the experience with which it seems to correlate. Only when we have some minimal satisfaction concerning these things will we be able to ask the first pertinent question of her postconversion poetry: What is it that has been transformed?

The reading of *Winter Sun*, even when focused on that book's nonreligious aspects, leads most readers to the conclusion that Avison's poetry, from the very beginning, is at least implicitly religious in character.[3] The issue of change in her poetry following her experience of conversion is thus not one we may expect to be defined in terms of a sudden shift in basic human concerns or ostensible subject matter. The track between "Identity" (*Winter Sun*, 70) and "The Two Selves" (*Dumbfounding*, 102), for example, or "A Conversation" (*Winter Sun*, 79–80) and "The Earth That Falls Away" (*Dumbfounding*, 131–39) is a nearly unremarkable continuum. As David Kent has aptly observed, "the pre-conversion poetry is deeply moral, and it is committed to 'recreation' of the self and to responsibilities that were engrained in Avison during her Christian childhood."[4]

Whether focused on the self or on society, Avison's reflections on nature and human nature probe through the flesh to a desired transcendence, through object to meaning. Overwhelmingly driven to acquire clearer vision, she reflects again and again on the imagination of ultimate perspective in "One, in a patch of altitude . . . / Who sees, the ultimate Recipient / of what happens, the One Who is aware" ("The Apex Animal," *Winter Sun*, 11). And though some of her reflection concerns the achievement of perspective as a kind of mastery ("Dispersed Titles," *Winter Sun*, 13–17), there is also a

---

3. See Daniel W. Doerksen, "Search and Discovery: Margaret Avison's Poetry," *Canadian Literature* 60 (1974): 7–20.

4. David A. Kent, from an essay on Margaret Avison in *Canadian Writers and Their Works*, Poetry Series 6 (Toronto: ECW Press, 1989).

persistent theme of seeking and yearning after the transformation of habit-locked subjectivity.

In "Prelude," we can see a little of what, in *Winter Sun*, Avison hopes for, and for the most part what sort of transformation she imagines may be possible; the aspiration—and its attendant uncertainty—is cryptic in her rubric:

> *The passive comes to flower, perhaps*
> *a first annunciation for the spirit*
> *launched on its seasons.* ("Prelude," epigraph; italics in the original)

This poem is representative of her early work in its keen dissociation of darkness and light and transvaluation of the latter. "The turning-point is morning" (line 1), the light diurnal light, and it creates such meaning as the world affords in history and in memory; its shadowed delineation is shaping the meaning in each recollected image. This demarcation is evidently both an opening and a closing:

> The honeycombing sun
> opened and sealed us in
> chambers and courts and crooked butteries,
> cities of sense. ("Prelude," lines 20–23)

Already in this poem we see Avison's profound sense of an incompleteness of understanding in what light shows: objects, like the poetic language in which they are reflected, both clarify and obscure:

> Sparrows in the curbs
> and ditch-litter at the
> service-station crossroads
> alike instruct, distract. ("Prelude," lines 28–31)

As if by the same token, repositories of collected human wisdom offer uncertain reclamations of light's values, "palaces of sense . . . / patchy after years of hopeless upkeep" (lines 38–39). It is as though light, when so "locked in" by the pursuit of enlightenment, can hardly touch the ordinary world. Avison expresses in this poem her desire for a simple experience of light that transforms the ordinary. In the probing eyes of the poet, even unreflecting consciousness and the objects of institutional art ("The stone lip of a flower," line 32) "suffer the cryptic change" when the rising sun sweeps away shadow and

> The turning-point of morning, and the
> unmerging child,
> like the sadness of the summer trees,
> assert their changelessness
> out of this day-change. ("Prelude," lines 51–55)

What is revealed in the transformation wrought by light is, if not as radical a renewal as the "sea-change" sung by Shakespeare's Ariel, at the very least a prospect of it:

> Light, the discovering light, is a beginning
> where many stillnesses
> yearn, those we had long thought long dead
> or our mere selves. ("Prelude," lines 56–59)

Not in the Shakespearean but certainly in the Wordsworthian sense, "Prelude" is a "Romantic" reflection—and an affirmation of transvaluing perception. It recognizes the troubling limits of subjective vision, but holds out for a somehow-transcendent valorization of a personal view of things, where "in each at least light finds / one of its forms / and is" (lines 69–71). This is the theme that rises to its high point of confidence in "Snow" (*Winter Sun*, 27), with its call for the venturing optic heart. But in "Snow" also is added the attendant doubt, reflected in Avison's paradoxical challenge to the reader, in which we are warned that within the burgeoning of life that light reveals are also shadows of death: "The rest" (what follows, and our inevitable repose) may signal another, less-splendid transformation.

Doubt and Self-Scrutiny

All of Margaret Avison's poetry is marked by a persistence in self-questioning, by a desire for honesty that goes beyond the merely intellectual but that is profoundly intellectual in character. This alone sets her apart from many of her contemporaries. From the point of view of her poetic, in which "Prelude" is the central early document, this means that she is continuously subjecting to scrutiny not only history and the world but also the virtues of language, metaphor, the conventional forms of poetry, and even her very vocation as a poet. "Butterfly Bones" (*Winter Sun*, 29) is in this sense more than a principled questioning of the high traditional artifice of the sonnet; it is also a disturbing query concerning the value to perception of trophied language—even, perhaps, of any kind of language. Avison is primarily concerned here not with the atrophy of poetic idiom, I take it, but rather with the failure of language as an instrument, and so she expresses her consistent worry that poetry, like criticism, might become "the kind of story that kills what it conveys." This line ought to be read in the context of Avison's growing concern, from her early poetry on, to practice poetry as a means and not as an end. Just as light for her is the means whereby the world is known, so poetry, as a refracted experience of light, is to be valued only in proportion as it illumines. The final question of this sonnet—

> Might sheened and rigid trophies strike men blind
> like Adam's lexicon locked in the mind? (lines 13–14)

—is thus a question of profound concern not only for her poetic but also for her poetic language.

Avison's central image in this poem is, of course, far from insignificant. The butterfly, a symbol of the psyche since the ancients, is also a primary symbol for psychic transformation or, as Ovid suggested, for the concept of imaginative metamorphosis. For Avison, as for Ovid, poetry is about metamorphosis. The concern of the poet is with transformation—not only of the poet's mediating perspective but of all of life. Avison cannot detach her Romantic aspiration for transformed personal vision from her conviction—equally Romantic, even as it is morally "Christian"—that a transformation of vision ought to be able to change something in the world. In this sense too she appears almost Words-worthian. If poetry is a means, and light exists to enlighten, to "light up the terrain" (*Winter Sun*, 73), then what is effected by light—and by poetry—is to be asked about very carefully. Avison asks, and sometimes comes to disturbing and unflattering answers. In "Grammarian on a Lakefront Park Bench" she expresses her frustration in passionate language reminiscent of Hopkins:

> Skewer my heart and I am less transfixed
> than with this gill that sloughs and slumps
> in a spent sea. Flyspecked and dim
> my lighthouse signals when no ships could grind.
>   (lines 1–4; *Winter Sun*, 35)

How can she signal meaningfully to a world not in tempest but stagnation? Rejecting for herself the role of a midway prophet, she is overwhelmed by color washes from an unknowing world and disturbed by her inability to place upon that reality a satisfactory light or perspective.

Here, then, is a poet whose concern is with what in general terms we regard as spiritual values, who offers a Romantic poet's celebration of personal vision and subjective light, and yet who feels increasingly frustrated, in doubt that the encoding of her personal vision can communicate meaning to anyone else (see "Extra-Political" [*Winter Sun*, 54] and "Intra-Political" [*Winter Sun*, 55–57]). How should a poet face this perhaps inevitable dilemma, when Romantic subjectivity is coupled with a persistent desire for truth in the "outer" world? "The Swimmer's Moment" (*Winter Sun*, 47) is one instance in Avison's early work of an almost Kierkegaardian intensity to these questions. But in *Winter Sun* there is no dramatic existentialist resolution, no plunge into the Devil's Hole or the swimmer's abyss. Rather, there is at last a resignation, a concession to isolation, to alienation and silence. Whereas early in the volume Avison's verse is brilliant with definition, it later expresses in shadowed translucence her deepening skepticism. In "Identity,"

> Half-sleeping, unbewildered, one accepts
> The countless footsteps, the unsounding thud,
> Not even asking in what company
> One seeks the charnel houses of the blood. (*Winter Sun*, 70)

Here, even her identity as a person is in question ("The presence here is single, worse than soul"), though finally her cynicism will attach itself more firmly, if reflexively, to persona and vocation:

> So pressed, aloft, the errant angel sings.
> Should any listen, he would stop his breath.

This returns us, reflecting on *Winter Sun*, to one of Avison's plainest-speaking poems, "Voluptuaries and Others" (*Winter Sun*, 73). Because it so succinctly summarizes her evaluation of the poet's enterprise at this point in her career, I quote the entire first stanza:

> That Eureka of Archimedes out of his bath
> Is the kind of story that kills what it conveys;
> Yet the banality is right for that story, since it is not a communicable
>   one
> But just a particular instance of
> The kind of lighting up of the terrain
> That leaves aside the whole terrain, really,
> But signalizes, and compels, an advance in it.
> Such an advance through a be-it-what-it-may but take-it-not-quite-as-
>   given locale:
> Probably that is the core of being alive.

The speculation is not a concession
To limited imaginations. Neither is it
A constrained voiding of the quality of immanent death.
Such near values cannot be measured in values
Just because the measuring
Consists in that other kind of lighting up
That shows the terrain comprehended, as also its containing space,
And wipes out adjectives, and all shadows
    (or, perhaps, all but shadows). (lines 1–18)

"Lighting up the terrain" is here not at all a high-flown advertisement for the triumphs of poetry, but rather a kind of admission of limit, barely compensated for by that last tentative saving of the appearances: general recognition, at least, is communicable, and "that story about Archimedes does get into public school textbooks." (Avison had prepared such a text for Ontario public schools at the time this poem was written.)[5] Here, the Romantic poet's self-refulgent "Eureka" has certainly vanished; the poem is intensely self-ironic. The quest for self-achieved enlightenment and the poetic drive to climb up out of Plato's cave of conventional representations into the Light have been severely disappointed. "The floor of heaven is really / Diamond congoleum," she writes ("R. I. P.," *Winter Sun*, 74), and though "All of us, flung in one / Murky parabola, / Seek out some pivot for significance" ("The Mirrored Man," *Winter Sun*, 81–82), in fact, "the long years' march deadens ardour, a little," until finally "no sun comes / Beyond the yellow stoneway" ("The Agnes Cleves Papers," *Winter Sun*, 96–97). The day-change no longer seems to illumine: "The wild smell is the other side / Of the impenetrable world of stone" (*Winter Sun*, 98). Avison, superbly accomplished as a poet, sets her hand to the last pages of this remarkable first volume as one disappointed in poetry. Already she seems to have suspected that the inefficacy for real transformation in the subjectivism she had espoused was somehow inherent in it from the beginning, encoded in its very premises.

Poetry as a Means of Light

Avison's poetry after *Winter Sun* undergoes a profound transformation, a conversion both of sense and sensibility. Nonetheless we may recognize as incorporated into this conversion a finely spun thread of persistent inquiry. In

5. Margaret Avison, *History of Ontario* (Toronto: Gage, 1951).

her poetry she moves from delight in the thing seen to ambivalence concerning the possibility of precision in capturing it, always subtended by careful meditation on the medium by which she sees (and by which, as she later affirms, the objective world lives at all)—Light.

In her early work, light and poetry are nearly synonymous. The emphasis on seeing is an emphasis on the poet, on poetic vision. Avison's poetic had been implicitly a version of the Romantic *poeta nascitur* (the born poet). After her religious experience, which she dates precisely to January 4, 1963, the development of this poetic takes a dramatic turn. Light does not at all disappear as a value, but rather is clarified. Light is now the Apex; poetry is reflective understanding. The transformation is rendered explicit in *The Dumbfounding*, but it is helpful to contextualize it with her own perspective on her conversion experience.

Avison's cryptic and pseudonymous spiritual autobiography discusses an early desire to "have her cake and eat it too," to revel in gifts of "music, libraries, and winter mornings burning with cold beauty" as if these were intrinsic to her own personality, and without admitting to herself their otherness and "that these things fade if not acknowledged."[6] What she talks about in this almost innocuous little essay echoes many of the "re-evaluations" in *The Dumbfounding*. The problem she sees in her earlier intellectual and spiritual life is a subversive lack of any transpersonal reference for ultimate meaning—implicitly, a tendency to solipsize, a subjectivism that localizes all reference in the self while imagining otherwise. Of this phase she writes,

> I wish I had known that although thinking, comprehending, understanding, probing, are good—faculties God gave to us human beings—yet these faculties are given so that we can come to some notion of His unapproachably beautiful thinking, comprehending, understanding, and probing, even of me, my feelings and contacts and plans and responses to situations and openings from moment to moment in history (a history which, too, He comprehends).[7]

She goes on to consider her opacity to the higher Light she finally came to recognize. In their informality, these words make all the more plain, perhaps, that Avison's religious reassessment and her reassessment of her place as a poet are not really separable:

6. Angela Martin (pseudonym), "I Wish I Had Known That . . . I Couldn't Have My Cake and Eat It," in *I Wish I Had Known: Thirteen Christians Describe Misunderstandings They Had about the Christian Way of Life* (Grand Rapids: Zondervan, 1970), 90.

7. Martin, "I Wish I Had Known," 91.

I see how grievously I cut off His way by honoring the artist: the sovereignty of God was the real issue for a long time, for me. Of course I rue the years when I confused conscience with adapting to what certain approved people expected of me. I wanted to be liked, and on the basis of "genuine merit" too! In the arts I had my touchstone for scope and vividness—and poetry seemed to promise aliveness too. But this orientation allowed me to neglect or distance some real elements of humanness as alien to my own sense of what mattered. In questions of behavior, too, my priorities were confused. A social gaffe could make me burn with shame upon every remembrance. Yet on ethical issues, I tended to generalize.[8]

Her observations also bear fairly on the poetry of *Winter Sun*. Despite her desire for uniqueness of vision, Avison says, she felt overwhelmed by pressures to conformity in the world of her peers. In her remembrance one finds easily enough a correlative to the pervasive spirit of many of the later poems in that first volume—a lack of conviction, skepticism, a self-protective drawing down of the blinds.

One had to try to serve the general interest—stuffing envelopes in some chilly committee room on into the evening, or working up copy for leaflets and mimeographed magazines. Gradually, a malaise, a false peace, settled in. Persons, events, and my own responses grew more and more indeterminate, lost the bite of uniqueness. I was going down into living death.[9]

Then came the dramatic change. While reading the fourteenth chapter of John's Gospel, Avison was suddenly and decisively moved to a self-abandoned reordering of priorities for her whole life. In the following two months she wrote compulsively, drafting most of the poems that make up *The Dumb-founding*.[10] (*Winter Sun*, elegant testimony to the modern *poeta nascitur* that it is, had taken by contrast more than fifteen years to assemble.)

> Word has arrived that
> peace will brim up, will come
> "like a river and the
> glory . . . like a flowing stream."
> So.
> Some of all people will

8. Martin, "I Wish I Had Known," 92–93.
9. Martin, "I Wish I Had Known," 93.
10. Harry der Nederlanden, "Margaret Avison: The Dumbfounding," *Calvinist Contact*, October 19, 1979, 1; also Merle Shain, "Some of Our Best Poets Are . . . Women," *Chatelaine*, October 1972, 104.

> wondering wait
> until this very stone
> utters. ("Stone's Secret," lines 33–41; *sunblue*, 21–22)

What was being transformed? The poems in their own way best make this clear. Hanging over *Winter Sun* from the outset there had been a sense of the poet's isolation, her alienation from any enduring community of like or unlike mind and prospect. The poems are solitary, their voice a single voice. But in *The Dumbfounding*, as in *sunblue*, the heretofore impossible "many" of human otherness enters almost immediately into possible dialogue. Even as the dominant array of winter images yields to the fragrance of spring's and summer's color, so the "newspaper house" ("Chronic," *Winter Sun*, 18) gives way to a deepening "heart's room" ("Many as Two," *Dumbfounding*, 115): a community takes shape. Dialogue springs up on the pages; living conversation enters into poem after poem. For Avison there is beauty in the irony that it should be an "outcast's outcast" ("The Dumbfounding," *Dumbfounding*, 153) who makes relationship possible, even as he is bringing stillness to a clatter of words that are forever asymptotic, always falling short of their imagined relational effect.

There is in *Winter Sun*, especially in the last poems, a sense of oldness and of growing old, of unconsummated life and withering leaf as the twilight fades. Such tranquility as is felt is like composure before death, a resignation to the lengthening shadows. In *The Dumbfounding* there is, by contrast, a kind of recovery of childhood, a trustful openness, a simple desire to be whole that makes healing possible. In "A Child: Marginalia on an Epigraph" (*Dumbfounding*, 101) and "Unspeakable" (*Dumbfounding*, 188) and in *sunblue* the theme is recurrent. It is consistent with the richness of vernal imagery in these volumes and with the passage from city to garden, from sterility to fecundity, and from ice to flowing water ("SKETCH: Thaws," *sunblue*, 9 [cf. "Thaw," *Winter Sun*, 50]; "Released Flow," *sunblue*, 24; "Stone's Secret," *sunblue*, 21–22, and so on).

In *Winter Sun*, as we have seen, Avison had begun in a fascination with light and with poetry as a kind of light, its choicest words as amiable sunbeams. She then began to lose confidence in language and to drift toward shadow and silence. Now, confronted by Light in a way she had not imagined, the "Light that blinded Saul" ("Branches," *Dumbfounding*, 140), she finds herself reduced to silence in a strikingly different way, speechless and "dumbfounded." The new posture is neither one of skepticism nor of defeat; it is one of humility, and perhaps its most concise and beautiful realization comes in the graceful poem ". . . Person *or* A Hymn on and to the Holy Ghost" (*Dumbfounding*,

147): "How should I find speech / to you, the self-effacing," she asks, "to you whose self-knowing / is perfect" (lines 1–2, 5–6). To the Holy Spirit, the "unseen," she prays:

> to lead *my* self, effaced
> in the known Light,
> to be in him released
> from facelessness. (lines 13–16)

What she asks for is not, as we might casually expect, Light to see by and words to better write about it, but rather to be herself led into the Light so that, listening to Light "articulating," she may come to know herself as one who is seen; instead of imagining herself to be doing all the interpreting, she herself asks to be read out and interpreted. It is a courageous prayer. What she longs for, then, is to be able to "show him visible"—not at a comfortable aesthetic distance, but in life, in the difficult places where he "(unseen, unguessed, liable / to grievous hurt) would go" (lines 18–19). Avison spent most of her subsequent life in inner-city social work and modestly paid labors as a secretary in the Toronto office of a Southeast Asia mission. The personal evasion of ethical issues with which she charged herself before her conversion came quickly to be redressed in personal action, not just in the articulate social criticism in her poetry ("Of Tyranny, in One Breath," *Dumbfounding*, 162–67; "July Man," *Dumbfounding*, 116; "Needy," *sunblue*, 78, and so on).

In all of this change we see that her fascination for Light continues, but that her sense of what Light can do is radically transformed. From the beginning she had resisted the notion that light experienced passively—even as enlightenment ("Prelude")—could be sufficient. Now she comes much further, to say that the experience of light worth having is the one that cannot be achieved by mastery or merit, because it shines beyond (and in spite of) poetic inspiration or bootstrap ambitions for a self-induced epiphany. Avison, in her early poetry, had always been a seeker after truth in the legitimate sense: her obsession with light was not merely an absorption in poetry, but also represented a desire to see and to know. But in her troubled days after *Winter Sun*, she took refuge in the "heart's room" spoken of in John 14, and it led her to an encounter with God not as abstract idea or, as she says in "Strong Yellow, for Reading Aloud" (*sunblue*, 40–41), as mere "Possibility," but as Person. "Let not your heart be troubled," says Jesus in the opening verse of John 14. "Ye believe in God, believe also in me." He goes on to offer not only comfort but the Comforter: "Even the Spirit of truth; whom the world cannot receive, because it seeth him not, neither knoweth him" (v. 17). Avison seems to have always been the sort of person who could identify comfort with the truth. Here, at the turning point in her life, she reached for the Comfort and found it Light.

It is apparent to a reader of her poetry that this is Light strikingly mediated by language; indeed, at its own highest reach of biblical metaphor, it is explicitly juxtaposed with the Word. From the point of view of her poetic, Avison's transformed understanding of Light from a natural to a spiritual aesthetic has immediate roots in the Gospel she was reading at the time of her conversion. That Gospel begins, of course, with a statement about creation, one in which the medium reveals its message unqualifiably: neither invented nor inventable, it is itself all-creating. The Word creates life, and it is this life that then becomes Light to the world:

> In the beginning was the Word, and the Word was with God, and the Word was God.
> The same was in the beginning with God.
> All things were made by him; and without him was not anything made that was made.
> In him was life; and the life was the light of men.
> And the light shineth in darkness; and the darkness comprehended it not.
>   (John 1:1–5)

The image of creating Light, central to John's Gospel (and Epistles), is developed there in a way that parallels the relationship of Light to Word in Avison's imagination. She further reflects the spirit of John's prologue (John 1:1–18) in dissociating the prophet (or poet) from the Light itself (1:8), and in seeing prophetic (or poetic) words as a witness to a Word they cannot contain, a "Word made flesh" (v. 14). By analogy, the poet's words do not create. The Word that creates life—or more properly, is life—is before and beyond poetry, and thus is not finally utterable. Rather, it is, as for John of the Cross, a word known in silence—not a silence of despair, but a stillness of waiting.[11]

This relationship of Light to Word well underscores the poetic expressed in Avison's three-poem sequence "Light I; II; III" (*sunblue*, 59–61). The first poem begins with a statement that dramatically undermines a traditional Romantic perspective:

> The stuff of flesh and bone
> is given, *datum*. Down
> the stick-men, plastiscene-

11. The signal lines are: "The Father utters one Word and that Word is his Son, / and he utters him forever in everlasting silence / and in silence the soul has to hear him."

people, clay-lump children, are strewn,
each casting shadow in the eye of day.

Then—listen!—I see
breath of delighting rise from
those stones the sun touches
and hear a snarl of breath
as a mouth sucks air. And with
shivery sighings—see: they stir
and turn and move, and power
to build, to undermine, is theirs,
is ours.

The stuff, the breath, the power to move even thumbs
and with them, things: *data*. What is
the harpsweep on the heart for?
What does the constructed power
of speculation reach for?
Each of us casts a shadow in the bewildering day,
    an own-shaped shadow only.

The light has looked on Light.

He from elsewhere
speaks; he breathes impasse-
crumpled hope even
in us:
that near. (lines 1–27)

The poet does not invent the world, nor reinvent. She sees it now as a given: Light makes her listen. In each of us who move in the Light, she says, there is the power to speculate or to hide; the wonder of creation is our freedom to will. Self-shaped shadow fables, seeking an invented, not a created, world. Light needs to look upon Light before Light speaks. "Any shadow," she says, is "self, upon / self" ("Light [II]," lines 5, 7–8). To overcome that self-clouding, she adds, one needs to "look to the sunblue" (line 16). In "Light (III)," the whole cosmos is transformed in this knowledge; the whole sky has become Light. Under it one accepts that seeing leads to hearing, and hearing to self-knowledge. The poet's role is not at all that clichéd Blakean proclamation of unique vision and special revelation—far from it. It is a view of the poet still seeking after truth, now in petition, listening, for eternal wisdom:

Because I know
the voice of the Word

is to be heard
I know I do not know
even my own cast burden,
or oh, the costly load
of knowing undisturbed.
There is a sword
enters with hearing. Lord,
who chose being born to die
and died to bring alive
and live to judge
though all in mercy, hear
the word You utter
in me, because I know
the voice. ("Listening," *sunblue*, 58)

Avison is no longer *poeta nascitur*, nor, as we might fear, some television evangelist's "Eureka" version of *poeta re-nascit*, but—astonishingly—simply *poeta fit*, the poet who harkens, who makes and is made.

To be sure, Avison's *poeta fit* ought not to be construed in narrowly neo-classical terms; she means something more. Yet her poetic now is far more akin to neoclassical than to her erstwhile Romantic premises. There is a new openness to a community of understanding for self-knowledge, to the past as a relevant authority for the present, and to the time-honored classical convic-tion that it is not just we who interpret or "create" but that it is we who are being interpreted by the light we walk in and the texts we read. This poem intends a commentary on the Epistle to the Hebrews 4:12; Avison's sword that "enters with hearing" is the same two-edged sword that "is a discerner of the thoughts and intents of the heart" (cf. her use of this epistle in "For Tinkers Who Travel on Foot," *Dumbfounding*, 130). But it also bears reading in the light of Psalm 19. The plea that the Lord who is the Word may "hear / the word You utter / in me" parallels the plea of the psalmist at the conclusion of his meditation, which is also that the Word may interpret him, so to speak, rather than the other way around: "Let the words of my mouth, and the medi-tation of my heart, be acceptable in thy sight, O LORD, my strength, and my redeemer" (Ps. 19:14). Just as an emphasis on visionary light is normative for the *poeta nascitur*, so is the wisdom of the word inspiration to the *poeta fit*.

Avison in *sunblue* is a craftsman keenly aware of herself also as a creature. She makes because she is first made in the image of a Maker. Creation and creativity are indissolubly linked; the poet who strives for truth is no Faustian inventor of ungiven worlds. Rather, she is herself a reader, ferreting truth and artistic form out of a world already charged with meaning: "The word read by the living Word / sculptured its shaper's form. / What happens, means" ("The Bible to Be Believed," *sunblue*, 56–57). "Creative Hour" (*sunblue*, 99), even in its opening image of the child with coloring book, satisfactorily encodes her statement about a converted poetic. For her, finally,

> The evasive "maker"-metaphor,
> thank God, under the power
> of our real common lot
> leads stumbling back to what it promised to evade.
>
> There is no one reviewed, no viewer,
> no one of us not creature;
> we're apparently at work. But nothing is made
> except by the only unpretentious, Jesus Christ, the Lord.

Here, the statement of faith is a rejection of conventional Romanticism and, however atypically, a modern critique of post-Romantic aesthetics. The Maker is the model for making (*poesis*), the begetter of the possibility of every art. In her shift of images from seeing to listening, we are drawn from the conventions of prophetic vision to a poetry of meditation.

In the *Winter Sun* phase of Avison's reflections on the art of poetry, we recognize her exuberance in the light of nature, her careful reification of moments of acute perception in precisely chosen words that acknowledge even as they celebrate the subjectivity of her perception—what later she calls "self-shadow" (*sunblue*, 60). By the end of that volume we can anticipate in her growing skepticism and the character of her habitual restraint a movement toward silence. By the end of *The Dumbfounding* and all through *sunblue*, however, we not only anticipate but also experience an entirely different kind of silence. It is not a mere hesitancy to speak. What Avison calls "dumbfounding" and "silencing" (*sunblue*, 57) involves a death to the insistent self that, like the passage of seed into earth, becomes a passage to new life ("A Story," *Dumbfounding*, 120–23). This new kind of silence is contemplative, really a stillness, a stillness that allows hearing and that, as in the case of Bunyan ("For Tinkers Who Travel on Foot"), nourishes creativity. Though it may have suffered "deaf and dumb months," the imagination may be brought to life once it has consented to Life.

The quietness we find in Avison's early work is thus profoundly transformed, transmuted to a stillness that is expectant, listening for the voice of the Creator. The poetry such stillness breathes is deep, clear, and tranquil, almost anomalous in the insistent, self-glorifying hullabaloo of our time, in which even poetry is often mere talkativeness. Perhaps one of the most valuable aspects of Avison's total contribution is to remind us that, as Kierkegaard once put it, "Only some one who knows how to remain essentially silent can really talk—and act essentially."[12]

Margaret Avison's poetic canon is not large.[13] She is no more on paper than she was in person one who could be described as "talkative." But such a witness resides in her quietness, and in her stillness such a refuge for our badgered senses, that she has earned a respectful hearing from fellow poets and readers alike—even from those who cannot yet share with her the still center of her vision, or who can at best lay claim to viewing it from afar. Avison's succinct poetry remains as witness to a remarkable transformation of an inner life, and the "talk" it offers is an exquisitely lucid distillation, a bequest of whispered gold.

No thoughtful assessment will dismiss Avison as a mere votary, let alone a voluptuary of her calling. In her later poems the same patient inquiry after truth persists; in fact, in some respects it becomes stronger than ever.[14] The dialogue poems allow her to air her doubts, to debate with her fellows or with Scripture or with God himself in pursuit of resolution to her questions. In some of her early Christian poems she openly resents the intrusions of responsibility or the persistence of her singleness—running away from comfort even as she is seeking comfort. But what had perhaps been evasion, and fear of "that turned-to-marble chase" made so memorable by Bernini's magnificent sculpture ("Research," *sunblue*, 100), in the later poems is reconciled by an irony that is pivotal to her "Searching and Sounding" (*Dumbfounding*, 154–56), a joyous reversal in which self-knowledge deepens:

> And as I run I cry
> "But I need something human,
> somebody now, here, with me."
> Running from you.
> The sunlight is sundered by cloud-mass.

12. Søren Kierkegaard, *The Present Age*, trans. Alexander Dru (New York: Harper and Row, 1962), 69. The passage in context is: "What is *talkativeness*? It is the result of doing away with the vital distinction between talking and keeping silent. Only some one who knows how to remain essentially silent can really talk—and act essentially. Silence is the essence of inwardness, of the inner life."

13. In addition to the volumes discussed here, see *No Time* (Hantsport, NS: Lancelot Press, 1989), *Not Yet but Still* (Hantsport, NS: Lancelot Press, 1997), *Concrete and Wild Carrot* (London, ON: Brick Books, 2002), *Momentary Dark* (Toronto: McLelland and Stewart, 2006), and the posthumous collection *Listening: The Last Poems of Margaret Avison* (Toronto: McClelland and Stewart, 2009).

14. Bowering, "Avison's Imitation of Christ the Artist," 60–61; cf. Doerksen, "Search and Discovery," 15–17.

The Daphne images echo Thomas Carew's response to the same transfix of wood and willfulness converted (ironically and passionately) in acceptance:

> Daphne hath broke her bark, and that swift foot
> Which the angry Gods had fast'ned with a root
> To the fix'd earth, doth now unfettered run
> To meet the embraces of the youthful Sun.[15]

Nescis, temeraria, nescis, / quem fugias:[16] running—to embrace the Sun from whom she had originally fled. In a seventeenth-century poet's image, perhaps, is the meaning of Avison's conversion, the metamorphosis of her poetic, and the transformation of her psyche.

Conclusion

We can hardly appreciate the impact of Avison's conversion upon her work without recognizing that she has by now become a significant poet in the English meditative tradition. Quite naturally she joins ranks with Herbert and Hopkins (whom she had always admired), remaining closer to them than to Eliot (about whom she always had deep reservations).[17] This is not to say that she is not as "modern" as Eliot, but that her poetry is much more a species of prayer, dialogue with God. Some of the prayer, too, is even a kind of "Intercession." In her poem of that title she commends one not identified, who prays and waits:

> The old saint, because of her
> long hours not spent afield
> therefore with searching force
> waits it out, for us:
> wounded, and healed. (lines 13–17; *sunblue*, 69)

One is moved to wonder whether such words might not be applied to Avison herself. In her poetry, she offers herself to us as one who waits hopefully, and

---

15. "A Rapture," in *The Poems of Thomas Carew*, ed. Rhodes Dunlop (Oxford: Clarendon, 1949; 1964), 52.

16. "You don't know, thoughtless girl, whom you flee" (Ovid, *Metamorphoses* 1.514–15).

17. I am agreeing here with Lawrence M. Jones, "A Core of Brilliance: Margaret Avison's Achievement," *Canadian Literature* 38 (Autumn 1968): 50–57, and Doerksen, "Search and Discovery," who makes the connection with Herbert in an especially attractive way. The fullest treatment of the matter, and best contextualized, is still Ernest Redekop's seminal monograph *Margaret Avison* (Toronto: Copp Clark, 1970).

listens, by her craft interceding between our rumbling darkness and the Light for which she would have us listen too. It takes, of course, an unusual stillness for that, and faith. Yet in the conversion of Margaret Avison's imagination, even the secret locked in stone is one day to shine forth in purest speech. Against that day, in the incarnation of transformed imagination that is her work, she enacts a generous commitment to our attunement, a graceful preparation of her reader's hearing.

ten

MEDITATION AND GRATITUDE

The Enduringly Beautiful Changes of Richard Wilbur

Richard Wilbur (1921–2017) was a two-time Pulitzer Prize–winning poet (1957, 1989) and was named poet laureate of the United States in 1987. He had a continuously productive career as a poet and translator. One reviewer called him "the Grand Old Man of American poetry." Born on March 1, St. David's Day, his fruitful life spanned the decades of America's most illustrious rise, greatness, trial, and now perhaps demise as an imperial power. Wilbur himself, despite his laurels, was anything but an imperial poet; indeed, despite his youthful leftist views (during World War II he was removed from the intelligence service on suspicion of disloyalty), on balance he could hardly even be said to have been a political poet. Yet few (conceivably none since his friend and predecessor as laureate, Robert Frost) so perfectly exemplified the natural and apolitical American voice—perhaps the quintessence of all that sets America apart among the literary cultures of the modern world—in poetry. There were odd patrician ironies contesting with this apparently authentic vernacularity; Wilbur, though himself of modest means, was an eleventh-generation New Englander, and in that sort of remarkable coincidence that often attends intellectual life among the denizens of Harvard Yard, his friendship with the much older Frost at Harvard was aided by the unlikely fact that his wife's father had been the publisher of Frost's early poetry.

Anterooms

Wilbur's last volume of poetry, *Anterooms*,[1] reflects in its title poem and several others the perspective of his old age, wise and full of years. That the tone of this work is free of strident egoism, cynicism, bitterness, or even the slightest hint of self-pity distinguishes it still further from the work of many another modern writer who has sensed the inevitable approach of mortal silence. The governing image in the title poem is archetypal—a garden in winter in which a sundial emerges from a snowdrift slowly, recrudescent as the returning springtime sun begins to warm the stone. Wilbur plays upon this image, reflecting the intersection of cyclical time with mortal limit, time and eternity, a boundary not met here in our world except in dreams, he says, which foreshadow that ethereal intermingling

> Where, before our eyes,
> All the living and the dead
> Meet without surprise. ("Anterooms," lines 19–21)

Wilbur's tone throughout *Anterooms* is one of "Reckoning," as he calls it, less a retrospect than an examination of conscience that readily acknowledges the existence of words and deeds he might wish to take back, but, seeing the futility of that desire, that he chooses instead to consign quietly to the vast and universal annals of life's inevitable imperfections. As for his life's work as a poet, he writes here no retraction in the manner of a Chaucer or an Augustine, but rather a more placidly elegiac *apologia*, "Ecclesiastes 11:1," in which he describes his own particular vocation as being subject to the common lot by which we all are obliged at last to "*cast our bread / Upon the waters*" (lines 1–2, italics in the original). Shifting the image again to winter and transposing Qoheleth's waters therefore to snow, he throws out his crumbs into the almost forgotten garden beneath the drifts and makes a less ambitious and more poignant wish

> That birds will gather, and that
> One more spring will come. ("Ecclesiastes 11:1," lines 17–18)

It is characteristic of the gentle but unmistakably Christian character of Wilbur's poetry that he should include in this volume a "Psalm" of gratitude for life, both its joys and its sorrows. Even "House," the exquisitely beautiful postmortem love poem to "Charlee" (his wife, Charlotte Hayes Ward, who

---

1. Richard Wilbur, *Anterooms* (Boston and New York: Harcourt Houghton Mifflin, 2010).

died in 2007), conjuring as it does a longed-for future shared awareness, is poignant with the still-vibrant intimacy of a life lived out in love and even now unclouded by despair despite the magnitude of her loss. Such thankfulness, everywhere in his poetry, forbids morbidity. In his gently whimsical "A Measuring Worm," in which an inchworm working its way up a window screen reminds him, in each ingathering, of the Greek letter *omega*, he is able to intuit his own prospect of "Last Things." He is unafraid: hunched up with the accumulation of his own ingathered strength, he senses just beyond this window frame the light of an approaching universal metamorphosis of which this inchworm is a humorous sign: "He will soon have wings." Echoes of St. Paul's citation of the poetry of Isaiah lie just below the surface of such deceptively simple lines: "Eye hath not seen, nor ear heard, neither have entered into the heart of man, the things which God hath prepared for them that love him" (1 Cor. 2:9; cf. Isa. 64:4; 65:17)—and an attuned ear can catch its memorable phrasing, subsumed in the circumspect last lines of this poem:

> And I too don't know
> Toward what undreamt condition
> Inch by inch I go. ("A Measuring Worm," lines 13–15)

The balance of advantage and disadvantage in living long is tilted toward the good, most Christians have tended to think, when one has lived well, not clinging to some version or other of a desperate immortalism. This wisdom, expressed variously in other Christian poets such as T. S. Eliot, W. H. Auden, and Wendell Berry, emerged in Wilbur as a deep contentment pervading with convincing seamlessness the whole of his poetry, almost from the beginning. The very peaceableness of so much of his verse reminds us that Richard Wilbur was always a wisdom poet. There is a sense of consistency in his work that owes not only to his craftsmanship as a poet but also to his constancy as an affectionate observer of creation, both nature and human nature. Thus, the masterful lyricism and theological clarity of his earlier masterpiece, "An Event," a poem that appeared in 1956 in his volume *Things of This World*,[2] finds a symmetrical recension in "Mayflies," the title poem in his volume of 2000.[3] The theme of both poems is the almost ineffable mystery of pattern, of design in the life of things, as in the breathtakingly fluid art of winged myriads aloft:

2. Richard Wilbur, *Things of This World* (Boston and New York: Harcourt Brace, 1956); reprinted as *Collected Poems: 1943–2004* (Orlando, FL: Harcourt Harvest, 2004), 347.
3. Richard Wilbur, *Mayflies* (Boston and New York: Houghton Mifflin Harcourt, 2000); cf. *Collected Poems: 1943–2004*, 36.

> As if a cast of grain leapt back to the hand,
> A landscapeful of small black birds, intent
> On the far south, convene at some command
> At once in the middle of the air, at once are gone
> With headlong and unanimous consent
> From the pale trees and fields they settled on. ("An Event," lines 1–6)

In "Mayflies," where he observes "a mist of flies / In their quadrillions rise," the mystery is not lessened but renewed: "It was no muddled swarm I witnessed," he writes, for the patterns, as if choreographed in a "great round-dance," lead him to characterize his poet's calling in relation to the eternal cosmic jig or reel as "one whose task is joyfully to see / How fair the fiats of the caller are." The unseen caller and tiny dancers cooperate to create a fluid, moving art at which normative observation and reflective thought can only be amazed.

Wilbur is not here debating the fine points of intelligent design but, in the manner of the psalmist or the authors of Proverbs and Ecclesiastes, simply marveling at an intricacy of wondrous beauty that makes his own art a species, as J. R. R. Tolkien once put it, of refracted subcreation. The human artist will inevitably be limited in how he or she may respond to the glory that "the heavens declare" and the firmament proclaims (Ps. 19), but this hardly diminishes pleasure in a poetry of call and response that, precisely because it overflows with gratitude for the gifts both of creation and creativity, can with a touchstone word or poignant phrase bring tears unbidden to our eyes:

> Delighted with myself and with the birds,
> I set them down and give them leave to be.
> It is by words and the defeat of words,
> Down sudden vistas of the vain attempt,
> That for a flying moment one may see
> By what cross-purposes the world is dreamt. ("An Event," lines 19–24)

No sensitive reader of Wilbur's poetry from any stage of his long and productive life can fail to see that his wonder, crafted into art, is a kind of worship, often a hymn of thanksgiving.

A Living Legacy

Dana Gioia, who bids himself to have one day a claim to such a distinction, wrote just before Wilbur's ninetieth birthday that "Wilbur is America's preeminent living Christian poet." The qualifying adjective might by itself have seemed to make him marginal in a post-Christian literary environment, such as that in which now we find ourselves. But there is much more that is countercultural in his art, and Gioia has described this as well as anyone by speaking of Wilbur's poetic effort as an "ironic achievement"—namely, "to excel at precisely those literary forms that many contemporary critics undervalue—metrical poetry, verse translation, comic verse, song lyrics, and perhaps foremost among these unfashionable but extraordinary accomplishments, religious poetry."

One of Wilbur's poems has become a hymn, in fact; it appears in the 1982 hymnal of the Episcopal Church, with a musical setting by David Hurd.[4] As with all of Wilbur's poems in which the Bible plays a visible part, "A Christmas Hymn" reflects an immersion in Holy Writ far deeper than any notion of mere allusiveness or portentous reference can suggest. The epigraph, for example, is a quotation (from the King James Version) of that passage in Luke's Gospel that describes a demand of some Pharisees near the gates of Jerusalem that Jesus should silence his exuberant disciples (Luke 19:39–40). The point of Wilbur's juxtaposition may be to say that in our time things are much the same. This moment in Luke's text is freighted with a significance that these Pharisees from their perspective quite reasonably construe as political, for, entering Roman-occupied Jerusalem on that first day of what now we call Holy Week, Jesus' disciples are strewing their cloaks and palm branches over the road, crying out before him, in the words of Psalm 118, "Blessed be the King that cometh in the name of the Lord: peace in heaven, and glory in the highest" (Luke 19:38). This *introitus* is not, however, political in the worldly sense, but an acknowledgment of transcendent and hence apolitical cause for rejoicing. It is clear to Wilbur that the words of the disciples' reflexive acclamation, recalling as well the angels' song to the shepherds in Luke 2, add a powerful frisson to Jesus' reply, "I tell you that, if these should hold their peace, the stones would immediately cry out" (Luke 19:40). Wilbur's poetic juxtaposition of these passages forms a beautiful meditation on the wondrous intricacy and grace of the divine Poet's redemptive artistry, by which a stable lamp, lighted in a humble Palestinian stable for the improbable birth of the King of kings; the quaint and clichéd crèche at which we sing our carols; the Palm Sunday hosannas that declare "his kingdom come"; and yes, the agony of that terrible Friday we dare to call Good all are woven together to charge the Bethlehem moment with a timeless significance:

4. *The Hymnal 1982: According to the Use of the Episcopal Church*, 2 vols. (New York: Church Publishing, 1985), no. 104.

> But now, as at the ending,
> The low is lifted high;
> The stars shall bend their voices,
> And every stone shall cry.
> And every stone shall cry
> In praises of the child
> By whose descent among us
> The worlds are reconciled.[5] ("A Christmas Hymn," lines 25–32)

This poem/hymn articulates as well as anything in historical exegesis of the nativity account one central concern of Luke's Gospel—namely, to show how political power is typically inclined to suppress transcendence, to miss that the "good" in the evangel has to do with the reconciliation of fallen humankind with its divine Author. Wilbur's poem, like the gospel itself, foregrounds the primacy of truth and love, qualities to which politics is often both deaf and blind.

Wilbur is no naïve pietist. An explicitly biblical poem such as "Matthew VIII," voicing the cynical rejection of Jesus by the Gadarenes following the loss of their swine, is in this respect akin to others of his biblical poems; each in its own fashion "Eve," "Peter," and "The Water Walker" (about St. Paul) reveals Wilbur's deep appreciation for the irony of narrative voice so prevalent in the Bible itself. Nor does Wilbur retouch with some metaphorical airbrush the harsh angularities in his religious portraiture, even of the apostles. His Saul, converted to Paul, still "wasn't light company," he observes drily, and in his "Peter" the voice of the apostle himself reports a confession to the reader of the severest failings—his neglectful sleep at Gethsemane, his intemperate and misguided sword blow at the high priest's servant, and the abiding ignominy of his denial of the Lord three times. Wilbur marvels that our flawed mortality can, despite such failures, somehow come to reflect the greater glory of God (e.g., "Gnomons," on the Venerable Bede, or "John Chrysostom").

Yet if we are to deduce a theology from Wilbur's poetry (though it would be presumptuous to go too far in this direction), surely it would not mislead to say that his work is suffused with the spirit of Psalm 19, reflecting thus a deep pleasure with creation and yet, simultaneously, his resignation concerning the limits of poetic language to do much more than hint at its higher meaning. This does not lead Wilbur into abstraction, something he has said he "always turned from . . . at school and at church." In the *Image* interview[6] with fellow

---

5. Wilbur, reprinted in *Collected Poems: 1943–2004*, 347.
6. Paul Mariani interview of Richard Wilbur, *Image: A Journal of Poetry and the Arts* 12 (1995).

poet Paul Mariani in which he made this remark, he went on to say that as a poet he identifies more with Hopkins than with Eliot because he (Wilbur) is "the sort of Christian animal for whom celebration is the most important thing of all," and that at Mass he prefers—even to the theology he affirms in the Nicene Creed—that simple responsive moment when the call comes to "Lift up your hearts!" His use of the Bible in his poetry is a reflection of that celebratory *Sursum corda!*—it is responsive, not doctrinal, and refreshingly unpretentious. Reminding us in this way of Margaret Avison, Wilbur shows himself to be keenly aware that even where Scripture is to be voiced, a prudent poet is gravely in need of self-restraint and the grace of a higher translation (cf. Ps. 19:14). Otherwise there is a risk of telling lies. Three lines from his poem "Lying" might readily serve as an epigraph for much in his larger view on this matter of the poet's merely apparent originality:

> In the strict sense, of course,
> We invent nothing, merely bearing witness
> To what each morning brings again to light. (lines 16–18)

His little poem "The Proof," in a similar vein, tactfully expresses in four couplets his gratitude for God's patience with him.

> Shall I love God for causing me to be?
> I was mere utterance; shall these words love me?
>
> Yet when I caused his work to jar and stammer,
> And one free subject loosened all his grammar,
>
> I love him that he did not in a rage
> Once and forever rule me off the page,
>
> But thinking I might come to please him yet,
> Crossed out *delete* and wrote his patient *stet*.[7]

No one who is not a mature and contented poet, quite unashamedly indebted, personally and poetically, to the gift of Scripture and its tradition, could write in such whimsical self-effacement and gratitude all in the same breath. We are reminded of Herbert, as well as of the Psalms.

What shall we say of Wilbur's beautiful love poems to Charlee, or his lovingly funny verse for children, old and young, his playful riddles and his elegant though puckish whimsy? That he makes us laugh, and in our laughter

7. Copyright © 1963 by Richard Wilbur. See *The Atlantic Monthly*, March 1964, 62. https://www.theatlantic.com/magazine/archive/1964/03/the-proof/308475/.

we learn once again to love things we ought not to have forgotten. And what shall we say of his superb translations, especially of so many French and Russian poets, by which he made much of his daily bread? That he is uncannily gifted (and patient), able to hear another's voice, to love the art of another poet for itself and to convey even its particular cadences to us so that we too can "hear" what many a lyrical prophet has spoken almost as if in that poet's own accents. This thoughtful attunement of the ear, for Wilbur, has been the obligatory response to all species of the prophetic voice, whether in sacred or in secular scripture. He has been the very opposite of the itinerant or television prophet he satirizes in "Advice to a Prophet"; he does not break in upon his readers, "mad-eyed from stating the obvious." Rather, he tells us of the beautiful world created for our use and adoration, and how, by our reemergence in it, we might come to be grateful, even as he is grateful, for the becalming Art of it all.

Perhaps this is no more than to say that all of Richard Wilbur's poetry is, in some splendid sense, love poetry—poetry born of love for the things of this world, and love also for things of a world unseen, somehow held aloft together, harmonized by a voice so unmistakably authentic and unaffected that, were it not so beautiful, we might take it to be that of an ordinary dear friend, speaking among us quietly, as if on our porch as the sun is setting over our own garden.

But we ought not to be so deceived. Richard Wilbur is not in the least "ordinary." The great trick of a master poet such as himself is a wondrous misdirection of our leaden preconceptions, teaching us by precisely chosen words to see the golden echo in all that surrounds us and to love it even as— being mortal—things change before our eyes. The last stanza of an early poem, "The Beautiful Changes," in this way anticipates an enduring virtue in all of Wilbur's work: his gracious clarity of observation of the gift given, and, in a superlatively ordered form of words, his generous and persuasive gentleness of gesture in holding life out, like a bouquet from the original garden, freshly picked for us. Receiving his *florilegium*, the gift of his verse, we might, perhaps as in a toast, say to him and of him what long ago he said to another:

> Your hands hold roses always in a way that says
> They are not only yours; the beautiful changes
> In such kind ways,
> Wishing ever to sunder
> Things and things' selves for a second finding, to lose
> For a moment all that it touches back to wonder. (lines 13–18)

More than any American poet of our time, Richard Wilbur teaches us to open ourselves to wonder. In this he has been a prophet and more than a prophet; for those with eyes to see and ears to hear, he has been a bearer of comforting words in the manner and mode of Isaiah. Though he is indeed the "Grand Old Man of American poetry," his voice remains that of America's younger self, a self still open to the beauty of a world renewed and ever-new, and with the presence of mind to be thankful for it.

eleven

EPIPHANIES OF A FATHER'S LOVE

Anthony Hecht and Gjertrud Schnackenberg

L ike many academics, I am a bit of a pack rat. One of the things I have allowed to collect dust is a box of old vinyl LPs from the 1960s. On the back of one of these faded jacket covers is a photograph of a young pop/rock balladeer slumped in an evidently British stairwell, back against the wall by a cast-iron downspout. Beside him stands a tousled, smiling child of four or five years of age, hands folded together, almost as if in prayer, resting upon the singer's knee: a child and her father. It is a beautiful image and, in context, incongruous. The singer is Phil Ochs, the album *Pleasures of the Harbor* (1967), and the liner notes beside the photograph are in the form of a poem weighty with the singer's ambivalence about returning to the United States and the demands of his recording studio:

> To face the unspoken unguarded thoughts of habitual hearts
> A vanguard of electricians, a village full of tarts
> Who say you must protest you must protest
>   It is your diamond duty . . .
> Ah but in such an ugly time the true protest is beauty.

Protest—sharp, abrasive questioning of authority—was then the watch-word. Its missionaries included Ochs's touring friends and fellow balladeers Bob Dylan, Joan Baez, and T Bone Burnett, each a kind of prophet against a culture they saw as too easily anesthetized by American Beauty, each singing against the grain of musical and cultural cliché, often raspy and nasal-toned in their resentment and disdain. In this one album Ochs, however, broke step; he paused to reconsider the prospect of beauty, of healing, and notably, of the persistence of a father's love. It wasn't to last long, and it didn't set a trend. Ochs returned to rebellion rock and fell into self-destructive drinking and manic depression. He took his own life in April 1976, at the age of thirty-five.

Few now remember *Pleasures of the Harbor*, or other music akin to it in the work of T Bone Burnett (e.g., "Truth Decay," "The Power of Love," "Hefner and Disney," and "Trap Door"), or even Bob Dylan's memorable lament "I Dreamed I Saw St. Augustine" (*John Wesley Harding*), which echoed throughout his flirtation with Christianity (one thinks here of the last song on Dylan's album *New Morning* [1970], "Father of Night, Father of Day"). Those who do may recall that there were strong notes of ambivalence regarding the love and wisdom of fathers in this musical movement, despite the dominant acrimony and conventional disdain for authority. One of the most important of these intermittent notes now seems to have been struck from a deep nostalgia, a yearning after spiritual fulfillment, for a lost beauty paved over, an ache for a love that somehow got lost through the willed or unwilled absence of fathers. There is a strong undertone of poignancy in much of this music that runs counter to the self-assertive mainstream drift of much of early twentieth-century poetry and songwriting. When in 1955 Pete Seeger took up Robert Lowrie's 1869 hymn "How Can I Keep from Singing?," he was not a practicing believer, but he could certainly hear "that real though far-off hymn / that hails a new creation," and his version, though more secular, tried to re-create its source of hope.

Lost Beauty, Rejected Authority

The culture of modernism has been defined by a resistance to authority of all kinds. Famous literary examples abound: from certain Victorian and turn-of-the-century writers, such as Samuel Butler (*The Way of All Flesh* [1903]), whose entire life's work was motivated by hatred of his father and then, subsequently, of his self-appointed surrogate fathers, to James Joyce, who, in *A Portrait of the Artist as a Young Man* (1916) and *Stephen Hero* (1944), extends his hatred to the Catholic Church and all paternity. Fathers had become by the end of World War II the representative enemy of freedom—political freedom, artistic freedom, and, perhaps above all, sexual freedom. The Death of the Father (Freud), the Death of God (Nietzsche), and the Death of the Author (Barthes) reflect a common and widely colloquialized impulse toward the rejection of any authority beyond the self. Intellectual formulations aside, fatherhood became unfashionable for many less-than-intellectual reasons, among which were its implications regarding taking responsibility for others, a necessary exercise of sexual restraint, and, perhaps, its tacit confirmation that aging is inevitable, that others will succeed us, that we too shall someday die.

The antipatriarchal impulse persists in many forms, not least in religious contexts. Certain strains of postmodern feminism have taken up where classic modernism left off, and a rejection of fathers and fatherhood now obtains fairly widely in liturgical revision and biblical translation as well as in fiction and poetry.[1] One novelistic evocation of the general ethos is Barbara King-solver's *The Poisonwood Bible* (1998), in which a mostly invisible and faceless Baptist missionary pastor provides an incontrovertibly stupid and ugly foil against which each of the women in his life struggles to find intelligibility, freedom, and, each in her own way, beauty.

Nevertheless, since the 1960s something else has been struggling to find its voice. If one were writing an American literary history of this liminal development, one would want to account for the gradual appearance of less totalizing and more ambivalent evocations of fatherhood. One might include the love-hate characterization of fathers by Chaim Potok in his *Asher Lev* novels or the unresolved yet largely fearful apprehension concerning the way in which father-love is expressed in such reminiscences of childhood as Theodore Roethke's poem "My Papa's Waltz." But few of these can be associated with simple affection for a father, let alone with appreciation for a father's affection for his children as, in its expression, something beautiful. That bête noire of early feminists, *Father Knows Best*, is kept in the public memory largely as a laughingstock; along with other dated idealisms, it is recalled as a quaint cultural stereotype that must be written off—the good father as at best a harmless incompetent. The eventual dismissal of such clichés in sitcoms gathered a darker edge in soap operas and laughable ineffectuality in such prime-time offerings as *The Simpsons* and *South Park*, finally giving way to indulgent second adolescence in *Modern Family*. Meanwhile, in fantasy films since the 1980s the father figure is often more malevolently dark—a Darth Vader, sinister and faceless.

With the sexual revolution in full sway, real-life fathers were abandoning their families in ever-larger numbers, while religious fathers, clergy, were falling prey to pornographic addiction and gross abuse of the vulnerable to the

---

1. A review of some of the most pertinent feminist liturgical and theological criticism may be found in chaps. 13 and 14 of my *Houses of the Interpreter: Reading Scripture, Reading Culture* (Waco: Baylor University Press, 2003).

degree that it became an international scandal. It has become clear that, in making sexual freedom the highest good, the *Playboy* generation had already begun to amass vast social costs in pursuit of its own gratification—and equally clear that it was all too willing to pass on the bills to the next generation. In the wake of such bitter consequences, as well as of so many lame or lamentable efforts to cope with these consequences, it must now seem almost an absurdity to seek in all that detritus exceptions, epiphanies of beauty, harbingers of a healthier, holier, self-transcending paternal love.

But they are there for the finding, and where they exist one frequently finds evidence of the fertility of Scripture for the poetic imagination, even in the waning of modernity. The signals are sporadic but powerful. Consider the worldwide response of youth to the aged and ailing Pope John Paul II as an exemplar of faithful and fatherly priesthood: in the closing years of the twentieth century, a massively popular recording of the pope in prayer ("Abba Pater") paralleled his extraordinary appeal to the young in youth rallies around the world. The equally countercultural recording by Cliff Richards of the "Our Father" or Lord's Prayer, sung to the tune of "Auld Lang Syne," was also a huge success in the marketplace of the young.[2] We might think also of the work of the Harvard professor turned apostle to the disabled, Henri Nouwen, SJ. In his *Return of the Prodigal Son* (1992)—a meditation on Rembrandt's painting as well as on the parable itself—he observes that "though I am both the younger son and the elder son, I am not to remain them, but called to become the Father." This slender volume continues to have an enormous influence, not least because it is, in the words of reviewer Luis R. Gamez, "a beautiful book, as beautiful in the simple clarity of its wisdom as in the terrible beauty of the transformation to which it calls us." At the heart of this beauty is a deeply countercultural presence—the loving father.

Though our focus here is on poetic imagination, one might adduce parallel examples in novels such as Leif Enger's *Peace Like a River* (2001), in which a self-denying father, accompanied by his other children, searches for his outlawed son and in the end quite literally exchanges his own life for the breath of life for his children. Nor can one overlook Marilynne Robinson's exquisitely crafted and Pulitzer Prize–winning *Gilead* (2004), in which the dying pastor-father of a young son sired in his old age writes an epistolary personal meditation on the fifth commandment, recollecting his own generational history so as to make of it in turn a gift, a legacy, blessing the son whose manhood he will not live to see. Each of these works is countercultural. Each, in the sense that Pope John Paul II's *Letter to Artists* (1999) suggests,

2. Both of these appeared in 1999, on the eve of the millennium.

affords an epiphany of beauty—in particular, a glimpse of the beauty of that fatherhood for which the apostle Paul once declared "the whole family in heaven and earth is named" (Eph. 3:15). There is much more of this sort of epiphany than Hollywood and the critics would like to think, and much of it rises well above the level of Disney's *Finding Nemo*—though it is certainly there too. As a plaintive note, a poignant admixture of nostalgia and regret, or perhaps in some cases a conscious sign of hopeful contradiction, these recent artistic depictions of a loving fatherhood merit reflection, for in virtually all of them there is a gesture toward Scripture, a remembrance of its consolation prompting the poetic imagination.

A Different Beauty

Overwhelmingly, the most perdurable images of tender parental affection in art and literature depict a mother and child. Many of these are truly beautiful; one thinks of the Madonnas of Botticelli, Piero della Francesco, Roger Van der Weyden, and Leonardo da Vinci as representative universals in this regard. With fathers and children, not so many examples come to mind. But in late modernity there are a host of poetic representations of fatherhood in which the love of a father for his child becomes a thing of beauty, beauty mixed with nostalgia because there is in the deep memory of many of them a tinge of longing for something not yet complete. Different from the familiar nurturing mother image, these representations can nevertheless achieve a true beauty— just not in quite the same way. "Everything is beautiful in its own way," the familiar Ray Stevens pop tune says, with its chorus of children singing the refrain. Actually, the biblical passage half-remembered here is considerably more potent than the song allows. From Ecclesiastes 3:11 (NKJV), it reads:

> He has made everything beautiful in its time. Also He has put eternity in their hearts, except that no one can find out the work that God does from beginning to end.

In this evocative biblical text, temporal beauty is described as proportionate to a divine creativity so fundamental to our human nature that it calls forth a yearning for beauty's source. The word here translated "eternity" is *ha'-olam* (also "the universe"), a term provocatively associated with God's fatherly love and provision in that most familiar of Jewish thanksgivings: "*Baruch 'atah adonai, elohenu melech ha'olam, ha-motzi lechem min ha-aretz*" ("Blessed are you Lord Our God, King of the universe, who has brought forth bread from the earth"). To such an infinite longing, "eternity in their hearts," our prayers of thanksgiving quite intimately correspond; the ache in the heart for the infinite is indeed for the "end beyond"—not merely for the gift but for the Giver, not merely toward beauty but toward the divine Artist.

And yet our longing for embrace with the eternal must now in some measure remain unsatisfied; the beginning and the end are beyond our time-locked reach. As the pre-Socratic philosopher Alcmaeon of Croton put it, this is the very definition of mortality: "Men perish because they cannot join the beginning and the end."[3] Accordingly, mortal longings have limit. Even the desire to shape our own life story is constrained by gaps in memory. Yet candid recognition of this limit sets us up, so to speak, to comprehend the definitive, ultimate epiphany: "I am Alpha and Omega, the beginning and the ending" (Rev. 1:8; 22:13). The annunciation to John on Patmos of the final revelation of Christ declares an end-term for each incomplete narrative and the closure—and disclosure—of the overarching story into which all other narratives fit. Only the divine Author may consummate his work of art—beginning and end are to be joined in him—and the contention of Scripture is that this is the ultimate closure toward which all our human poems and stories, wittingly or not, and whether of agony or of ecstasy, strive and yearn: "Even so, come, Lord Jesus" (Rev. 22:20).

In St. Augustine's formative view (e.g., *Confessions* 7.9.15; 13.20.28; *On Christian Doctrine* 2.40.60), our innate yearning for beauty is redeemed by being directed through and beyond the beauty of creatures and their art to "that Beauty which is above our souls." In such a scheme of reference, it turns out that we may be liberated, in fact, to see in works of artistic beauty or the beauty of creation an epiphany, a revelation of something higher—a "grace beyond the reach of art" (*pace* Alexander Pope). When Jacques Maritain speaks of the "end beyond" art, "of which beauty is the correlative,"[4] he implies that the ultimate locus of beauty is not the work of art itself but that toward which its beauty points and yearns. All this the biblical writers find poignantly embedded in our love of beauty and our desire for God. Each anticipatory glimpse of the author of the Big Story is thus an *epiphaneia*, epiphany; each vision of the final closure is an *apokalypsis*, a revelation, in all its polyvalent range of mystical meanings. On such a view, beauty is not perfection, perhaps because that would leave nothing to be desired. Occasionally, however, we are privileged with a sudden glimpse of the beauty beyond imperfection—in effect, an epiphany.

3. Hugh of St. Victor, in his twelfth-century book on literary instruction, held Alcmaeon to be the "first inventor of fables," and useful for understanding the primordial purposes of literary fiction (*Didascalicon: De Studio Legendi* 3.2).

4. Jacques Maritain, *Creative Intuition in Art and Poetry* (New York: Pantheon, 1953), 170.

Epiphanies of Beauty

Now, "epiphany," whether as used by a philosopher like Jacques Maritain or by the late Pope John Paul II, is a strong word. In the New Testament, "epiphany" (Greek ἐπιφάνεια, "manifestation" or "appearing") applies strictly to Christ. In such contexts it implies theophany. In more general anthropological usage, the term can apply to other divine beings, and what passes for theophany in one perspective may become at the least epiphany in another; in fiction, one may think here of the god Ungit appearing to Redival and then Orual in C. S. Lewis's *Till We Have Faces*.

Since James Joyce in *Stephen Hero*, the word "epiphany" in English literary texts has more commonly been used in a lesser, even desacralizing, way to describe a moment of realization or recognition—luminosity in a particular event, often of a quite mundane nature. By contrast, to speak theologically of "epiphanies of beauty," as did John Paul II, is all the more now to trope, to juxtapose two distinct orders of reality. (He too was a poet.) It seems that his intention was in fact to resacralize in art-language what has largely become emptied of divine reference or association in the language of art and poetry over the last century. This is to imply that beauty has still a potentially transcendent reference, dependent in part on attunement in the perceiver: one and the same perceptual event can have both a frightening and a comforting aspect. This double sense is captured by Lewis in his depiction of Aslan, of whom he has one of his characters say that, "as for Aslan himself . . . people who have not been in Narnia sometimes think that a thing cannot be good and terrible at the same time" (*The Lion, the Witch, and the Wardrobe*). Later, in *The Horse and His Boy*, we are told that from the Lion radiates a light so extraordinary that "no one ever saw anything more terrible or beautiful." In *The Last Battle*, we see the triumphant, returning Aslan "coming, leaping down from cliff to cliff in a living cataract of power and beauty."

Faces of the Father in Scripture

In the Hebrew Bible the term *hesed*, God's tender covenant love, is one of fourteen Hebrew words that may be translated as "beauty" or "loveliness" (e.g., Isa. 40:6), an astonishing semantic range compared to English. Context can make the luminosity of such beauty more evident: what to one person may appear to be the ugliness of a dangerous imposition can reveal to another the beauty of holiness. Confusion is possible. In the New Testament, theophanies are of Christ because the incarnation itself was expressly a revelation, an *appearing* in human form, of God the Father. To put this in Hans Urs von

Balthasar's way, "Jesus is himself the Father's assumption of form, the Father's *eidos*."[5] Jesus is not merely a sign or signal from the Father; he is "one with the Father" (John 1:1–4; John 17). Jesus speaks of himself repeatedly in theophanic terms: "He who has seen Me has seen the Father" (John 14:9 NKJV). In this way, the strict Old Testament limitation on human encounter with God—one breached only rarely for a singular Old Testament patriarch such as Abraham by the oak of Mamre, Jacob at the Jabbok, or Moses on the mountain—is here overcome.[6] The faithful Jew of antiquity typically dreaded to see God, as Jacob put it, *panim el-panim* ("face-to-face" [Gen. 32:30]), for fear of being struck dead for his lack of holiness. In narrative encounters with God in the Old Testament, there is thus always mediation, whether by angelic being, fire, cloud, or whirlwind. God the Father remains concealed more than revealed. In Christ there is suddenly a present means of imagining him, a presence realized differently but still powerfully now in the Eucharist. This is the basis for the Catholic conception of a "sacramental imagination."

The ideas, of course, are fundamentally biblical and permit our thinking about them in this directly textual fashion. In Jesus the normative Jewish expectation was reversed: many people now saw and bore witness to what their eyes had seen, their ears had heard, and their hands had touched (see 1 John 1:1). In the language of John's Gospel, "the Word became flesh and dwelt among us, and we beheld His glory, the glory as of the only begotten of the Father, full of grace and truth" (John 1:14 NKJV). Thus, for one familiar with the Hebrew Scriptures, a formidable paradox lies at the heart of the incarnation: "No one has seen God at any time. The only begotten Son, who is in the bosom of the Father, He has declared Him" (John 1:18 NKJV). And yet again, Jesus says to Philip, "He who has seen Me has seen the Father" (John 14:9).

Artistically speaking, among followers of Christ the strictures of the second commandment thus loosened. Michelangelo, like medieval dramatists and artists before him from Ravenna to the Netherlands, gives "a face [even] to God the Father" (Pope John Paul II, *Letter to Artists* II, 12). The Father could be portrayed as a mirroring of the Son in the Pantocrator, or more rarely as

5. Hans Urs von Balthasar, *The Glory of the Lord: A Theological Aesthetics*, vol. 1, *Seeing the Form* (San Francisco: Ignatius Press, 1982), 606.

6. Cf. von Balthasar, who takes the stronger Septuagintal reading of Numbers to say that "concerning Moses we have the testimony from God himself that he did not reveal himself to Moses as he had to the other prophets, in dreams and enigmas, but 'with him I speak mouth to mouth, with clear evidence . . . and not in riddles. . . , and he has beheld God's form (Septuagint: δόξα)'" (*Glory of the Lord*, 1:606). Von Balthasar's argument depends to some degree on this point. See also the useful article by Joseph Schwartz, "To Imagine Realistically," *Logos: A Journal of Catholic Thought and Culture* 1 (1997): 19–39.

the Ancient of Days in the Sistine Chapel or in the biblical illustrations of William Blake. Even those images that anthropomorphically suggest God's antiquity reveal him nonetheless in beauty and strength.[7] Yet over time, images of the Father became images of his revelation in Jesus almost exclusively.[8] "He who has seen me has seen the Father," repeats the Jesus of many of these paintings and icons (figuratively); "I and the Father are one." The poets and painters are confident in their remaining depictions of God the Father as a more physically massive, more beautiful and glorious perfection of that which is, as for example in Raphael's *La Disputa del Sacramento*, still recognizably Jesus. These redactions strive at—and often achieve—real beauty. In the medieval iconography of the Trinity, for example, the "Throne of Mercy" motif exemplifies a grace at once terrible and tender, a source both of heartbreak and of hope. In it God the Father cradles Jesus on his knee, but this is not the child Jesus of the Madonna icons; rather, it is the crucified Christ, offered as atonement—an unimaginably holy sacrifice for the redemption of an unholy world. This fatherhood is resplendent in the "beauty of holiness," a terrible reminder of the excruciating self-offering of a father's love for his children, even those who have turned away from him.[9]

Beauty and a Father's Love

I have suggested that Scripture provides us poetry and poetic imagination whereby we can envision something so culturally counterintuitive as a positive view of fathers—even the beauty in fatherhood. I want to consider, as concrete illustrations, two late twentieth-century American poems. The first, by the late Anthony Hecht, my onetime office mate and friend, provides the title of his Pulitzer Prize–winning volume *The Hard Hours*. It is dedicated to and named for one of his two sons. "Adam" has a biblical epigraph that comes not from Genesis, as initially the title might lead us to expect, but from the book of Job: *"Hath the rain a father? or who hath begotten the drops of dew?"* (Job 38:28).

7. Cf. Ps. 96:6. Herman Melville seems to have thought that the suggestion of strength was essential in divine beauty, and in *Moby Dick* he has Ahab comment on Michelangelo's depiction of God the Father in the Sistine Chapel in that connection (chap. 86).

8. Cf. Étienne Gilson, *The Arts of the Beautiful* (New York: Scribner's Sons, 1965), 162–63, who elaborates the incarnational theology that undergirds this emphasis.

9. Von Balthasar here adduces Karl Barth ("If we seek Christ's beauty in a glory which is not that of the Crucified, we are doomed to seek in vain" [*Glory of the Lord*, 1:55–56]) and Gerhard Nebel, who, in *Das Ereignis des Schönen*, responds to Rilke's phrase "For beauty is nothing but the beginning of the terrible," the *analogia eventus pulchri et Christi* (*Glory of the Lord*, 1:65), the very summation, temporally, of "the beauty of holiness" (Ps. 96:9).

"Adam, my child, my son,
These very words you hear
Compose the fish and starlight
Of your untroubled dream.
When you awake, my child,
It shall all come true.
Know that it was for you
That all things were begun."

Adam, my child, my son,
Thus spoke Our Father in heaven
To his first, fabled child,
The father of us all.
And I, your father, tell
The words over again
As innumerable men
From ancient times have done.

Tell them again in pain,
And to the empty air.
Where you are men speak
A different mother tongue.
Will you forget our games,
Our hide-and-seek and song?
Child, it will be long
Before I see you again.

Adam, there will be
Many hard hours,
As an old poem says,
Hours of loneliness.
I cannot ease them for you;
They are our common lot.
During them, like as not,
You will dream of me.

When you are crouched away
In a strange clothes closet
Hiding from one who's "It"
And the dark crowds in,
Do not be afraid—
O, if you can, believe
In a father's love
That you shall know some day.

> Think of the summer rain
> Or seedpearls of the mist;
> Seeing the beaded leaf,
> Try to remember me.
> From far away
> I send my blessing out
> To circle the great globe.
> It shall reach you yet.[10]

The first stanza is set in quotation marks, as if it were paroemia, a borrowed text, a voice separate from the narrator's. It offers no direct quotation, however, but a creative synthesis of many passages, a biblically informed imagination of the intention of the divine Father-Artist that generates alike human art and human offspring. It presents Adam to himself as one loved into being, as the image of a heavenly Father, and it affirms that all things of whose beauty we dream and on whose substance we live were themselves an act of divine love toward us, who are likewise of adam, *adamah*—of the earth, earthy—of the *humus*, human.

The second stanza goes on to relate the primordial Father's love to the love the poet feels for his own firstborn son, whom he in fact had named Adam. Here the quotation marks have fallen away; the poem becomes a type of haggadic commentary, a memory transcribed in words, as if it were a kind of living, present gloss on an absent though painfully recollected text. The poet, too, is a father—a Jewish father. As such he obeys the Deuteronomic injunction of the great *Shema* (Deut. 6:4–7; cf. Ps. 78:5–8). But the diaspora into which his son has gone, the result of marital separation and divorce, has opened up a great gulf. Of this child the poet has neither custody nor living conversation; his poem goes most probably unread and unheard, and he aches with an agonized father-love for a relationship gone wrong, for a denial of the possibility of communion and closure. A great emptiness eats at his heart.

The closing stanzas acknowledge that what are "hard hours" for a father will be echoed in hard hours for his son, and that out of them the son may have dreams of a father—a father *absconditus*—dreams far less untroubled than those of Adam's blissful sleep in the garden. The narrative voice anticipates fear, separation anxiety, the relentless pursuit of a mysterious, intergenerational tag-team curse—and yet urges this Adam to believe, if he can, "In a father's love / That you shall know some day." Whether that knowing is to be of this or of another, surrogate relationship, or transposed to fractured

10. Anthony Hecht, *The Hard Hours* (New York: Atheneum, 1967), 31–32.

father's love in another generation (as Adam takes his own turn, so to speak), hangs in painful ambiguity over the final two stanzas.

The last stanza borrows also, as does the epigraph, from Job and its poetic evocation of a beauty God alone can give. We realize that over the aching, heartbreaking incompletion of the poet's fatherly love arches the voice of God from the whirlwind, speaking to Job, calling him to reckon with his losses not as reducible to a formula, or to reason or analogy, but rather as *sub specie aeternitas*, beyond the reach of reason. Yet in the end, the divine voice offers consolation, comfort for a loss that must remain incomprehensible, since we are unable to conjoin the beginning and the end of our cosmic story. As another of Scripture's wisdom poets reminds us, "He has made everything beautiful in its time. Also He has put eternity in their hearts, except that no one can find out the work that God does from beginning to end" (Eccles. 3:11 NKJV). To this universal aporia the Master Poet will one day answer, "I am the Alpha and the Omega, the Beginning and the End" (Rev. 21:6 NKJV). We are inextricably middled; he is not. These are anchoring elements in biblical poetics.

And yet Hecht's poem concludes with an assurance of persistence in the father's love—and blessing—that will circle the earth, all diasporas notwithstanding, to find out the beloved child: "It shall reach you yet," the promise says; you will one day be restored to your father. All manner of biblical texts are here recollected, from the psalmist's intuition that no matter where on earth he hides himself, God will find him and know him (Ps. 139), to the Abrahamic covenant blessing (Gen. 12:1–3), to the words of the psalmist that remind us that messages of the Father's glory and beauty (Ps. 19:1–2) reach out into all the earth and echo in the poetry of all nations, whatever language may be spoken (19:3–6).

"Adam" is a heartbreaking poem of broken relationship—yet it ends in a promise of paternal love that, against all odds and all distance, will find out the beloved child and confer upon his own heartache the *hesed*, covenant love and promised blessing. Because Hecht's poem works on two levels, and with beauty recollects both a greater beauty and the end beyond the work of art, it successfully constitutes an epiphany of beauty, one that reveals something of the first Father's love, even though this poem is overwhelmed with its author's own mortal failure—in particular, the failure of fatherhood. Scripture enables a poetic imagination and hopeful creation that painful experience failed to give.

The other poem in my diptych is by Gjertrud Schnackenberg and likewise provides the title for her much-acclaimed volume *The Lamplit Answer*. It captures a childhood memory of her own father, a Lutheran pastor. From its triplet stanzas to its polysemous imagery and language, it is a deeply Christian and theological work, and aesthetically about as close to a "perfect" poem as one is likely to find in American literature of the last half century. It is titled "Supernatural Love":

My father at the dictionary-stand
Touches the page to fully understand
The lamplit answer, tilting in his hand

His slowly scanning magnifying lens,
A blurry, glistening circle he suspends
Above the word "Carnation." Then he bends

So near his eyes are magnified and blurred,
One finger on the miniature word,
As if he touched a single key and heard

A distant, plucked, infinitesimal string,
"The obligation due to every thing
That's smaller than the universe." I bring

My sewing needle close enough that I
Can watch my father through the needle's eye,
As through a lens ground for a butterfly

Who peers down flower-hallways toward a room
Shadowed and fathomed as this study's gloom
Where, as a scholar bends above a tomb

To read what's buried there, he bends to pore
Over the Latin blossom. I am four,
I spill my pins and needles on the floor

Trying to stitch "Beloved" X by X.
My dangerous, bright needle's point connects
Myself illiterate to this perfect text

I cannot read. My father puzzles why
It is my habit to identify
Carnations as "Christ's flowers," knowing I

Can give no explanation but "Because."
Word-roots blossom in speechless messages
The way the thread behind my sampler does

Where following each X I awkward move
My needle through the word whose root is love.
He reads, "A pink variety of Clove,

Carnatio, the Latin, meaning flesh."
As if the bud's essential oils brush
Christ's fragrance through the room, the iron-fresh

Odor carnations have floats up to me,
A drifted, secret, bitter ecstasy,
The stems squeak in my scissors, *Child, it's me*,

He turns the page to "Clove" and reads aloud:
"The clove, a spice, dried from a flower-bud."
Then twice, as if he hasn't understood,

He reads, "From French, for *clou*, meaning a nail."
He gazes, motionless. "Meaning a nail."
The incarnation blossoms, flesh and nail,

I twist my threads like stems into a knot
And smooth "Beloved," but my needle caught
Within the threads, *Thy blood so dearly bought*,

The needle strikes my finger to the bone.
I lift my hand, it is myself I've sewn,
The flesh laid bare, the threads of blood my own,

I lift my hand in startled agony
And call upon his name, "Daddy daddy"—
My father's hand touches the injury

As lightly as he touched the page before,
Where incarnation bloomed from roots that bore
The flowers I called Christ's when I was four.[11]

This poem hardly needs explication so much as a slow rereading, pausing perhaps over the symbol-rich imagery and philology that are part and parcel of its meaning as well as the vehicles for achieving that meaning. The lamp that evokes the Word (Ps. 119:105), the flower that invokes at once our flesh and the central Christian doctrine, the needle's eye through which every wisdom (including that of the poetic imagination) must stoop to pass, the butterfly psyche, the scholar's pondering of a tomb, the art that tries to spell out love's perfect text, the mystery of "Christ's flowers" that cannot be explained or given argument or proof any more than can the mysterious connectedness of verbal sound and deep, primordial, speechless longing—all are here unfolded, stanza by rhyming stanza, through the eyes of a little child who leads us. The needle moves through "the word whose root is love"; "the incarnation blossoms, flesh and nail." Her little injury brings home the greatest injury of all: the child calls out *Eloi, Eloi; abba, pater*. The father's hand touches the wound

11. Gjertrud Schnackenberg, *The Lamplit Answer* (New York: Farrar, Straus and Giroux, 1985), 81–83.

as tenderly as he touched the meaning in the words, and the memory of it, recollected in maturity, becomes likewise an epiphany of the beauty of the first Father's love, the "end beyond" all mortal beauty, invoking the ultimately ineluctable mysteries of the incarnation and atonement.

However paradoxical, for such great mysteries to grow their meaning in us, we must first become transparent to simplicity. "Except ye . . . become as little children" (cf. Matt. 18:1–6; 19:13–15) is a familiar injunction that, among other important things, reminds us that the uncomplicated character of a child's affection allows her to seek unselfconsciously her Father's love. In many an artist's image of Jesus with the children, we can find a deep register of conscious longing for the enduring beauty of protective love; even though most probably only subconsciously, it is reflected, poignantly, in the Phil Ochs album photograph. This is what a good father's love is like, say the images: warm, attentive, generous, gently teaching. And yes, of this image too the singer has our culture right: as often as not, the contemporary father is *pater absconditus*, with a legacy of recrimination and abandonment as a terrible consequence. The detritus has seeped into our culture at all analogous levels, provoking vengefulness and hatred as recurrent themes in popular music and poetry. So yes, "in such an ugly time the true protest is beauty," for nothing could be more contrary to the wreckage with which we live.

It is not true of matters of beauty to say that they cannot be reduced to words. However imperfectly, they can. But it *is* true, in respect of our glimpsing the way in which artistic beauty refers us to ineffable Beauty, that such matters can seldom so effectively be reduced to argument. That is why, in the kingdom of God and for the sake above all of our worship of God, we *need* poetic art: art allows us a special access to the holy; it is a handmaiden to faith. It is certainly not to be surmised on this account that art *in itself* is fully adequate to our search for the holy. But great art can give us a glimpse, when referred to its source, of the deep echo in beauty, especially in the beauty of a holy love, of the beauty of holiness, and thus of the love of our heavenly Father. Our reflection of that beauty, as Gerard Manley Hopkins so memorably put it, is necessarily partial, pied, and freckled. But when we can give glory to God for the dappled, even for the imperfect, for the antinomies of "swift, slow; sweet, sour; adazzle, dim," we may come to the true "end beyond"— that grace beyond the reach of art that prompts our worship.

> He fathers-forth whose beauty is past change:
> Praise him. ("Pied Beauty," lines 10–11)

EPILOGUE

Can Faustus Be Saved? The Fragile Future of Our Common Book

When I was growing up, my family was in the cattle and horse business. As a teenager, I was strongly inclined to keeping on in the same direction. One late spring day I was putting out hay for the cattle when my father came suddenly alongside and spoke to me. "See that bull over there?" He pointed to our first-string polled Hereford bull, probably the best we ever had and, as a four-year-old, certainly the biggest. Given the time of year, Bozo was itching to get out of his pen and on about the work we were paying him for; pawing the ground, tossing up the dust onto his back, he was throwing his head in the wind to catch a whiff of the possibilities. "Yes," I said, realizing that my father meant this as a teaching moment. "I see him."

"What's the difference between you and that bull?"

Now, a teenager can think up quite a few smart-aleck things to say in a situation like that, and I was thinking some of them. But if you had known my father, you would probably have responded pretty much the same way I did: "No sir," I said. "What's the difference?"

"That bull does not understand the principle of delayed gratification. You do."

This chapter is adapted from a speech I gave at the Modern Language Association in 2003 on the occasion of receiving a professional honor from the Conference of Christianity and Literature. In it I reflect not only on Marlowe's play but on the fading of biblical knowledge from the literary imagination of contemporary culture and the difficulty that creates for the study of great texts.

That, I realized only later, was to be my entire experience of "the talk." (I have always been grateful for the brevity of it.) My father was a man of few words; his language formed by the Bible, he took seriously the biblical adage that "he that refraineth his lips is wise" (Prov. 10:19).

He did not readily approve when I decided to go to college rather than buy some good bottomland not too far from the homeplace. His argument was typically succinct: "David, you show me a college-educated Baptist, and I'll show you a backslider." But I went, of course, and into a world of words, as he would say, in the multitude of which there "wanteth not sin" (Prov. 10:19). It is a source of relief to me, and of peace, that my father came in the end to accept my sense of calling—to work in which my tools would be books, and to neighbors who would be part of a quest for common understanding that has stretched much further than either of us could have foreseen.

Context and Appropriation

A most excellent benefit of membership in an academic community is that we continue, lifelong, to learn from one another. Iron sharpens iron. In literary study, this can be most richly evident when we are obliged to reconsider a favorite work in the light of fresh readings (or interpretations) offered by a sister discipline such as music, cinema, theology, or theater—or by a literary scholar whose perspective is sharply divergent from our own.

Just over a decade ago, I was asked to review the script and to offer an introductory lecture for the Baylor theater company's production of *Doctor Faustus*. The script proved rather forbidding. My colleague the director, in his effort to make Marlowe's sixteenth-century tragedy more accessible to twenty-first-century students and lay audiences, had interspersed (at some cost to the original counterplot burlesque) excerpts from the hellfire sermons of the eighteenth-century theologian and preacher Jonathan Edwards. He thought of this as a way to clarify the biblical content of Marlowe's play. To make the anachronism still more plausible to American students, he had moved the venue from Wittenberg to Yale and introduced, as fifth business and Professor Faustus's rector, Elisha Williams.

Now, howsoever much I strive to keep promises to my colleagues, I confess that I felt a certain doom settling upon me in this instance. In fact, my foreboding was such that I asked for my lecture to be scheduled for the afternoon following (rather than, as first planned, preceding) the opening-night performance. It didn't help much. Through the dim and strobe-lit chemical smoke, the dashing young Mercutio-like Faustus zipped through his speeches like an eager telemarketer. Mephistophilis appeared not as "an old Franciscan friar," despite the contention of Faustus that "that shape . . . befits a devil best," but rather as an extremely acrobatic young woman in a body stocking. Like W. C. Fields, and in contemplation of my assignment, I was beginning to think that "on the whole, I'd rather be in Philadelphia."[1]

Yet I tried to sympathize with the director and to think through Marlowe's play with his problems in mind. Among them, I realized, he would have to anticipate that, even in Baptist-dominated audiences, the play's crucial biblical references would go mostly unrecognized. Two examples from Marlowe's original text: when Faustus reads "The wages of sin is death," he stops mid-sentence and concludes prematurely, "Ha! The wages of sin is death? That's hard." Marlowe could count on his contemporary audience to know the rest of the verse. My colleague had to have his *ex machina* Rector Williams fill it in from across the stage: "but the gift of God is eternal life through Jesus Christ our Lord" (Rom. 6:23). Similarly, when Faustus reads "If we say that we have no sin, we deceive ourselves, and the truth is not in us" (1 John 1:8), he cuts off the text to interpose a preemptive inference:

> Why then belike we must sin,
> And so consequently die.
> Ay, we must die an everlasting death.
> What doctrine call you this? *Che serà, serà,*
> What will be, shall be? Divinity, adieu!

My colleague had Williams then intone the subsequent verse: "If we confess our sins, he is faithful and just to forgive us our sins, and to cleanse us from all unrighteousness" (1 John 1:9). Marlowe's point, evident to a biblically literate audience, was that Scripture seemed "hard" to Faustus precisely because he closed his eyes to its fullness—that is, because of his rejection of the "comfortable words" of the very same texts, the grace offered to reconcile our transgressions. Faustus, for his purposes, is from the outset interested only in half-truths.

But my colleague could not count on even a Baylor audience to fill in the rhetorical and theological blanks. In the Churches of the Blessed Overhead Projector, biblical literacy lags well behind that of the Elizabethan theater.

I thought for a while that might be the worst of my problem—but soon recognized that, in thinking so, I had undershot the mark. Nowhere in the play, despite a host of spectacular special effects Marlowe could not have

---

1. Fields used to quip that he'd rather travel to hell than to Philadelphia; the quotation is on his tombstone.

imagined at all, was there evoked anything like the sheer horror of hell necessary to constitute for our audience the devil's pact as the stuff of "tragedy"
or to render the final, long death speech of Faustus even plausibly terrifying.

So that is what I composed my talk about: the Renaissance's and Reformation's fearful imagination of hell and damnation. Since I was lecturing in the
theater, and from the set itself, I acted out Faustus's last speech, aided by the
presence and taunting last words of both the Good and the Bad Angel. My
effort was followed by a burst of uncomfortably enthusiastic applause. (Some
people are apparently pleased to see an old professor damned to hell; to see
it happen to a provost, as then I was, excites almost universal glee.)

It is quite difficult to get students in the twenty-first century to take hell
seriously. Its most familiar guise—that imprecation which makes "hell" a
direct object of the verb "to go," usually offered as a categorical imperative in
the second person—hardly now even counts as a real curse. It just encourages
the telemarketer to call on someone else, a colloquial vindication of Jean-Paul
Sartre's unduly famous remark that "hell is other people." (Anyone of my
generation who remembers being a child jammed in the middle of the back
seat between overstuffed and elbowy siblings on the way back from Christmas
dinner at grandmother's house could have as easily come up with that remark.)

But is this a hellish enough hell to make sense of *The Tragicall Historie
of Doctor Faustus*, Dante's *Inferno*, Milton's *Paradise Lost*, or even Charles
Williams's *Descent into Hell*, let alone the teachings of Jesus? I have serious
doubts. And worse still, without some sense of divine holiness, how are students to conjure with the agonized impatience of the reply Mephistophilis
makes to Faustus's literalistic question, "How comes it then that thou art
out of hell?"

> Why this is hell, nor am I out of it.
> Thinks't thou that I, who saw the face of God
> And tasted th'eternal joys of heaven,
> Am not tormented with ten thousand hells
> In being deprived of everlasting bliss?

How Now Shall We Understand?

It is a commonplace among those of us who teach literature that some of
the world's greatest texts are, by now, extremely difficult to teach to under-
graduates. While the reasons vary from text to text—premodern, early modern, modern, or postmodern—they usually implicate our students' lack of
linguistic amplitude or their want of literary foundations as a context for

approaching the works in question. There has been a certain amount of pious and quite futile hand-wringing about this and, much more commonly, an emphatic curricular exclusion of what is seen as culturally estranged literature.

Conceivably, I think, the preservation of some great vernacular works may depend upon scholars who are representative of subcultural communities—those whose call to learning comes in the context of personal religious formation. None who fail to value, or at least to understand, the religious significance of the conversation with biblical and theological foundations held by Dante, Chaucer, Marlowe, Sidney, Spenser, Shakespeare, Milton, Donne, and Herbert—let alone the Brontës, both Eliots, George MacDonald, David Jones, or R. S. Thomas (any even partial list would be very long)—can have so plausible a motive for preserving these authors as those who value their religious convictions and perspectives. Those disposed to take up this challenge rather than, as is more often the case, simply making gradual curricular concessions to fashions in the wider academy, have thus an opportunity to make vital contributions to general intellectual culture in years to come, when access to this literature may once again be desired.

But to accomplish this, they will have to do what all scholars who would preserve a great but unfashionable literature do, whether for their own purposes or for the common good of humanity. They will have first to read and teach with deep understanding the foundational literatures with which the subsequent great works hold conversation. Not even teachers in confessional colleges can count on the churches or departments of religion to have done this accountably.

We readily accept this intertextual necessity for literature composed in non-Christian religious contexts. Hence, the continuing pertinence of certain observations of Voltaire indicating the crucial role of foundational books for everything else in the literary cultures he identifies:

> The whole of Africa, right to Ethiopia, and Nigritia obeys the book of the Alcoran, after having staggered under the book of the Gospel. China is ruled by the moral book of Confucius; a greater part of India by the book of the Veda. Persia was governed for centuries by one of the books of the Zarathustras. (*Philosophical Dictionary*, "Books")

For teaching postcolonial or world literature, who would argue with this? Yet in our guild we have had an extreme scruple where "the book of the Gospel" and Western literature are concerned. Notably, professional aversion to our own "governing" book is proving to be coincident with an ongoing crisis of coherence for our literary profession, a discipline, of course, far younger than that of classics or any of the other core disciplines mastered and then rejected by Marlowe's Faustus.

English literature in particular became a university discipline only in the nineteenth century, and at least in part as a rejection of both classical and religious foundations. The genealogy is instructive. Though headmaster Thomas Arnold of Rugby remains almost as memorable for the power of his proclamation of traditional Christian verities as for his famous graduates, most of these better-known students—like Arthur Clough and Arnold's own son Matthew—soon departed from the senior Arnold's religious belief in order to embrace an ideal of culture from which the living faith had been largely excised. The first professor of poetry at Oxford to lecture in English rather than Latin, Matthew Arnold signaled the future of the discipline not only by focusing on *The Modern Element in Literature* (1857) but also by turning literary education itself toward social construction and explicitly away from biblical revelation. Yet in his revolutionary wish for the study of literature to provide an alternate clerisy and his desire to preserve the reading of the Bible not for religious but for literary purposes, he exhibited an unstable tension that has bedeviled our guild for one hundred and fifty years.

Justification for our place in the university depends upon more than simply teaching rudimentary skills on an order that, for the most part, would not have obtained a passing grade at Rugby. Our university prominence has depended more upon successfully ascribing high and (let us confess it) quasi-religious ideals to an increasingly low and secular reading practice. The advertised function of the practitioner is to make culture itself more widely available (in Arnold one moves from reading Homer in the original to comparing English translations of Homer), but by doing so ostensibly in search of a "grand style" expressive of a certain "nobility of the human spirit." If the poet "sees life steadily and sees it whole," the well-read critic all the more so. As poetry assumed the functions of religion among Arnold's successors, at least down to the New Critics and Northrop Frye, there was plenty of high-sounding stuff for its professors to sell to college administrators, regents, and many students. Arnold's "perfecting of a national right reason" worked together nicely with the later "pooled social intelligence" of John Dewey, as well as with numerous other identifications of salvation with the state and of virtue with a never-to-be-ended quest for poetic—hence, conveniently subjective—truth.

As we look over our shoulder, then, we can see how contentions that the classics are "the noblest recorded thoughts of man," the "only oracles which are not decayed" (Thoreau), reflect an archaic secular piety that did not long persist after the founding of our discipline. Nor was this reverence ever so fully extended to biblical literature in the modern university. For Matthew

Arnold, enamored of Goethe and the Romantics, traditional religion is already bankrupt; as he puts it in one of his more famous dismissals, "The strongest part of our religion today is its unconscious poetry" (*Study of Poetry*). Conscious poetry, especially that of the Romantics, he reckoned to possess a "higher truth and a higher seriousness." James Joyce simply echoes Arnold when Stephen, in *A Portrait of the Artist as a Young Man*, refers to literature as "the highest and most spiritual art."

These sentiments continued to be the prevailing secular pieties of our guild in the early 1960s in America. By the 1980s they too had been, of course, irrevocably interrogated, shaken down, and in some considerable measure dissolved. But the new revolutionaries were more than gradual secularists; among them a more candid apostasy was a requirement of the license to practice. They were thoroughgoing iconoclasts, and not in any sentimental sense worshipers. Their revolution has pretty effectively "done in" Arnold and, we might now suspect, most of the apostolic succession of his clerisy with him.

All across the English-speaking world, the formal study of literature is in disarray. Even when English departments focus on books of the most slender claim to nobility of thought, let alone grandness of style, pressing rather for what is taken to be more marketable fashion and relevance, students have continued to disperse to majors in communication studies, media studies, journalism, technical writing, cinema criticism, and cultural studies. Meanwhile, our discipline has acquired a popular notoriety for being the purveyor not of high and noble verities but of low and often trivial advocacies. Correspondingly, as the late Bernard Williams observed, even the primary literature itself has suffered from "some very reductive criticisms of traditional academic authority":

> If the canon of works or writers or philosophies to be studied, and the methods of interpreting them, and the historical narratives that explain those things, are all equally and simultaneously denounced as ideological impositions, we are indeed left with a space structured only by power.[2]

But such diminishment is hardly confined to the canonical status of texts (as deans of humanities and provosts will attest). The loss of literary authority to an utterly reductive account, as Williams further observes, deprives the critics themselves of sufficient power to sustain their enterprise. Put more crudely: the status of literary study as an apprenticeship to wisdom previously had the advantage of appearing, even to the unwise (e.g., administrators), to be a species

---

2. Bernard Williams, *Truth and Truthfulness: An Essay in Genealogy* (Princeton: Princeton University Press, 2002), 8.

of learning probably deserving of some environmental protection; but now, current rationalizations for literary study as a Saturday-night venue for avant-garde politics, competitive with the therapeutic social sciences, quickly lose traction.

Authority, notably, accrues to the possession of—or capacity for—truth of the high order that readers from Aristotle to Wordsworth (in the *Preface*) to Nietzsche ("Poetry desires to be . . . the unvarnished expression of the truth" [*Birth of Tragedy*]) have associated with the books most worth reading. Our modern discipline began with Arnold and the credo that religious truths had been, in literature, supplanted by the "higher truths" of nature, but we may well have approached the survival limit for our guild with postmodernist assertions that literature affords us no stable or shareable truths at all. In his provocative book *Truth and Truthfulness*, the philosopher Williams argues for a profound reversal of what he calls the "deconstructive vortex":

> If the passion for truthfulness is merely controlled and stilled without being satisfied, it will kill the activities it is supposed to support. This may be one of the reasons why, at the present time, the study of the humanities runs a risk of sliding from professional seriousness, through professionalization, to a finally disenchanted careerism.[3]

The drift of Williams's argument is toward a reassertion of that uncommon sense we still call "common," of a revaluing of pre-reflective openness to truth in relation to language, even of a sort of "primitive trust" in such "virtues of truth" as "accuracy and sincerity" and the "pooling of information" as a common good. There is more than a touch of Arnold here, but also a pointing to the need for something more basic than Arnold.

Williams's reflections correspond to my own (*People of the Book*; *Houses of the Interpreter*) in querying claims—albeit now enshrined as critical dogma—that there are no longer sustaining common stories or grand narratives. If we are thinking about the dissolution of modern European socialist agendas there is, of course, a certain rhetorical apropos to this claim; but if we are thinking of, say, African literature, it makes almost no sense at all. Among writers in China, whose formal Marxist grand narrative has also stuttered to a stop, many contemporary novelists have identified openly with religious story, and particularly the Christian grand narrative, among them Lao She, Xu Dishan, Bing Xing, and Mu Dan. There is a new literary style called Sheng Jing Te ("biblical") whose characteristics are described as "objective, truthful, terse."[4]

3. Williams, *Truth and Truthfulness*, 3.
4. David Aikman, *Jesus in Beijing: How Christianity Is Transforming China and Changing the Global Balance of Power* (Washington, DC: Regnery, 2003), 254.

However oddly for us, it is in parts of Africa, Asia, and South America that our own greatest older texts are now perhaps most carefully taught and intertextually reflected on. But I wonder if the pendulum may not yet swing here too, if only because our employment cannot much longer be sustained by the purveying of trendy ephemerality alone. To return to Williams, for us too

> the need to make sense of the past reasserts itself. It is particularly so when the smooth order of things is disturbed by violence, if only to answer the questions "Why" "Why us?" "Where from?" Communitarian politics (and, at the limit, renewed tribal wars) are one area in which the need is very much alive, and it appears, too, in the interest in current historical disputes. . . . The demand for an explicit and definite story about one's own people or nation is only one form of it, and that particular demand has been more urgent in some places than in others.[5]

And have we, here in the English-speaking countries, not now become one of those identity-distressed "places"?

Seeds of the Crisis

The present crisis for literary study has been long in the making; effectively, it is the outworking, I believe, of a congenital defect. For others it has been more attractive to think of it as merely an accidental disorder, the etiology of which has been examined—belatedly, and with eloquent alarm—by critics such as George Steiner (since the 1960s) and Terry Eagleton (beginning in the 1980s). In his essay "To Civilize Our Gentlemen," Steiner's nominal subject was arcane doctoral dissertations and thin literary journalism, but his underlying targets were the failed "rational and moral optimism" of I. A. Richards and Henry Sidgwick, which rightly he identifies as secondhand Arnold, and the aestheticism, however elegant, of F. R. Leavis and Arthur Quiller Couch. But Steiner's prescription for the ailing discipline, however much I affirm his notion of a multilingual *cortesia*, is by itself inadequate. Steiner asks, "Is it not as important for the survival of feeling today . . . to know another living language as it once was important for [someone] to be intimate with the classics and Scripture?"[6] To this I would answer no—that these sources of common understanding are not equivalent in value. Jews and Christians have reason to know that a secondary good cannot long be sustained without the

---

5. Williams, *Truth and Truthfulness*, 262–63.
6. George Steiner, "To Civilize Our Gentlemen," in *Language and Silence* (New Haven: Yale University Press, 1998), 85.

primary good from which it proceeds. For love of the neighbor to be sustained, we believe, it must grow out of love for God with all our hearts, souls, and minds (see Matt. 22:37–40). From this prior love, neighbor love obtains its true value, coherence, and credible modes of expression in whatever language lies mutually to hand.

For Terry Eagleton, a post-Catholic Marxist for whom the authority of his new religion lay precisely in its ethical rather than aesthetic claims, it was the failure of literary study following the 1960s to keep in the vanguard of socialist reform that occasioned his greatest anxieties; the "crisis" that he addressed (in 1983) was likewise a crisis of coherence. For Eagleton, the turn from literature to cultural theory has since then degenerated further into a socially acceptable yet entirely narcissistic self-preoccupation in which "quietly-spoken middle class students huddle diligently in libraries, at work on sensationalist subjects like vampirism and eye-gouging, cyborgs and porno movies."[7] His wrath rises proportionately to his sense that professional literary study has fled from public and political purpose to radically anarchic self-absorption: "The emancipation which has failed in the streets and factories" he writes, "could be acted out instead in erotic intensities or the floating signifier."[8] Yes. But is such an overdetermined diagnosis enough to chart a way out of our present malaise and toward a compelling public respect for the study of literature?

These are but two late twentieth-century realizations that formal literary study, in its pretensions to be a substitute for religion, has lost sight of the common good and become incoherent. One could cite others, including Jonathan Culler.[9] Culler's project has involved resuscitating the system of Northrop Frye (who was, of course, one of Arnold's most eminent twentieth-century disciples). Summarily, Culler sees that our professional position is untenable if we are unable to maintain even so much as a common ideal of literary value. It is difficult to disagree, however astonishing it is to reckon with Culler as the source of this appeal. His recommendation that we recover coherence by turning again to purely formalist concerns such as genre, mode, and archetype is in itself welcome—in my own way of thinking, even necessary. But resurrecting Frye—which is to say, resurrecting the twentieth-century Arnold—will not of itself save Faustus.

Steiner and Eagleton are types, respectively, of Kierkegaard's "aesthetic" and "ethical" man. Each laments but also remains locked into the Arnoldian legacy, despite ardent attempts to rise above it. We should empathize, but with

7. Terry Eagleton, *After Theory* (New York: Basic Books, 2004), 24.
8. Eagleton, *After Theory*, 29.
9. See Jonathan Culler, "Imagining the Coherence of the English Major," *Profession* (2003): 85–93.

a more self-examining circumspection. Steiner admits, correctly, that while "'art for art' is a tactical slogan, . . . pressed to its logical consequences it is pure narcissism."[10] Eagleton, while he recognizes the tactical advantage for radical social reform in coded discourse, is as appalled as Steiner at the loss of elegance and clarity in the wake of postmodern psychobabble. Each staggers under the professional burden of a discourse without rankable values, the Babel-effect of a secular religion gone wrong on all three measures of truth, the good, and beauty, and whose acolytes, cheerless in their alternate fits of denial and despair, discourse incommensurably even with each other, and hardly at all with an increasingly indifferent world. It is not surprising, on these accounts, that some of us are losing quorum in the classroom.

The parallels with the near-modern history of institutional religion, and in particular Christianity, are many—too many to explore here. The loss of any authority sufficiently transcendent to command a common allegiance and thus create a common discourse is but one of these parallels. It is no merely secular reflex, I think, that Steiner is made unhappy by that apparent permissiveness in the guild whereby we "can say any truth and any falsehood"[11] and get away with it; nor is it extrinsic to his radical-left social purpose that Eagleton now defends the idea of absolute truth and objectivity as fervently, if not as cogently, as does Bernard Williams.[12]

Since at least the time of Aristotle, who asserted in his *Poetics* that "fiction is truer and more universal than history," the hope for shareable truth has been an indispensable sustainer of the social authority of literature. One went to the theater at Athens because the truths made flesh on the stage were more than transient truths. This gave even to a dramatized *denial* of truth a terrible power to wound and heal. But just as with the religious plays of Aeschylus and Sophocles, Shakespeare and Marlowe, so for all literature that, in the end, bids to be taken seriously by the wider community of thoughtful minds: at bottom, the only guarantor of communal truth is transcendent truth; the only guarantor of authority is the near presence of an ultimate and abiding authority.

"If no authority, then only power."[13] Yet the power we in our discipline have wrested from authority is proving to be a rather feeble order of power—just how feeble, perhaps especially in straitened economic circumstances, the next decade will likely tell more completely. Put positively, it seems to me that the best hope for literature as a secular discipline is for it to reacquire its access to

10. George Steiner, *Real Presences* (Chicago: University of Chicago Press, 1991), 143.
11. Steiner, *Real Presences*, 84.
12. Williams, *Truth and Truthfulness*, 103, 105.
13. Williams, *Truth and Truthfulness*, 8.

some sort of moral and rhetorical authority; the rush to trade such authority for power has led to some very bad bargains.

Meanwhile, in communities of those who yet think there is truth and inquire after it, there remains more hope than despair and—accordingly, I believe—more hope for literature. That is because these communities know that for hope to persist, there is required a postulate of truth, and that correspondingly, in the words of the American novelist Leif Enger, "denying the truth is the beginning of death."[14]

In communities of those who yet think that truth has consequences—in time and out of it—there is also, however, the added obligation of neighbor love: to teach the great texts and to do so in a fashion richly affirmative of their relation to their respective founding religious texts. An advantage for readers whose common treasure is the Common Book, and for whom prayer and salvation are both desirable and not purely individual matters, is that they can become confident enough in their own identity to take the ultimate concerns of others, past and present, seriously. They should be able—if they have not entirely forgotten their calling—to give to older Christian literature an intellectually responsible treatment of its primary religious and moral as well as stylistic dimensions, as well as to deal candidly with contemporary literary works. I do not mean to say that none but denominational or confessional schools may provide such a context. I do mean to suggest that these are the schools in which, in this century in America, it ought to be most possible to teach premodern literature in such a way as to preserve its intelligibility. I want further to suggest that these institutions, accordingly, have a particular cultural responsibility to do just that.

Matthew Arnold thought that the spiritual capital of Christianity would readily transmute, at a comparably high value, to secular cultural capital, the prestige of its canons carrying over into a secular clerisy of the literate. Accordingly, he was happy for the grandiloquence of the King James Bible and the Book of Common Prayer to persist as some guerdon of their authority, and even to echo in the prose of literary scholars. But after one hundred and fifty years, that capital has been pretty well used up. Arnold and his successors were simply wrong to think that we could keep even these stylistic virtues without the high order of spiritual reverence to which they were attached.

Faustus, we may remember, was willing to go from half-truths and illusions about his own power to a kind of rabid incoherence in which he proved at

14. Leif Enger, interview by Mark LaFramboise, https://groveatlantic.com/book/peace-like-a-river/.

last to have no power at all. Having rejected the undergirding fullness of the Common Book, and believing himself superior to it in knowledge, wisdom, and mastery, he took up instead certain books of magic and necromancy by which, in his search for self-aggrandizement, he anathematized to himself the "New Testament and the Hebrew Psalter." In the end, in that last horrible scene, as the clock strikes and the demons draw nigh, he cries out in vain, "I'll burn my books!" His attempt at reformation, however, comes all too late. A Renaissance audience could see (can a modern audience perceive this?) that what Faustus most needed to do, at the very outset, was to tell "German Cornelius and Valdes," most emphatically, where to go.

Now, it must be said that in literature, hell is more full of notable academics, perhaps, than we should like. Among memorable examples are Dante's Brunetto Latini, for his reasons, and Charles Williams's Professor Wentworth (in *Descent into Hell*), for his. What these denizens have in common is a lifelong practice of retreat from the common good and of the concomitant, rationalizing away of any sense of accountability to the truth of the other. Perseverant egoism and almost absurd levels of narcissism are, in each case, made possible by a disdaining refusal of self-transcendent, mind-independent reality. Particular rationalizations for this or that denial are often, of course, ingenious; what gives each catastrophic fall its tragic dimension is the audience's appreciation that "rationalization is the homage paid by sin to guilty knowledge."[15] A literate audience—especially a biblically literate audience—will know it was a choice.

Coherence depends upon a common sense of objective value to which, communally, we may appeal. Language itself will not otherwise work. As Bernard Williams observes, "Children learn language in many ways and in many different kinds of situation, but one essential way is that they hear sentences being used in situations in which those sentences are plainly true."[16] In this respect also, "Whoever does not receive the kingdom of God as a little child will by no means enter it" (Mark 10:15 NKJV).

Can we bear the burden of obligatory clarity, even to preserve our livelihood, let alone the common good (the "commune profit," as Gower called it) of our students and neighbors? It may not seem obvious to many of us just how easy it is to make a pact with the devil only to belatedly regret it. Perhaps too few of us in this business now believe we have a soul to lose. Yet, for our discipline, there surely is a soul to lose. What I want to suggest is that for some of us who at least profess literature, "if sin by custom grow not

15. J. Budziszewski, *What We Can't Not Know: A Guide* (Dallas: Spence, 2003), 19.
16. Williams, *Truth and Truthfulness*, 45.

into nature," as Marlowe's Erasmian old man has it, it may not be too late to revive our options.

To wit: it may be that the fate of our profession still lies in our own power of decision—to want hope more than *wanhope*, to love health more than despair. This involves our willingness to locate literature in a real rather than in a purely chimerical notion of community—a community against and across time—and to be open to the full reality of our own immediate community of learning as much as that of any metaphorical "professional" community. As Wendell Berry has it, community life is by definition a life of cooperation and responsibility. People of the Book, it seems to me, are obliged to embrace their responsibility to community more readily than others; hence, they can—and should—work to preserve more credibly all literature that encourages future hope, for it is that literature alone that grants full human identity.

I am inclined to agree with Jacques Maritain (against Arnold) that "it is a mortal error to expect from poetry the supersubstantial nourishment of man."[17] That higher, more noble nourishment lies with the Greater Book, which in English literary tradition has been the most powerful source for the poetic imagination. At the same time, I also believe in the power of literature to enable our will to truth. And yet, I am convinced that without intellectually accountable access to the Greater Book, very many lesser, yet still very great, expressions of truth may go without understanding—unread and unreprinted. That would be for many others besides ourselves a tragedy; it might also, and perhaps irredeemably, further diminish the residual authority of our fragile discipline and indeed our wider culture.

17. Jacques Maritain, *"Art and Scholasticism" and "The Frontiers of Poetry,"* trans. Joseph W. Evans (New York: Scribner's Sons, 1962), 132.

INDEX

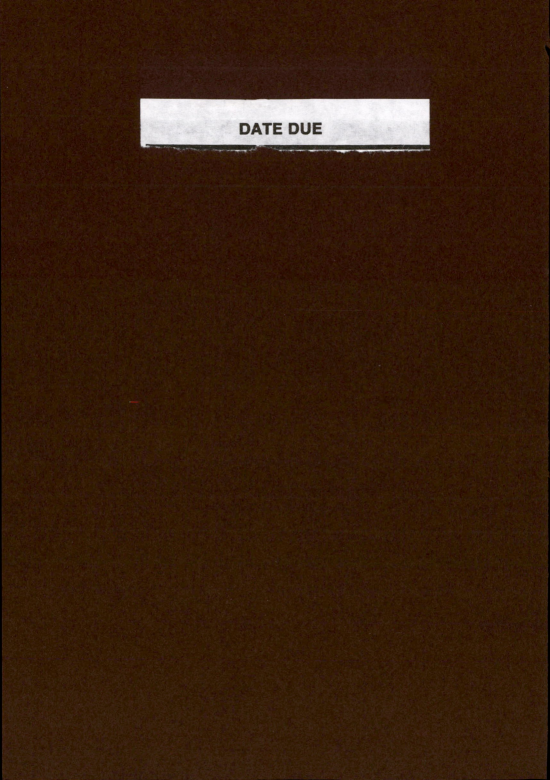
DATE DUE